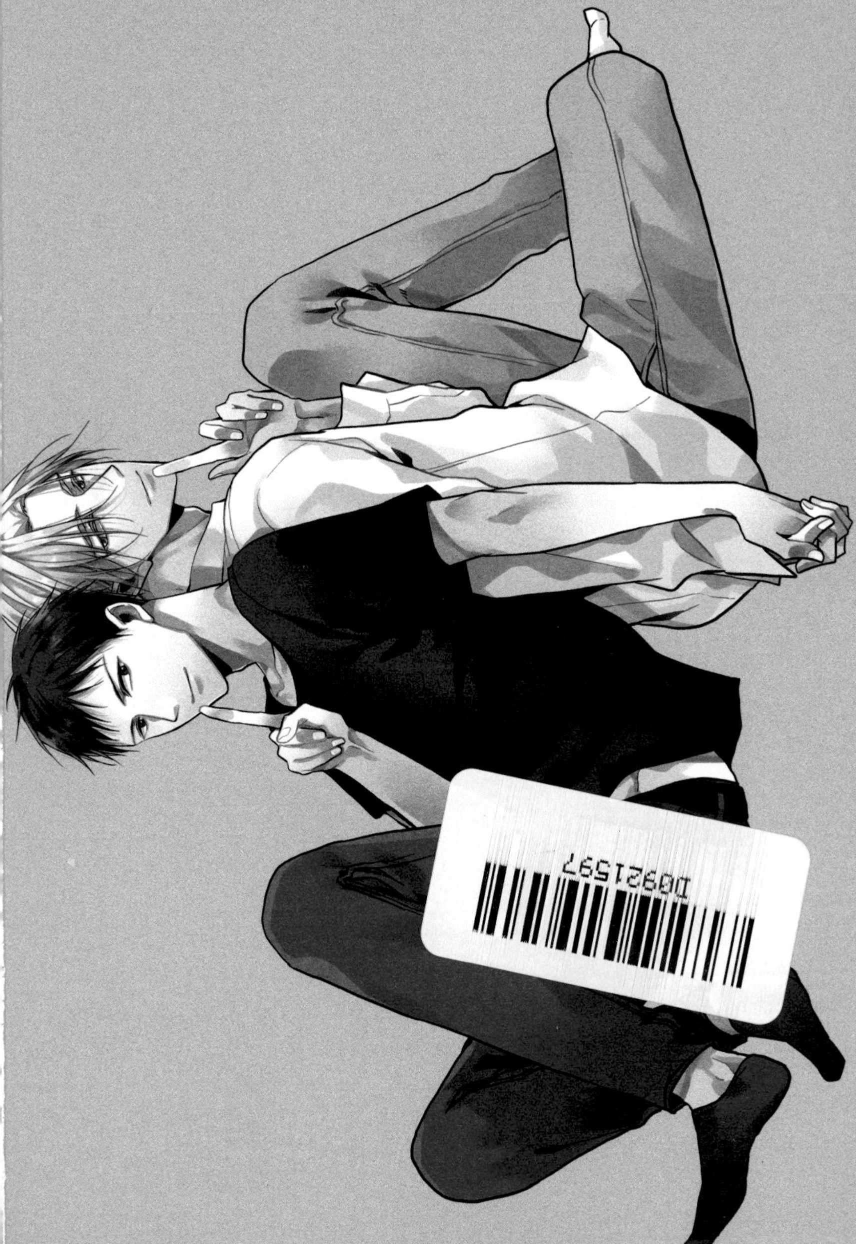

Contents

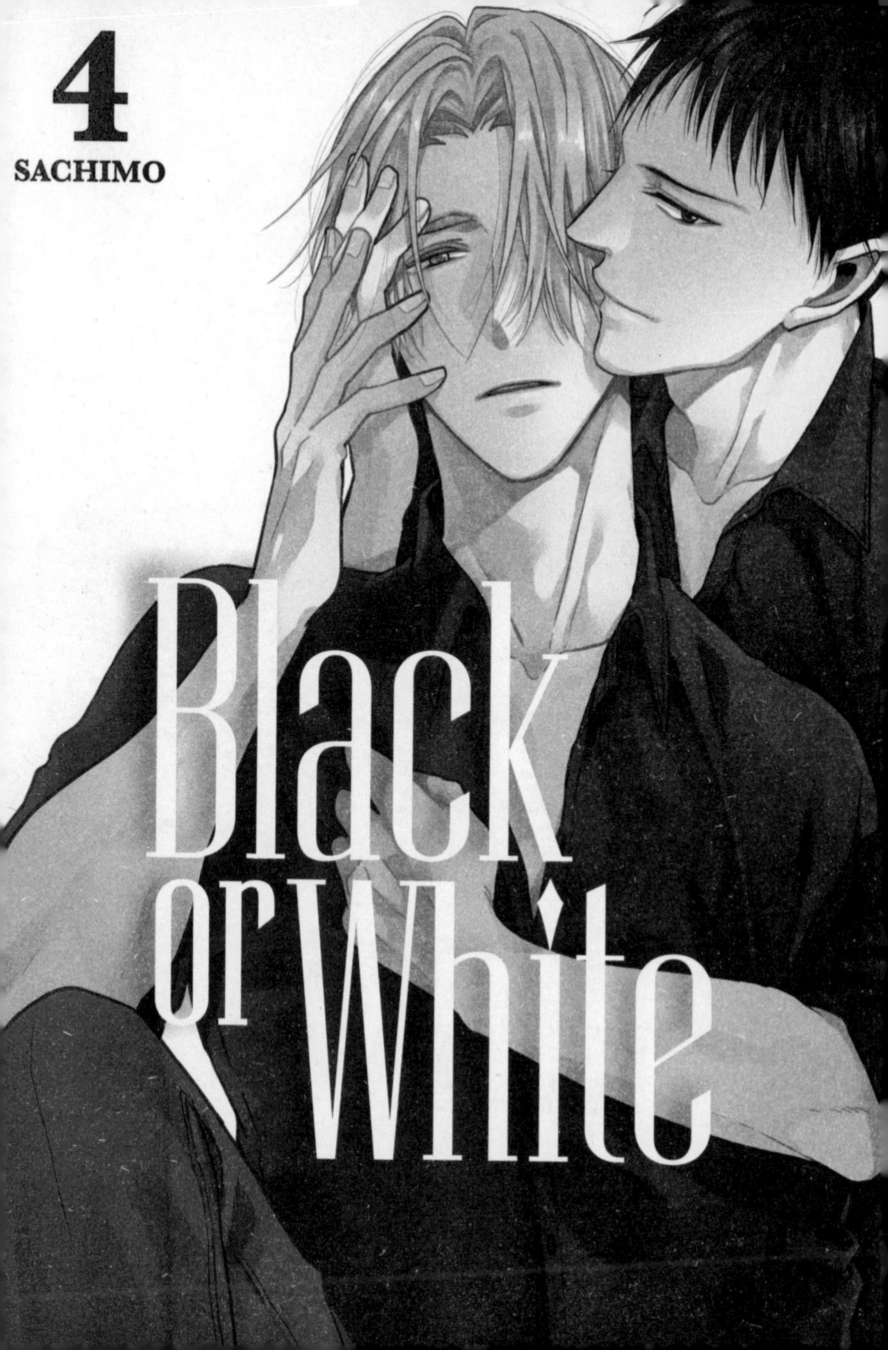
4
SACHIMO
Black or White

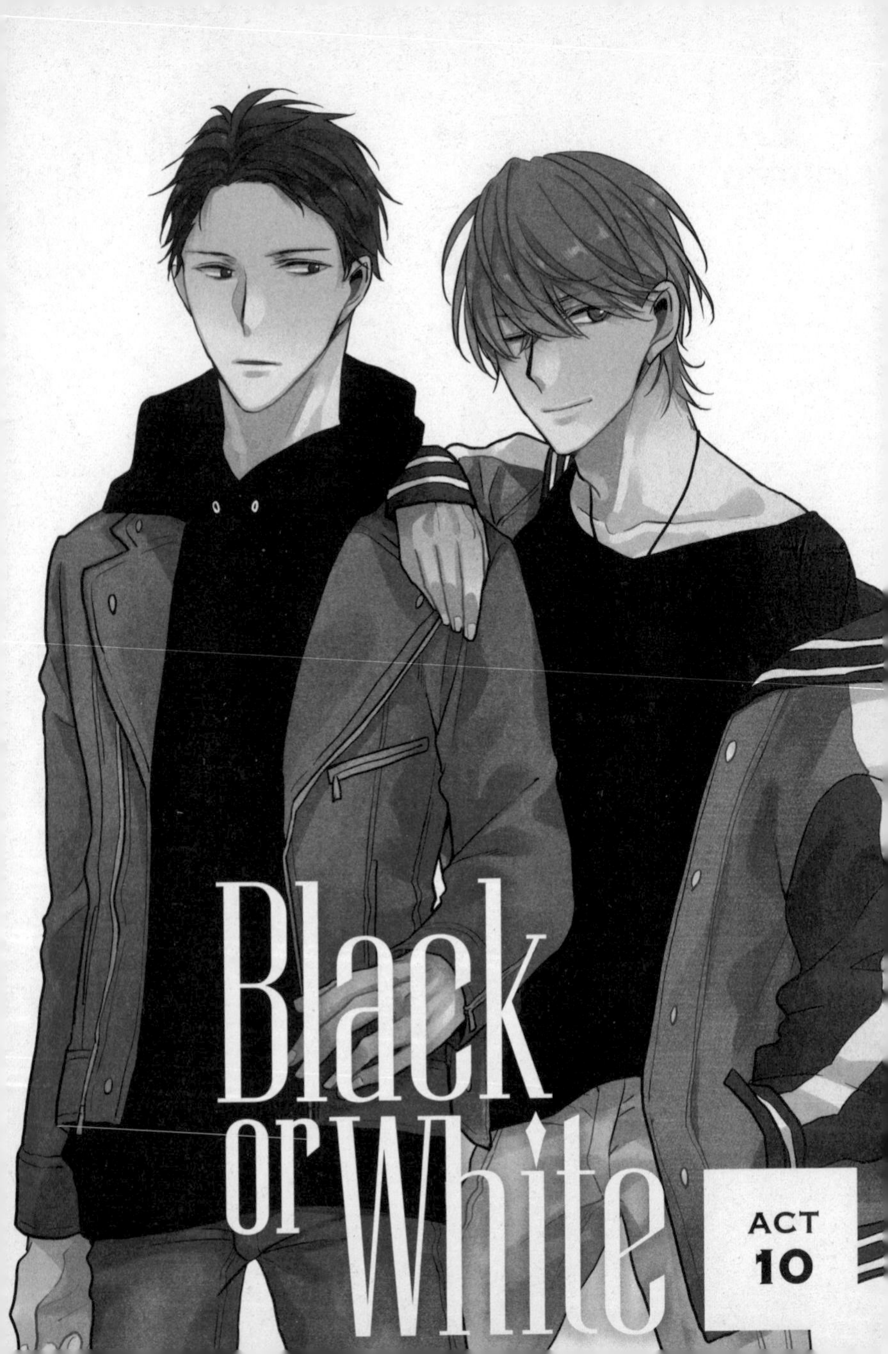
Black or White
ACT 10

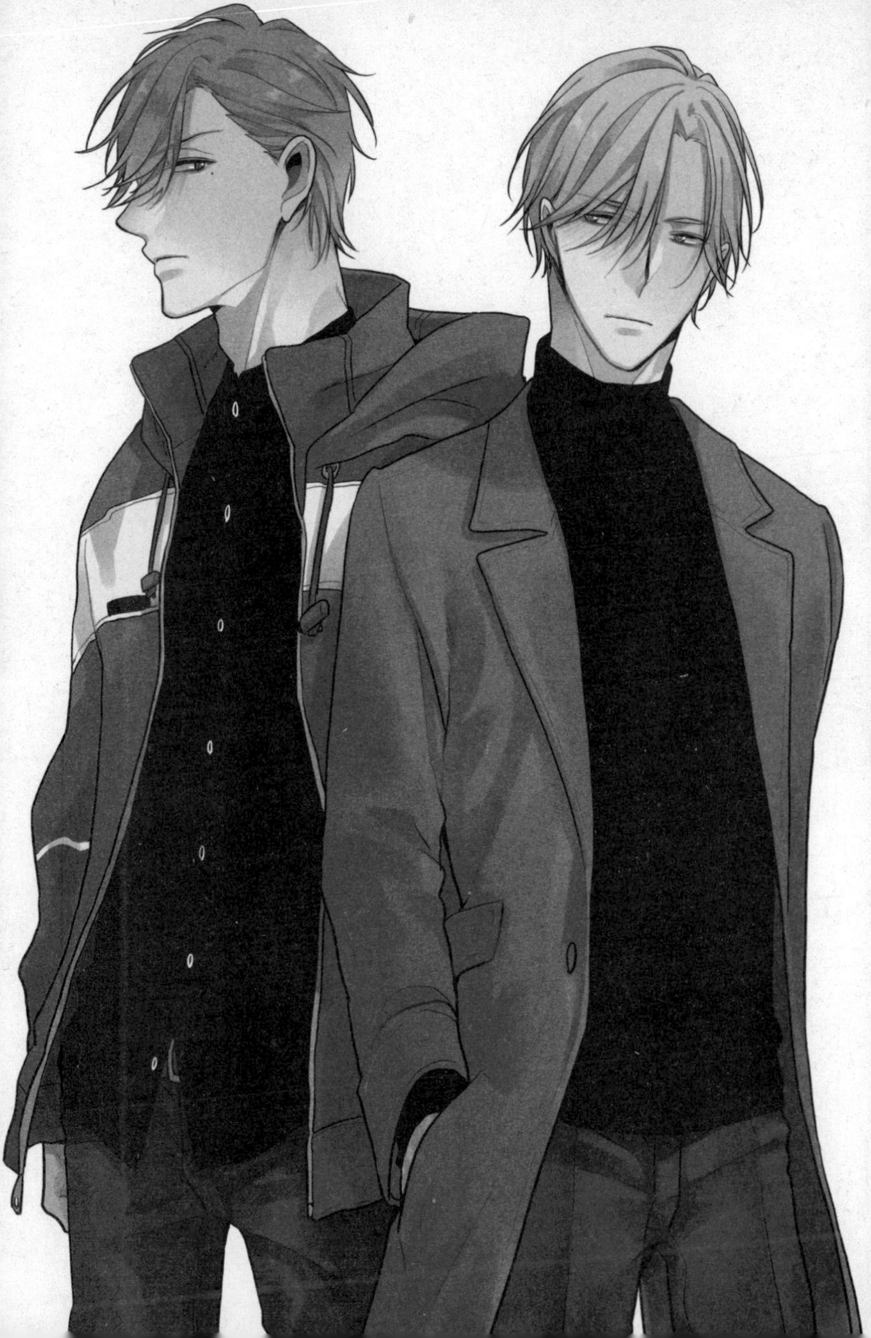

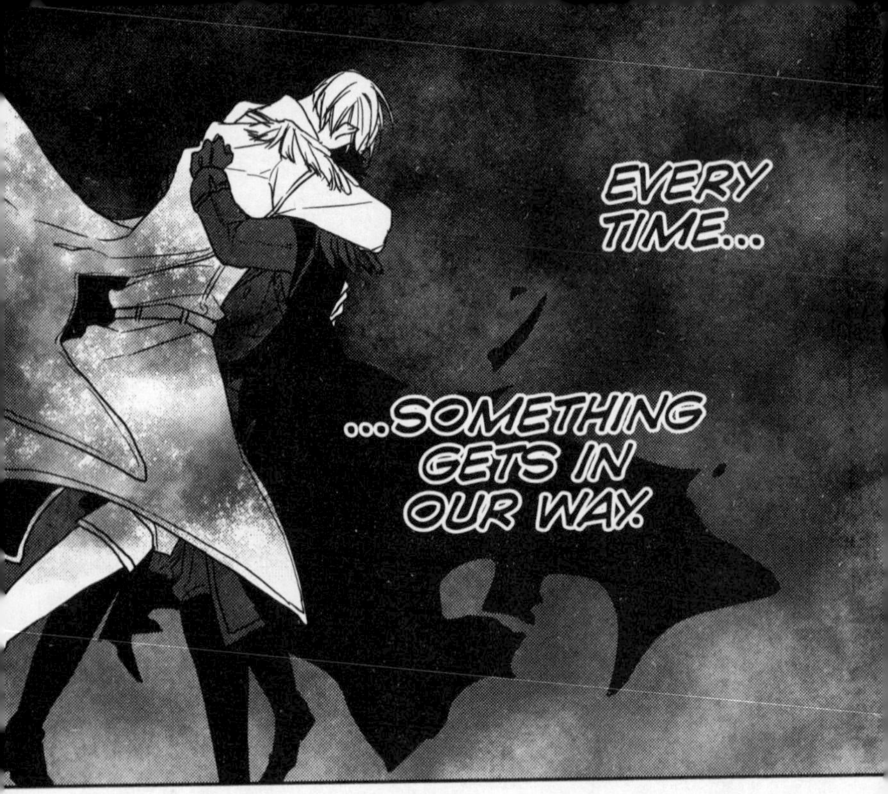
EVERY TIME...
...SOMETHING GETS IN OUR WAY.
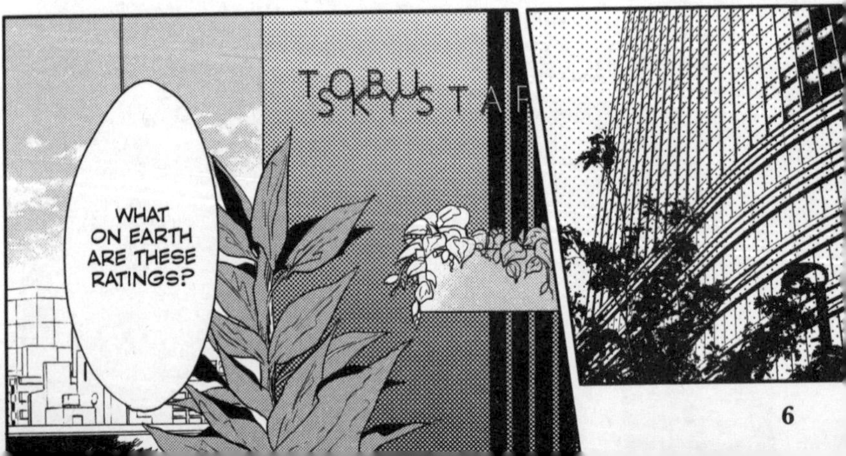
TOBU
SKYSTAR
WHAT ON EARTH ARE THESE RATINGS?

I'M SORRY, SIR.

THE REVIEWS ARE HARDLY STERLING EITHER.

THOUGH I WOULDN'T SAY IT'S ENTIRELY BECAUSE OF SHIGE...

SIIIGH...

KOSUGE?

SHUT UP.

THAT ROLE ON *OLDER WOMEN* IS ONE I PERSONALLY BROUGHT TO YOU.

I'D RATHER YOU NOT MAKE ME LOOK LIKE A FOOL FOR IT.

...

SORRY, SIR.

DOESN'T HE MEAN "BOUGHT" FOR YOU?

MUTR

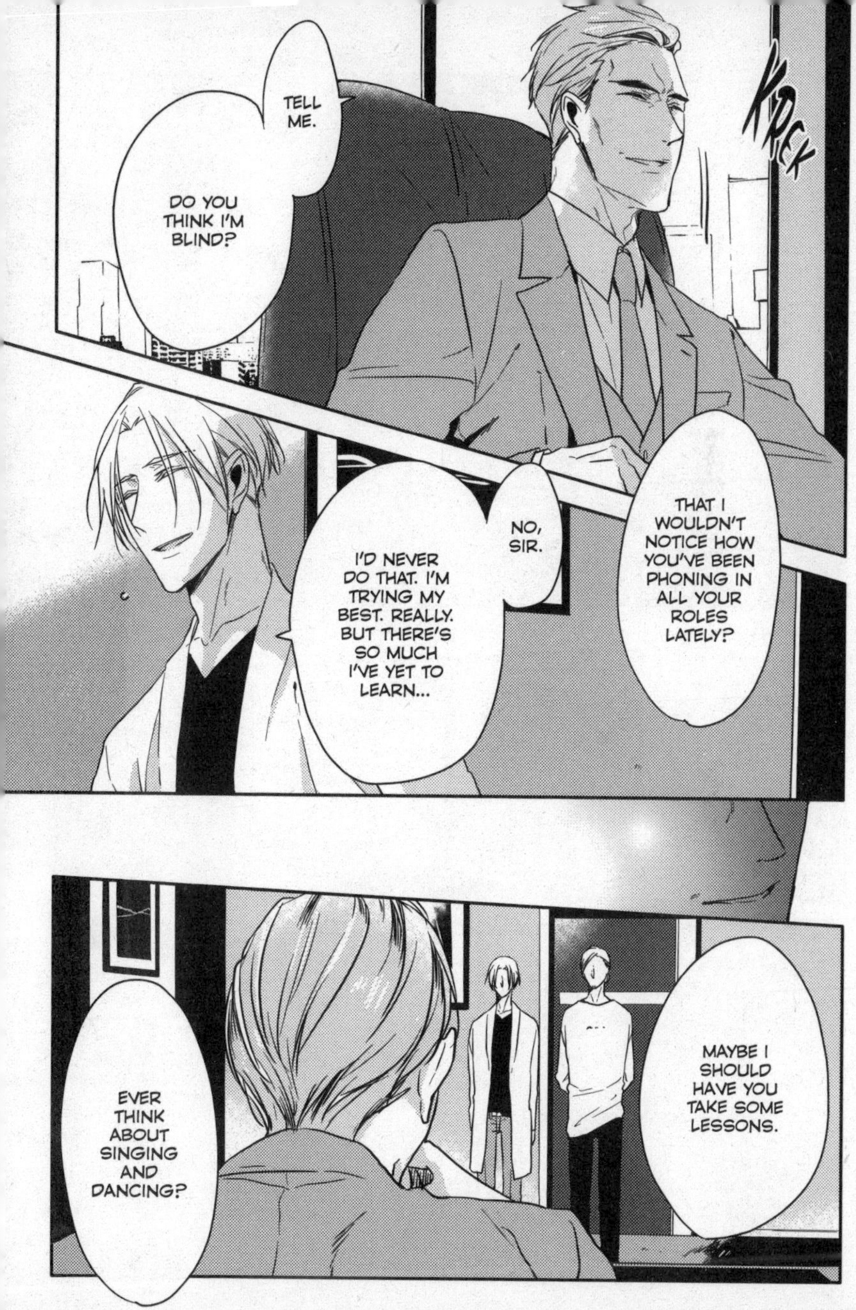
KRCK
TELL ME.
DO YOU THINK I'M BLIND?
THAT I WOULDN'T NOTICE HOW YOU'VE BEEN PHONING IN ALL YOUR ROLES LATELY?
NO, SIR.
I'D NEVER DO THAT. I'M TRYING MY BEST. REALLY. BUT THERE'S SO MUCH I'VE YET TO LEARN...
MAYBE I SHOULD HAVE YOU TAKE SOME LESSONS.
EVER THINK ABOUT SINGING AND DANCING?

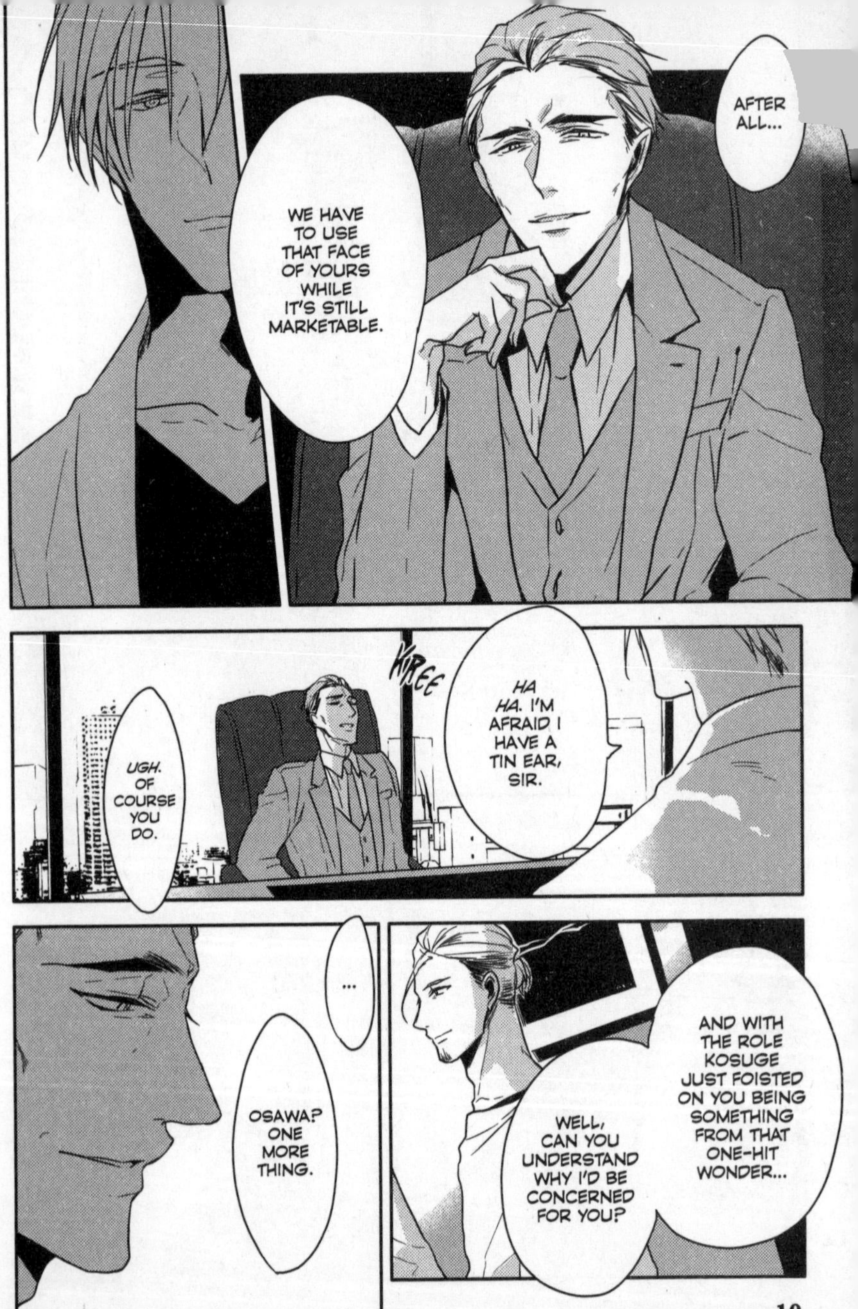
AFTER ALL...
WE HAVE TO USE THAT FACE OF YOURS WHILE IT'S STILL MARKETABLE.
HA HA. I'M AFRAID I HAVE A TIN EAR, SIR.
KIREE
UGH. OF COURSE YOU DO.
AND WITH THE ROLE KOSUGE JUST FOISTED ON YOU BEING SOMETHING FROM THAT ONE-HIT WONDER...
WELL, CAN YOU UNDERSTAND WHY I'D BE CONCERNED FOR YOU?
...
OSAWA? ONE MORE THING.

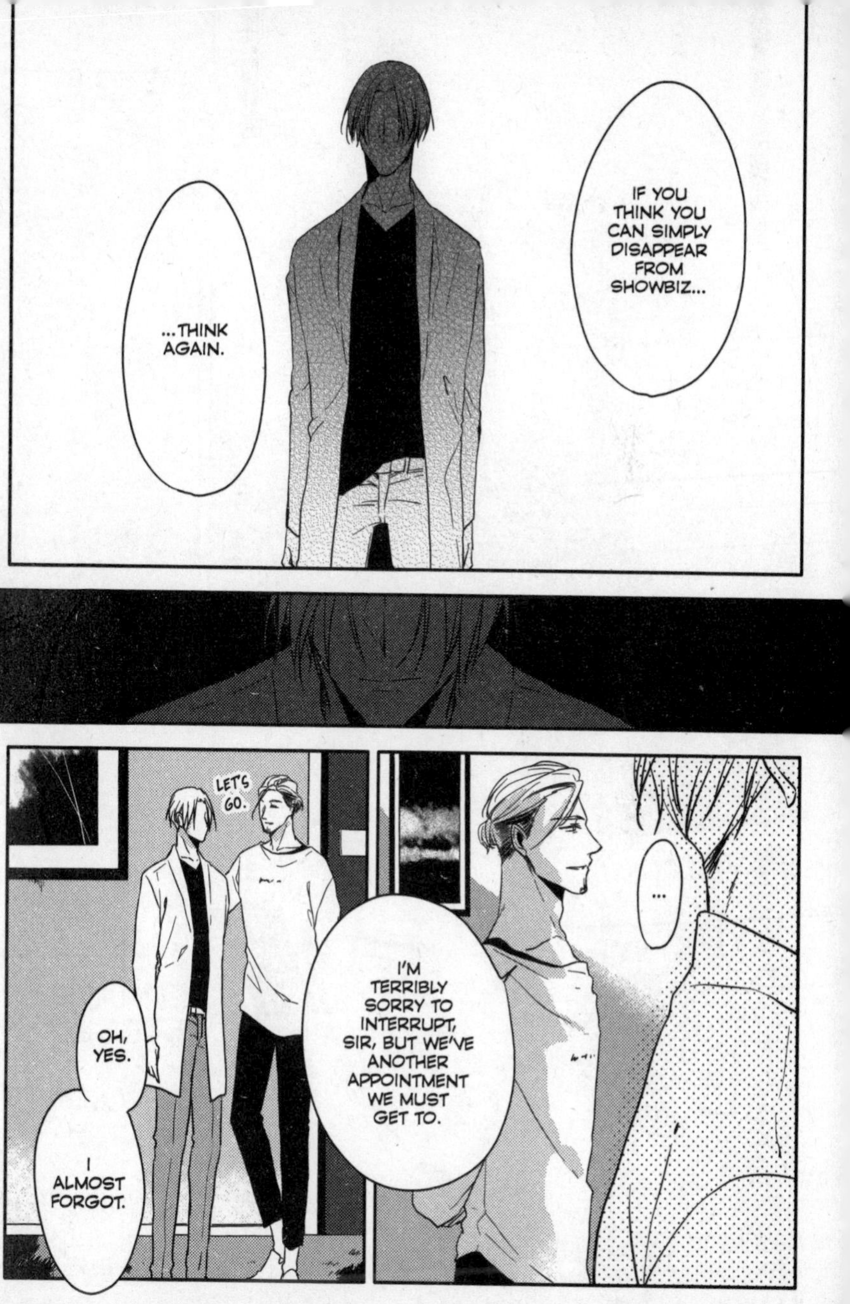
IF YOU THINK YOU CAN SIMPLY DISAPPEAR FROM SHOWBIZ...
...THINK AGAIN.
...
I'M TERRIBLY SORRY TO INTERRUPT, SIR, BUT WE'VE ANOTHER APPOINTMENT WE MUST GET TO.
LET'S GO.
OH, YES.
I ALMOST FORGOT.

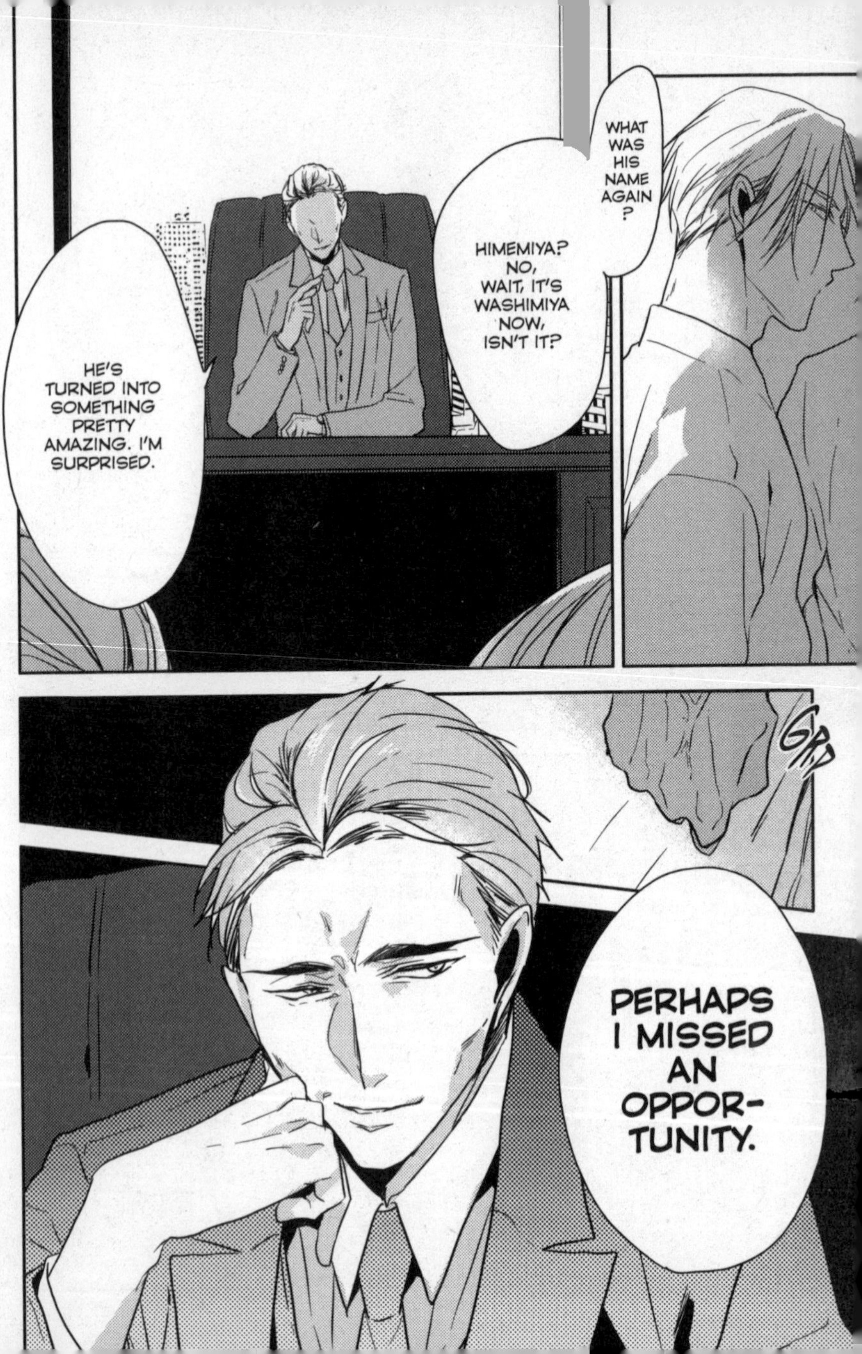
WHAT WAS HIS NAME AGAIN?
HIMEMIYA? NO, WAIT, IT'S WASHIMIYA NOW, ISN'T IT?
HE'S TURNED INTO SOMETHING PRETTY AMAZING. I'M SURPRISED.
GRP
PERHAPS I MISSED AN OPPOR-TUNITY.

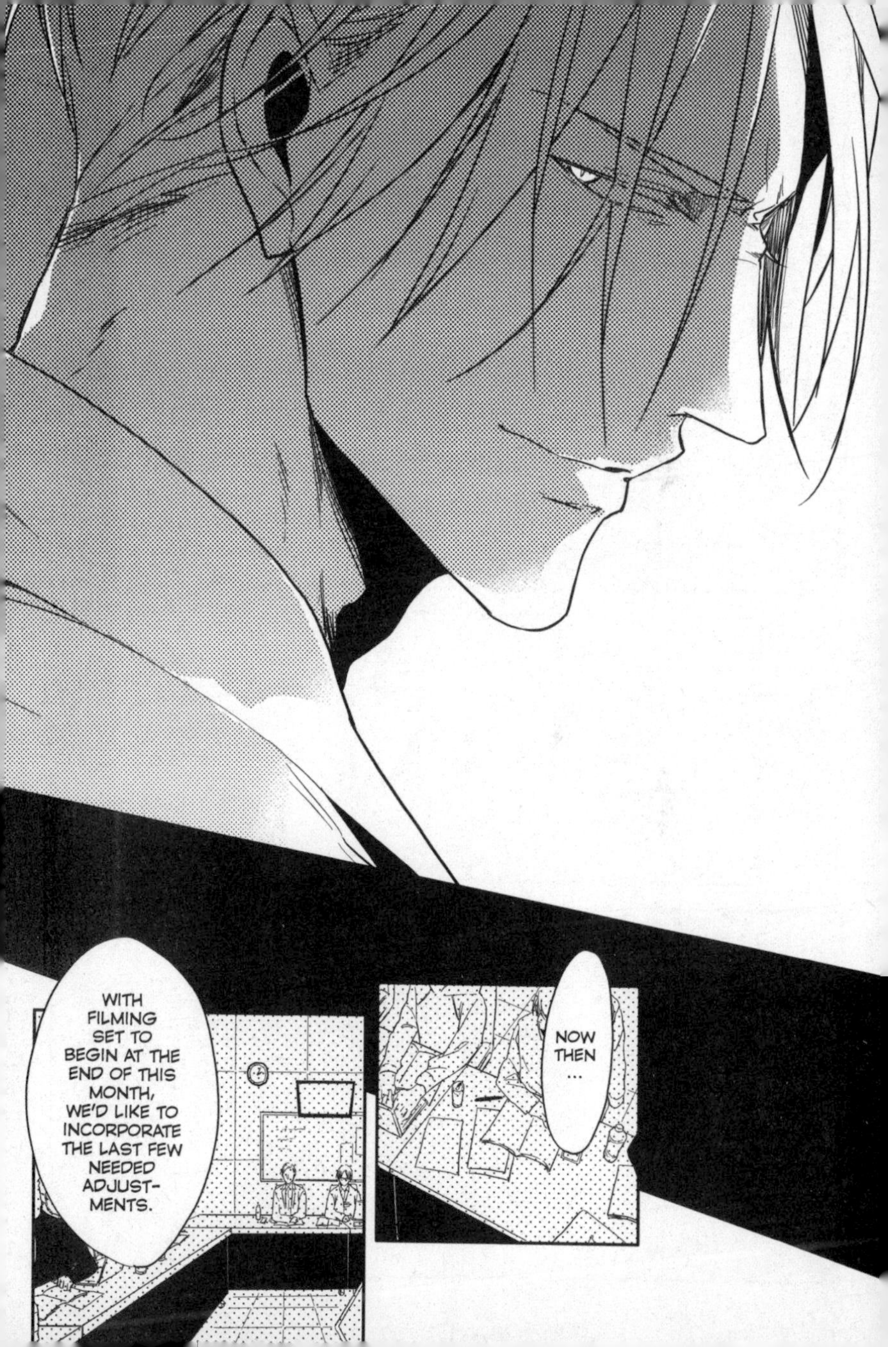
NOW THEN ...
WITH FILMING SET TO BEGIN AT THE END OF THIS MONTH, WE'D LIKE TO INCORPORATE THE LAST FEW NEEDED ADJUSTMENTS.

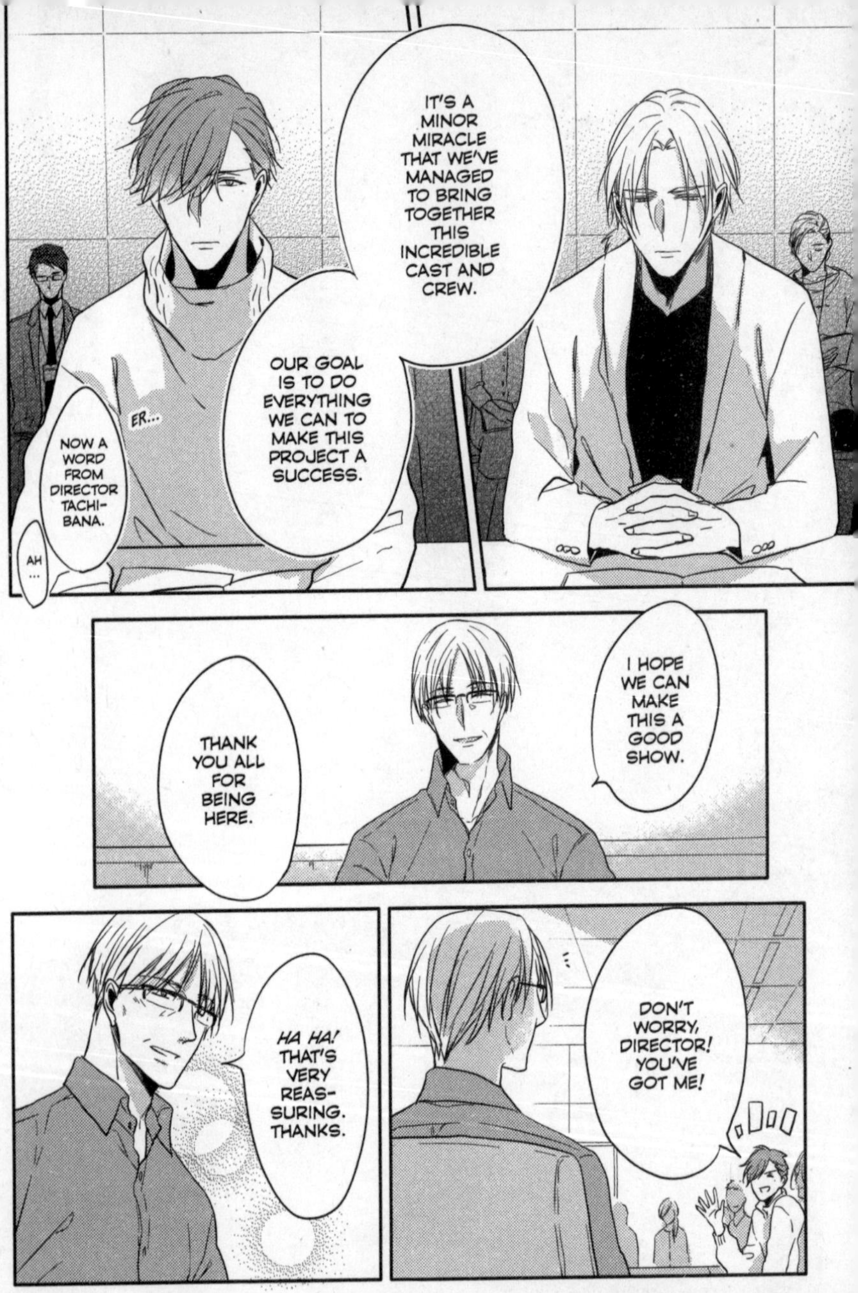
IT'S A MINOR MIRACLE THAT WE'VE MANAGED TO BRING TOGETHER THIS INCREDIBLE CAST AND CREW.
OUR GOAL IS TO DO EVERYTHING WE CAN TO MAKE THIS PROJECT A SUCCESS.
ER...
NOW A WORD FROM DIRECTOR TACHI-BANA.
AH ...
I HOPE WE CAN MAKE THIS A GOOD SHOW.
THANK YOU ALL FOR BEING HERE.
DON'T WORRY, DIRECTOR! YOU'VE GOT ME!
HA HA! THAT'S VERY REAS-SURING. THANKS.

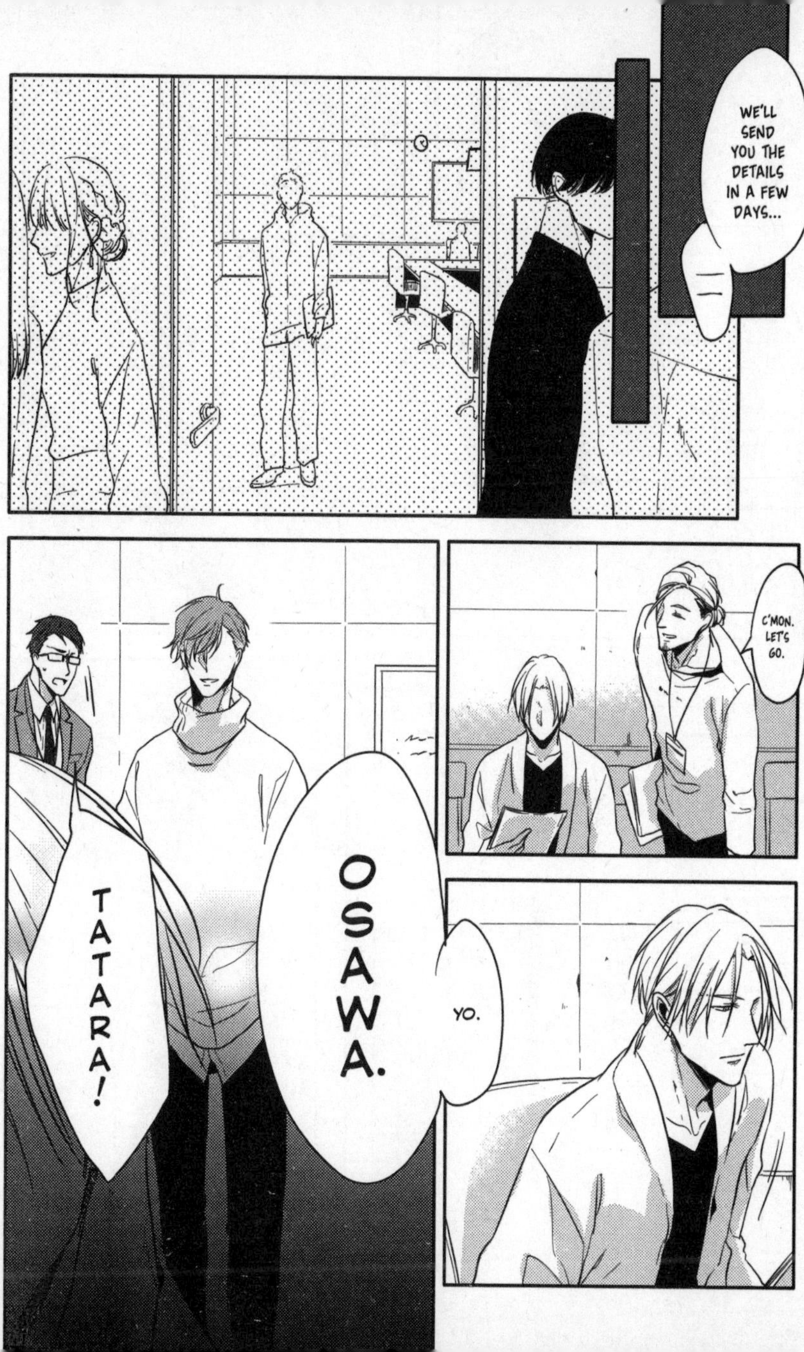
WE'LL SEND YOU THE DETAILS IN A FEW DAYS...
C'MON. LET'S GO.
YO.
OSAWA.
TATARA!

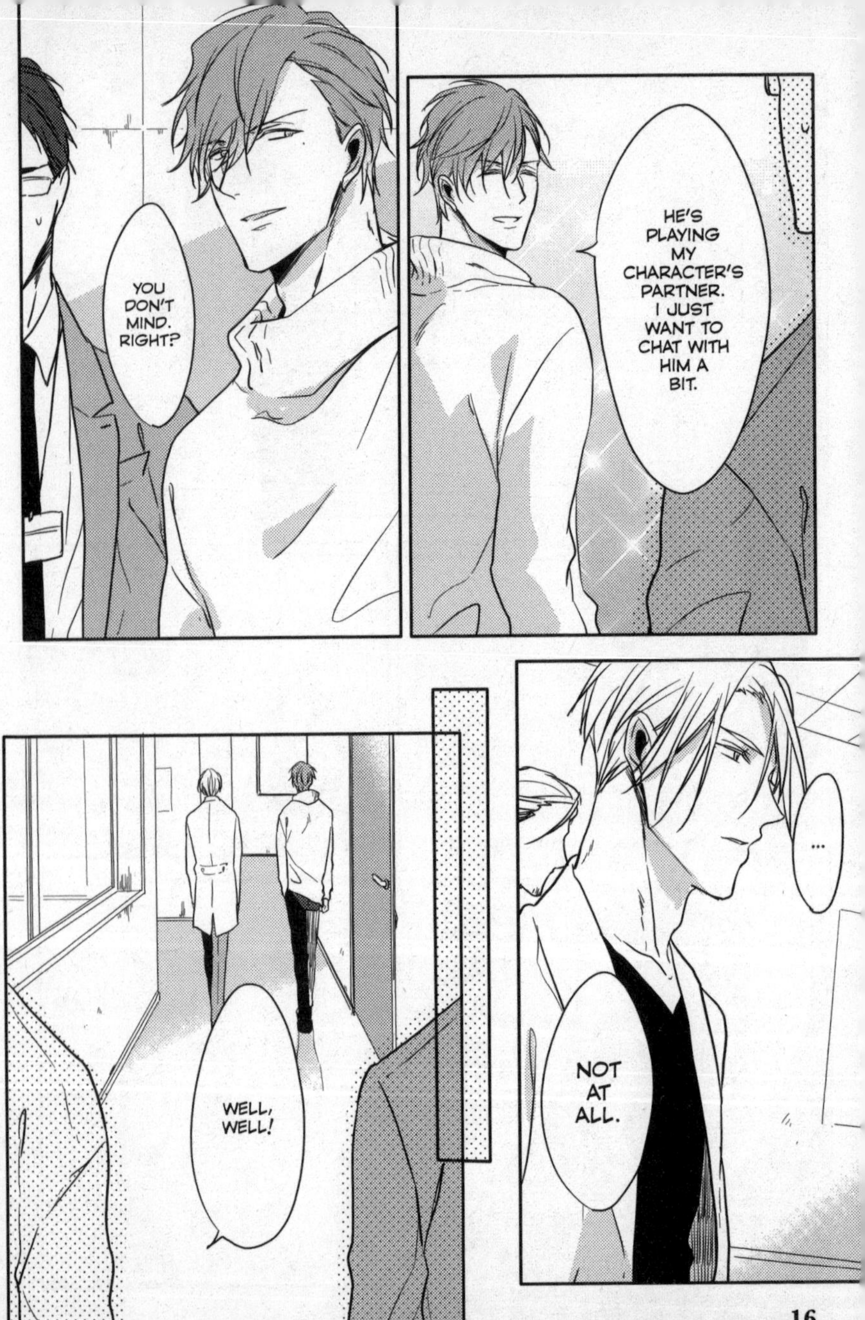
HE'S PLAYING MY CHARACTER'S PARTNER. I JUST WANT TO CHAT WITH HIM A BIT.
YOU DON'T MIND. RIGHT?
...
NOT AT ALL.
WELL, WELL!

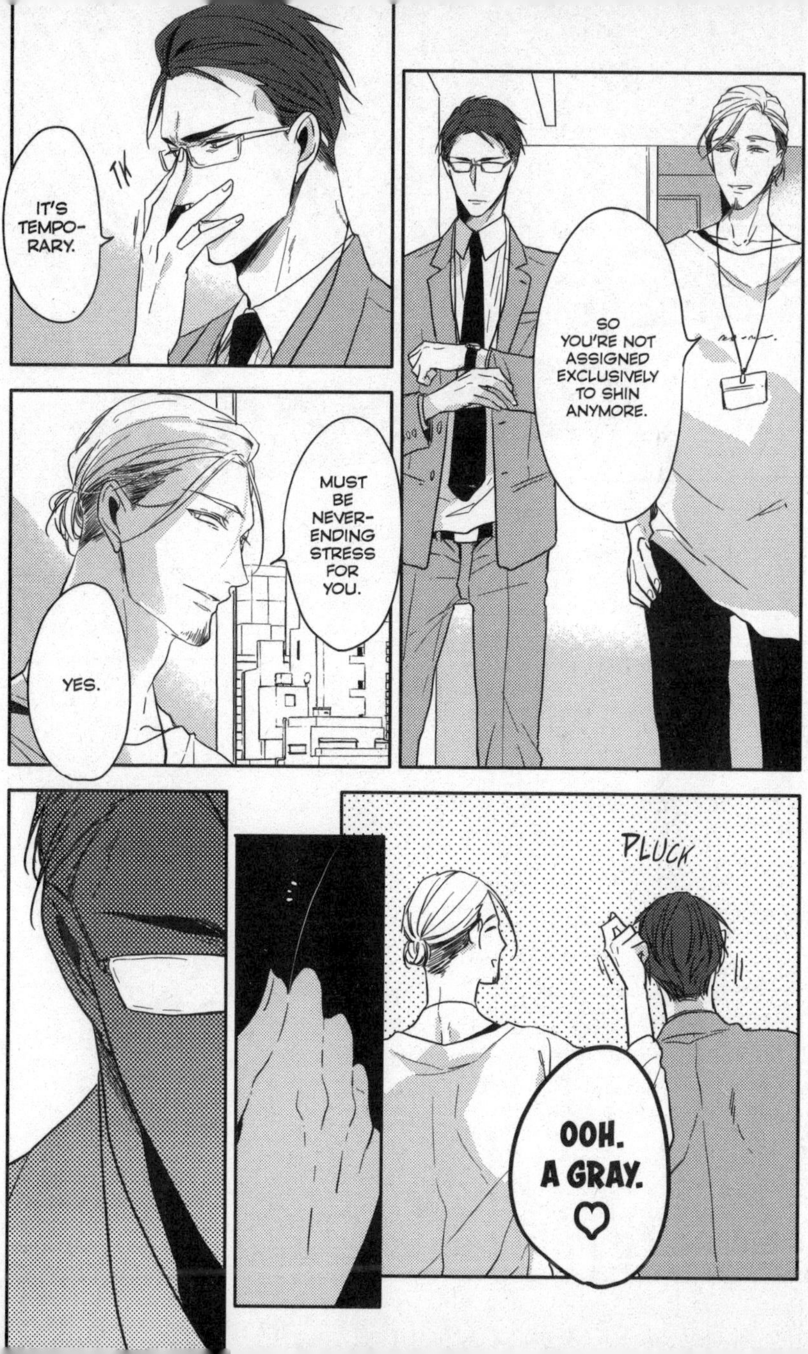
SO YOU'RE NOT ASSIGNED EXCLUSIVELY TO SHIN ANYMORE.
IT'S TEMPORARY.
TK
MUST BE NEVER-ENDING STRESS FOR YOU.
YES.
PLUCK
OOH. A GRAY. ♡
...

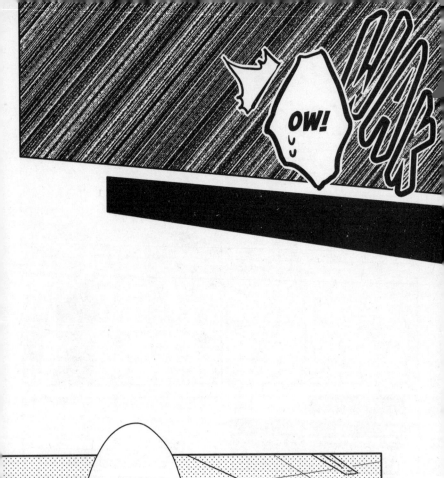

OW!

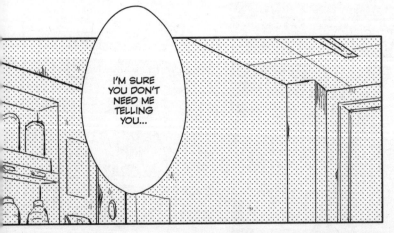

I'M SURE YOU DON'T NEED ME TELLING YOU...

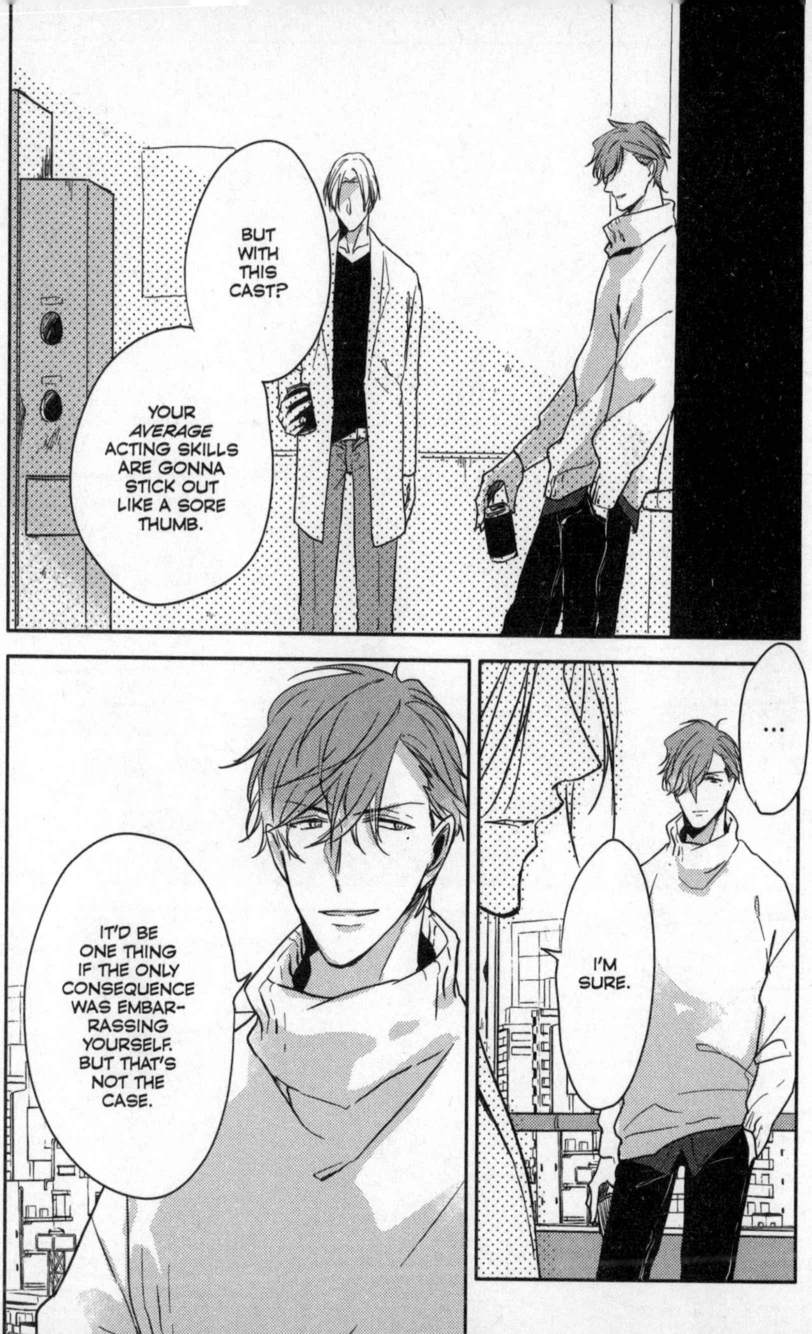
BUT WITH THIS CAST?
YOUR *AVERAGE* ACTING SKILLS ARE GONNA STICK OUT LIKE A SORE THUMB.
...
I'M SURE.
IT'D BE ONE THING IF THE ONLY CONSEQUENCE WAS EMBARRASSING YOURSELF. BUT THAT'S NOT THE CASE.

SEE...

Highest-Ra... TV Drama ...he Season Delinquent Detective.

o-and-Coming New St...

I OWE DIRECTOR TACHIBANA A DEBT OF GRATITUDE.

Tatara

THAT'S A HIGHLY PERSONAL REASON.

I'M NOT GOING TO LET THIS PROJECT FAIL.

YOU EVEN WENT AS FAR AS SWITCHING AGENCIES TO GET THIS PART?

I HEAR YOU'RE WITH ISE PRO NOW.

HAH!

CALL IT WHAT YOU WANT.

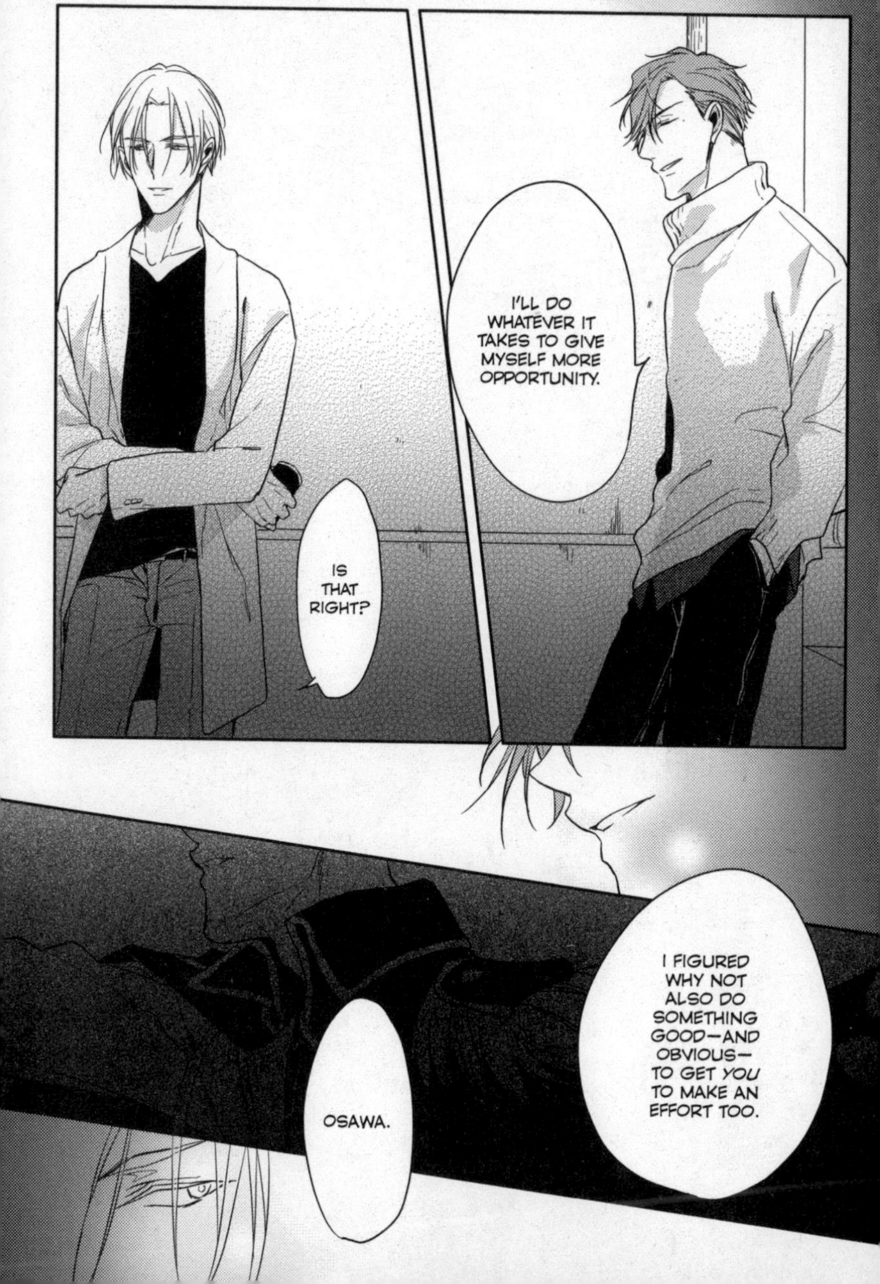
I'LL DO WHATEVER IT TAKES TO GIVE MYSELF MORE OPPORTUNITY.
IS THAT RIGHT?
I FIGURED WHY NOT ALSO DO SOMETHING GOOD—AND OBVIOUS—TO GET *YOU* TO MAKE AN EFFORT TOO.
OSAWA.

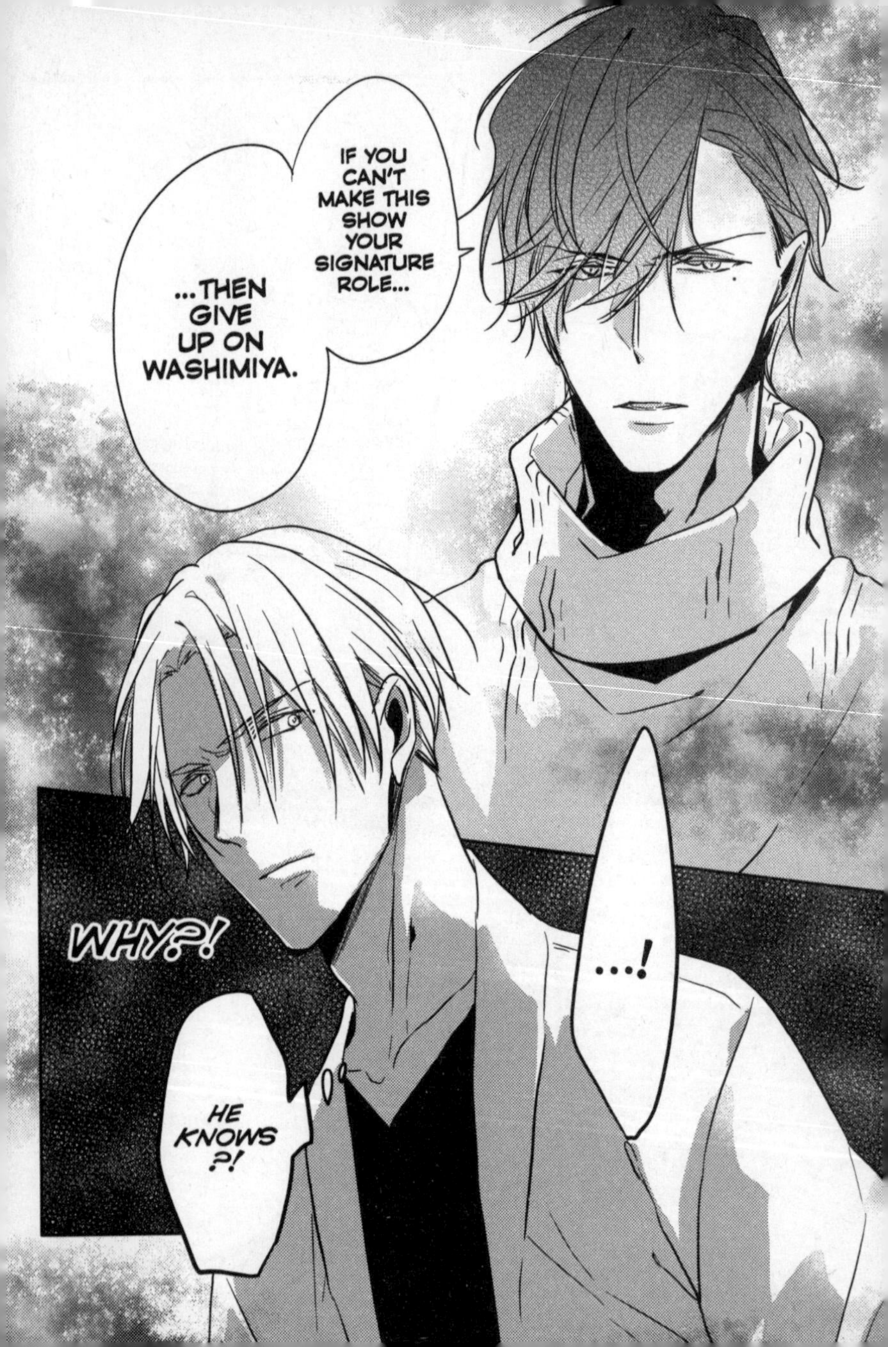
IF YOU CAN'T MAKE THIS SHOW YOUR SIGNATURE ROLE...
...THEN GIVE UP ON WASHIMIYA.
...!
WHY?!
HE KNOWS?!

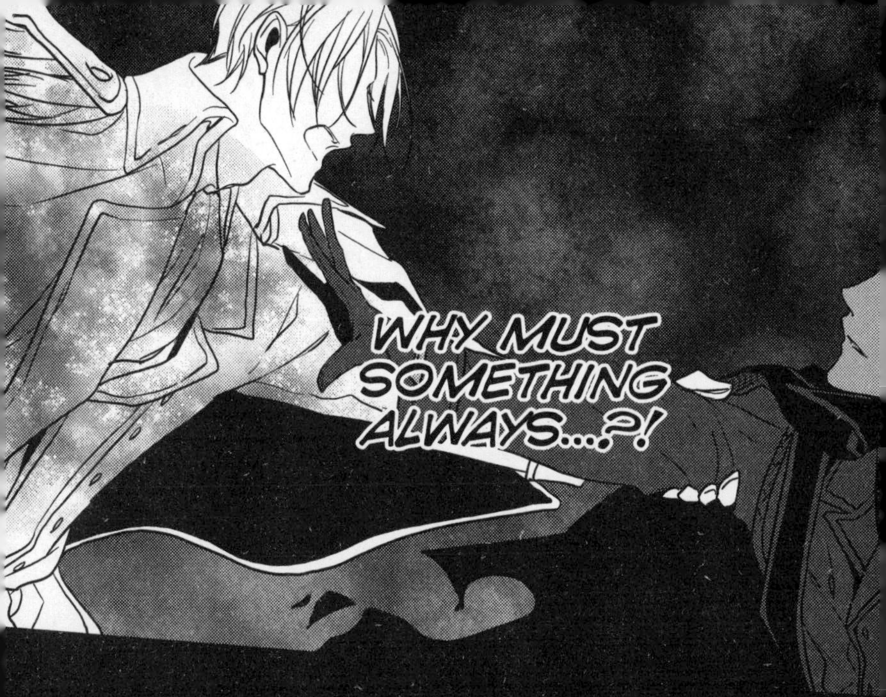
WHY MUST SOMETHING ALWAYS...?!
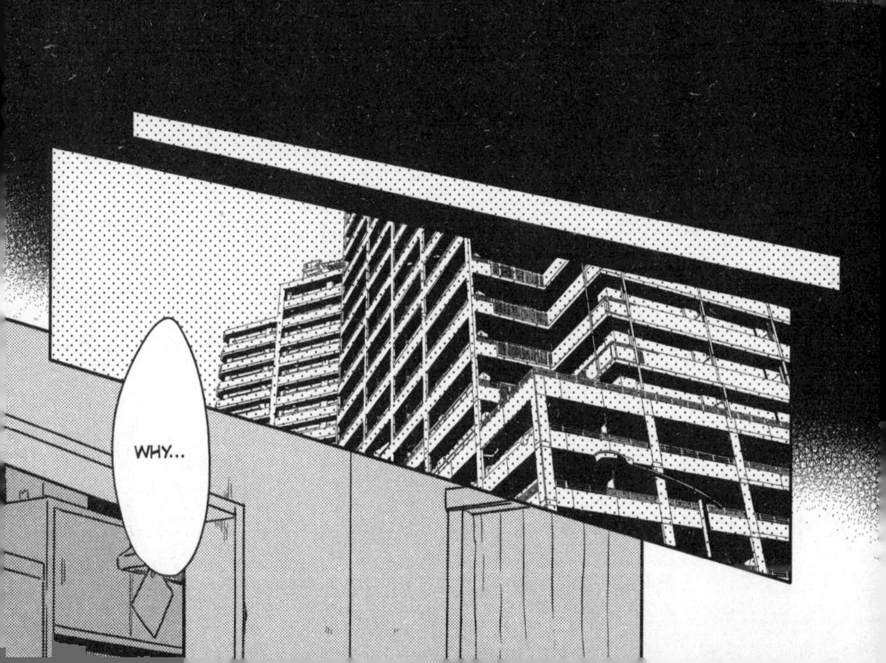
WHY...

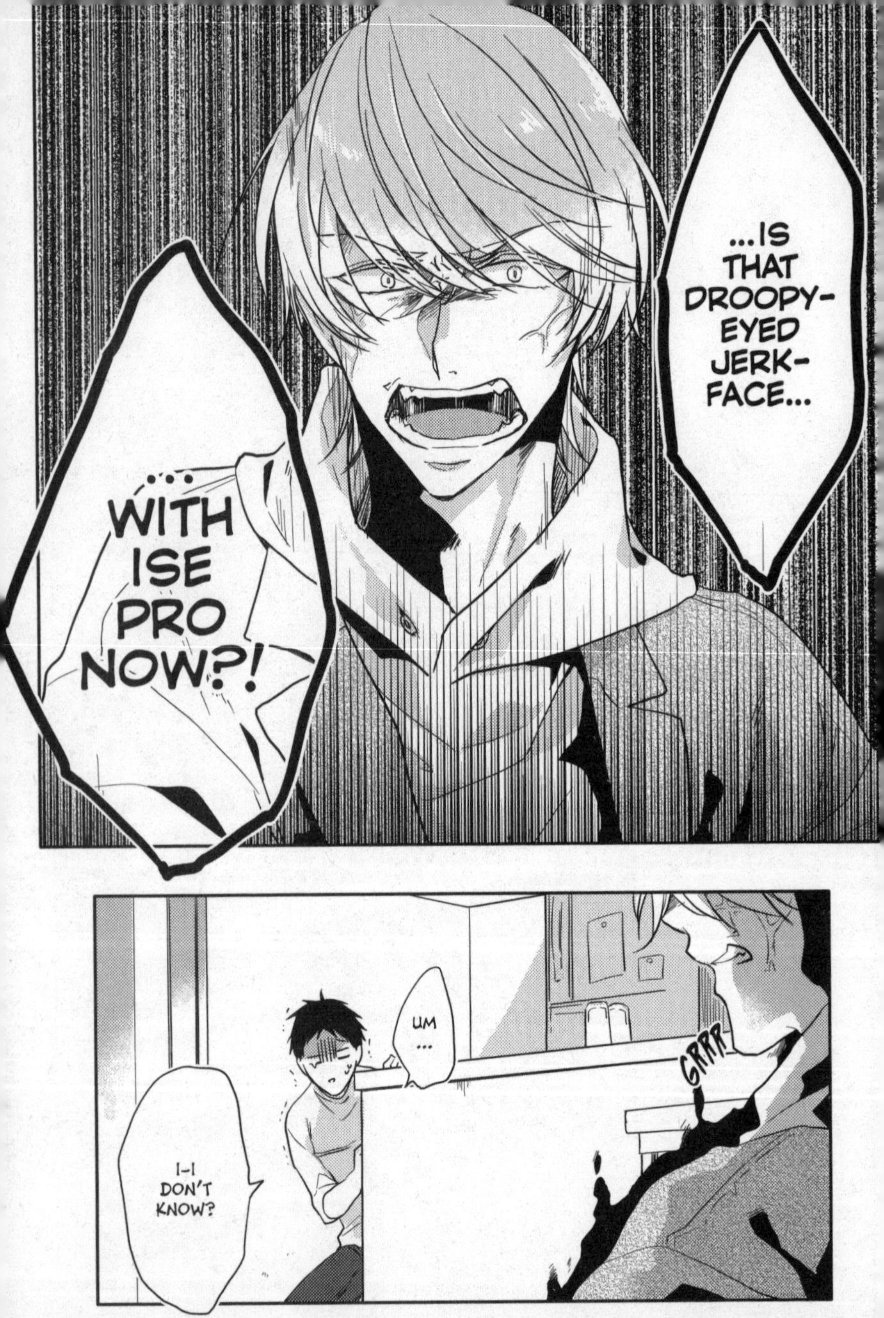
...IS THAT DROOPY-EYED JERK-FACE...
...WITH ISE PRO NOW?!
GRRR
UM ...
I-I DON'T KNOW?

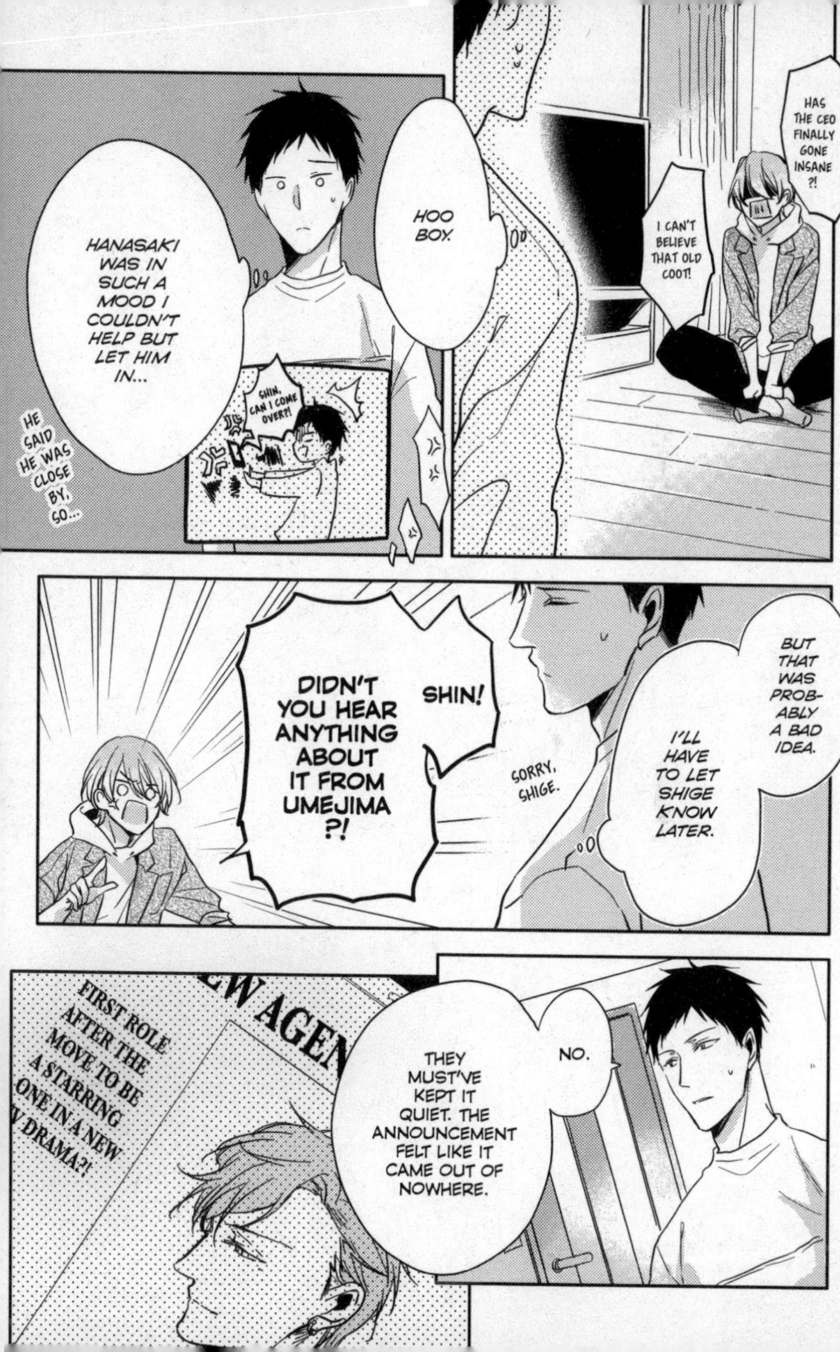
HAS THE CEO FINALLY GONE INSANE?!
I CAN'T BELIEVE THAT OLD COOT!
HOO BOY.
HANASAKI WAS IN SUCH A MOOD I COULDN'T HELP BUT LET HIM IN...
SHIN, CAN I COME OVER?!
HE SAID HE WAS CLOSE BY, SO...
BUT THAT WAS PROBABLY A BAD IDEA.
I'LL HAVE TO LET SHIGE KNOW LATER.
SORRY, SHIGE.
SHIN!
DIDN'T YOU HEAR ANYTHING ABOUT IT FROM UMEJIMA?!
NO.
THEY MUST'VE KEPT IT QUIET. THE ANNOUNCEMENT FELT LIKE IT CAME OUT OF NOWHERE.
EW AGEN
FIRST ROLE AFTER THE MOVE TO BE A STARRING ONE IN A NEW W DRAMA?!

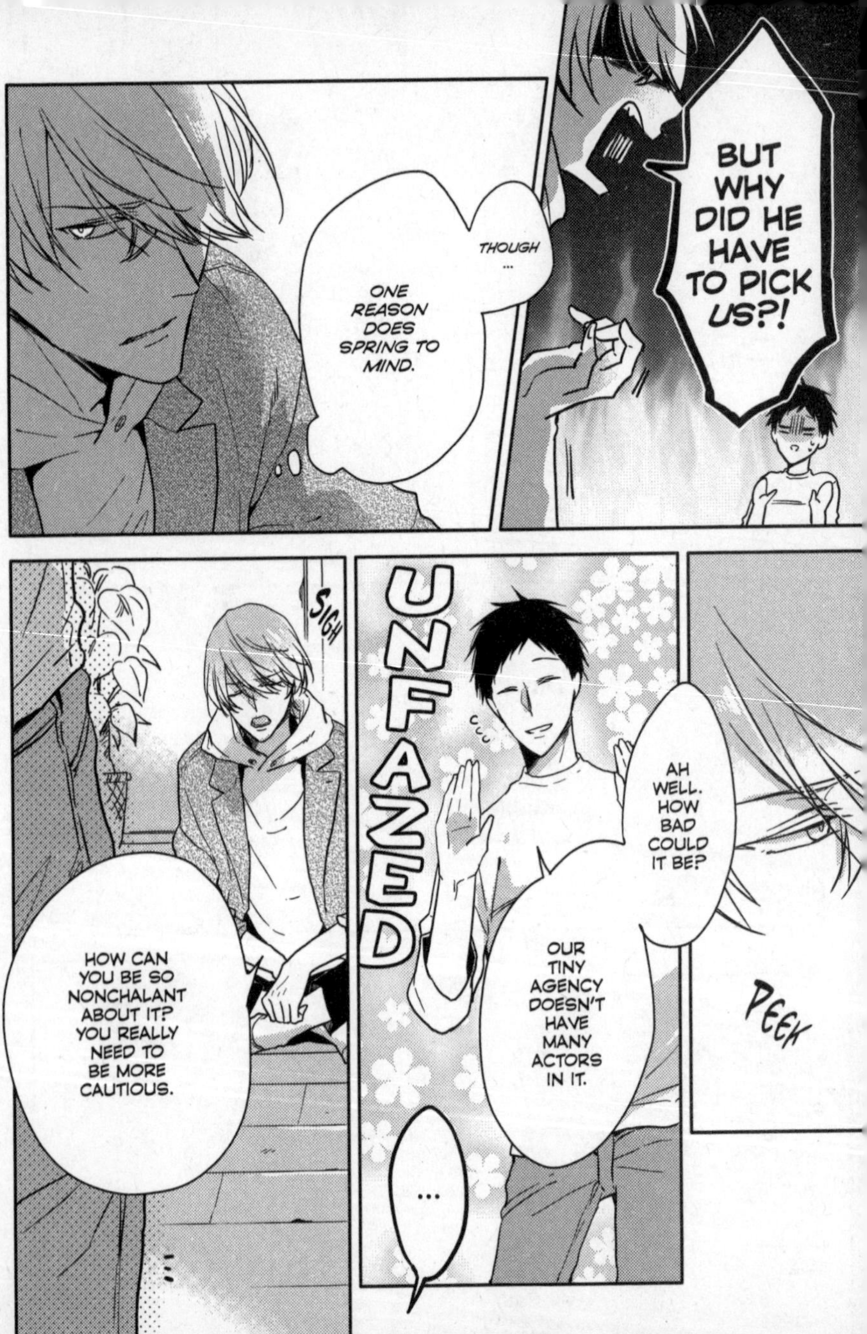
BUT WHY DID HE HAVE TO PICK US?!
THOUGH ...
ONE REASON DOES SPRING TO MIND.
PEEK
UNFAZED
AH WELL. HOW BAD COULD IT BE?
OUR TINY AGENCY DOESN'T HAVE MANY ACTORS IN IT.
...
SIGH
HOW CAN YOU BE SO NONCHALANT ABOUT IT? YOU REALLY NEED TO BE MORE CAUTIOUS.
...

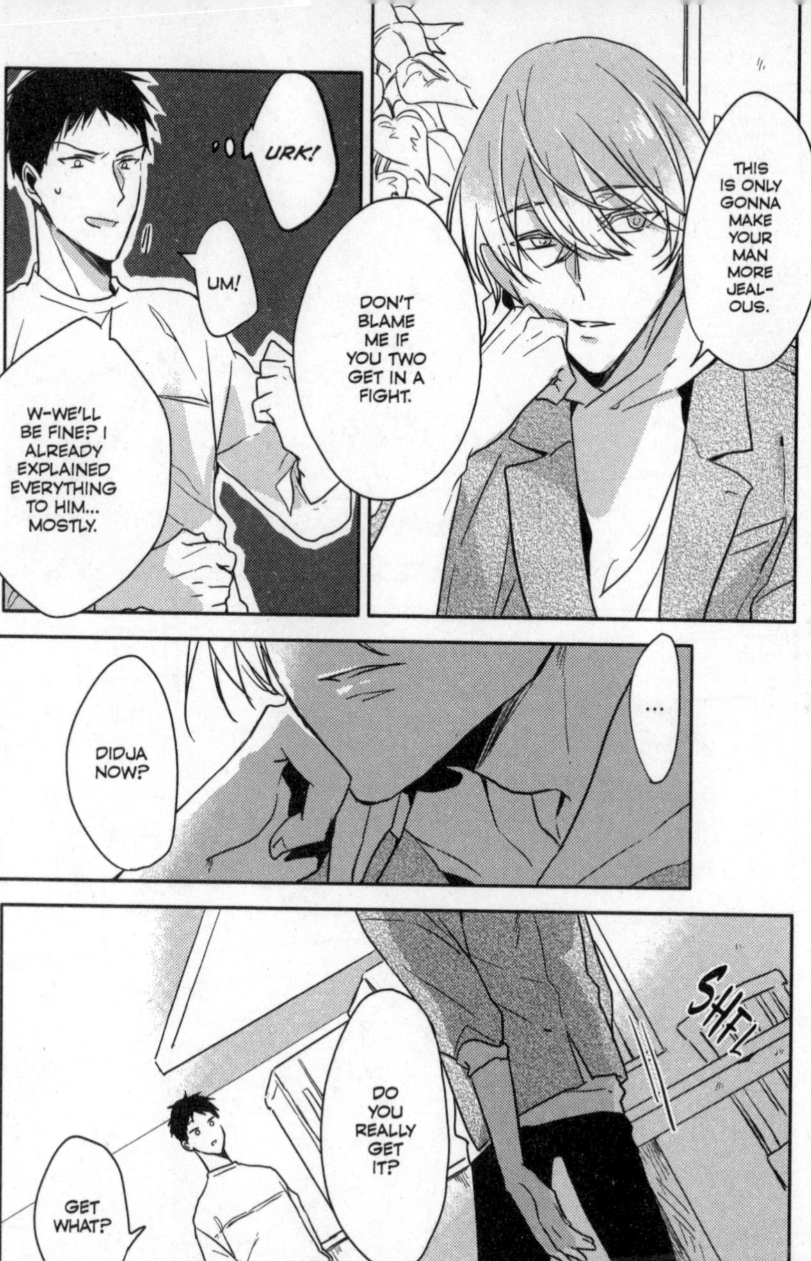
THIS IS ONLY GONNA MAKE YOUR MAN MORE JEAL-OUS.
DON'T BLAME ME IF YOU TWO GET IN A FIGHT.
URK!
UM!
W-WE'LL BE FINE? I ALREADY EXPLAINED EVERYTHING TO HIM... MOSTLY.
...
DIDJA NOW?
SHFL
DO YOU REALLY GET IT?
GET WHAT?

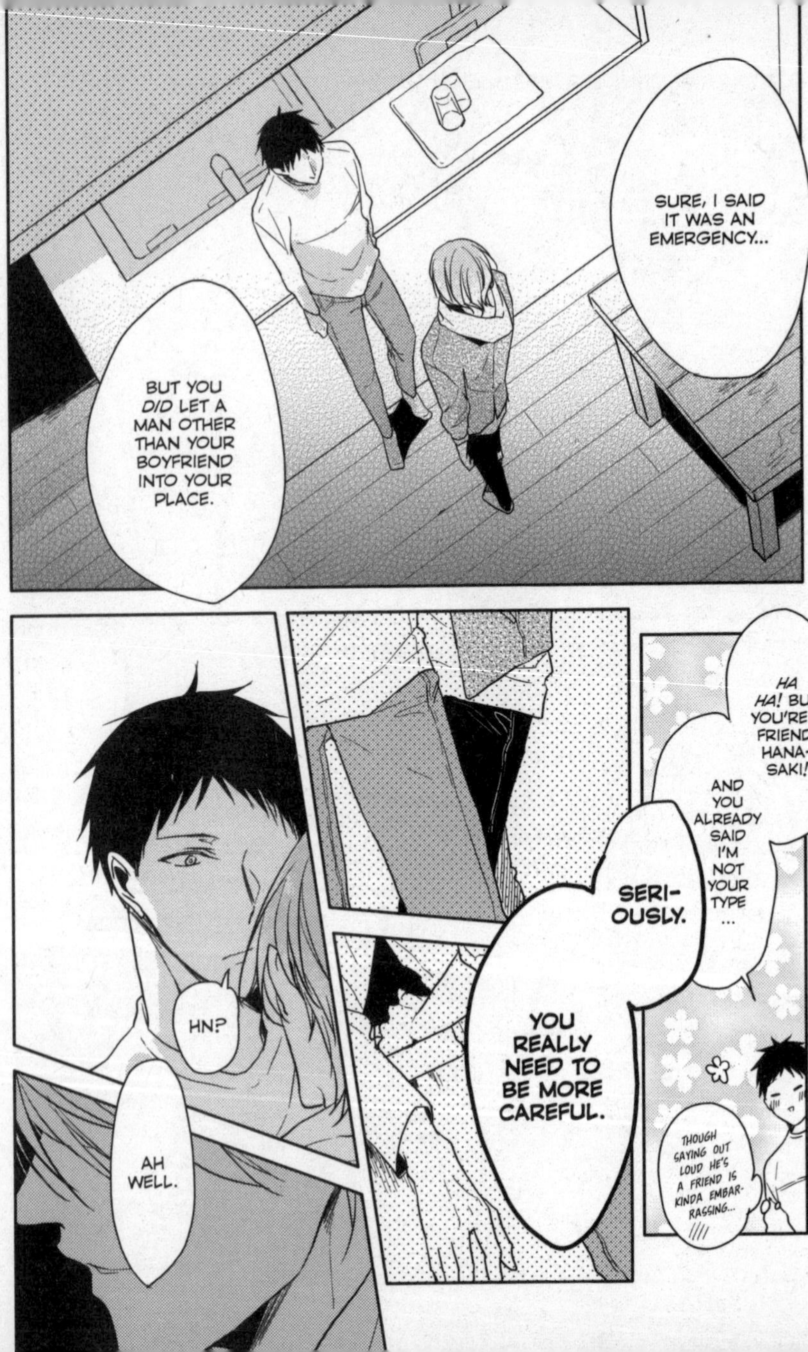
SURE, I SAID IT WAS AN EMERGENCY...
BUT YOU *DID* LET A MAN OTHER THAN YOUR BOYFRIEND INTO YOUR PLACE.
HA HA! BUT YOU'RE A FRIEND, HANA-SAKI!
AND YOU ALREADY SAID I'M NOT YOUR TYPE ...
THOUGH SAYING OUT LOUD HE'S A FRIEND IS KINDA EMBARRASSING...
SERI-OUSLY.
YOU REALLY NEED TO BE MORE CAREFUL.
HN?
AH WELL.

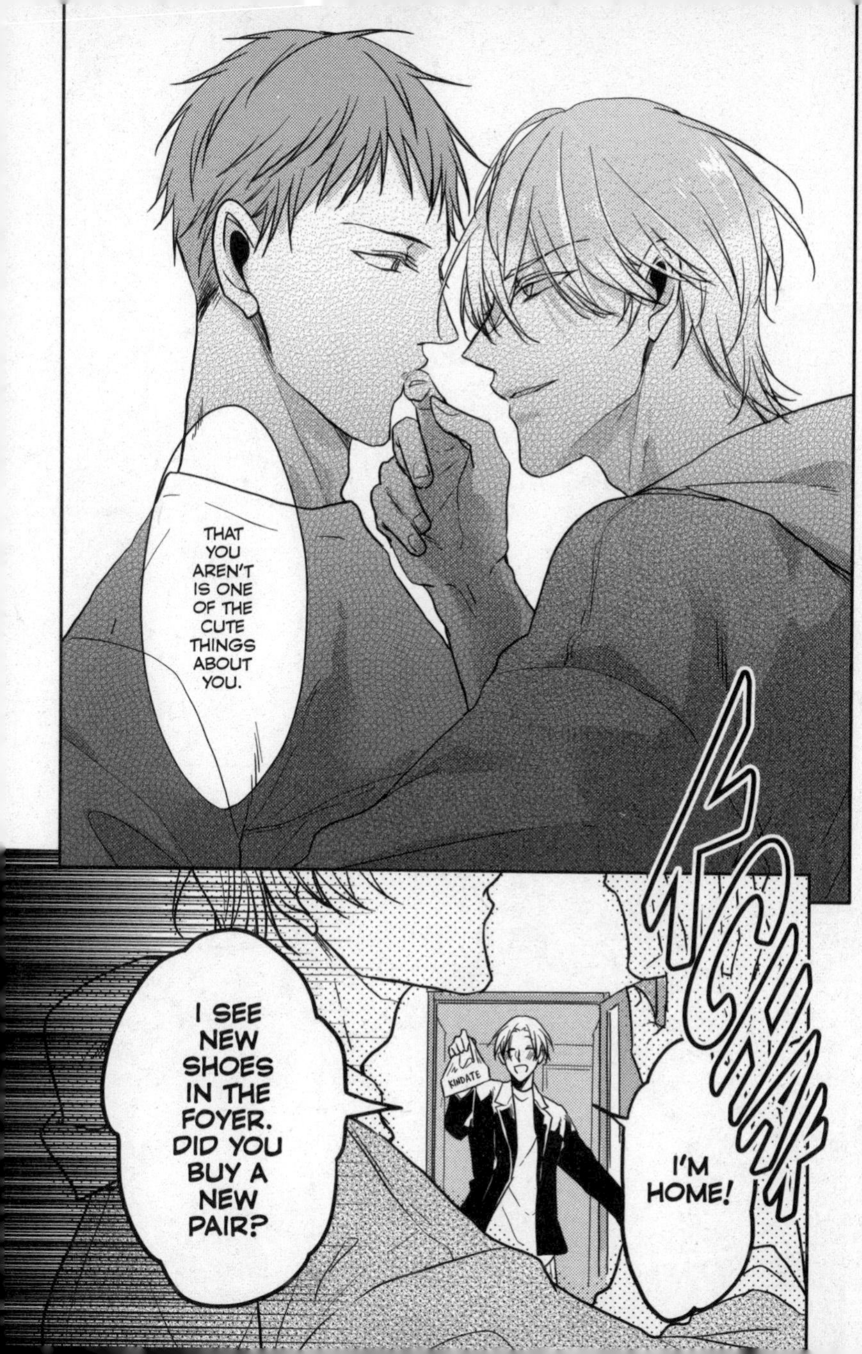
THAT YOU AREN'T IS ONE OF THE CUTE THINGS ABOUT YOU.
KCHAK
I'M HOME!
KINDATE
I SEE NEW SHOES IN THE FOYER. DID YOU BUY A NEW PAIR?

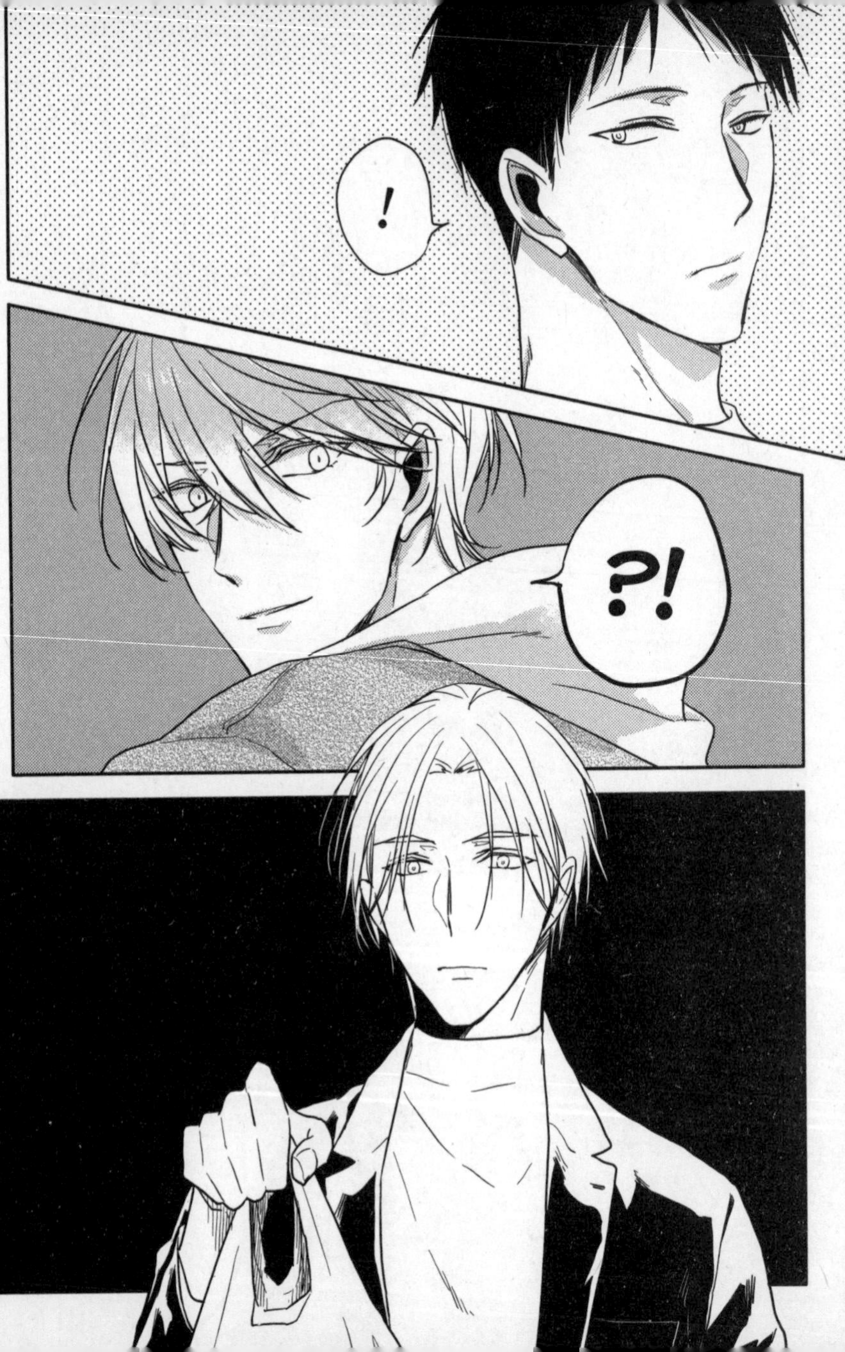
!
?!

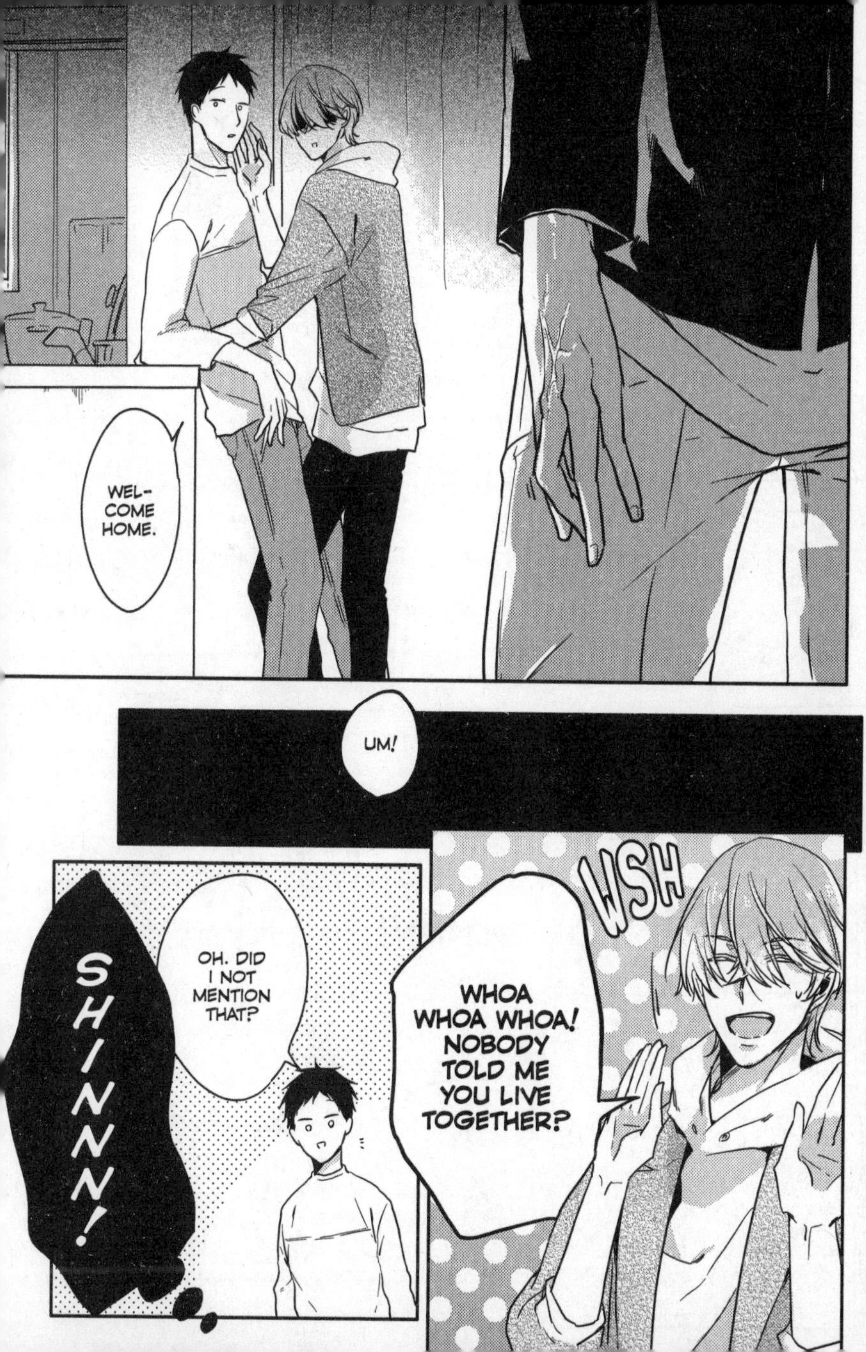
WEL-COME HOME.
UM!
WSH
WHOA WHOA WHOA! NOBODY TOLD ME YOU LIVE TOGETHER?
OH. DID I NOT MENTION THAT?
SHINNN!

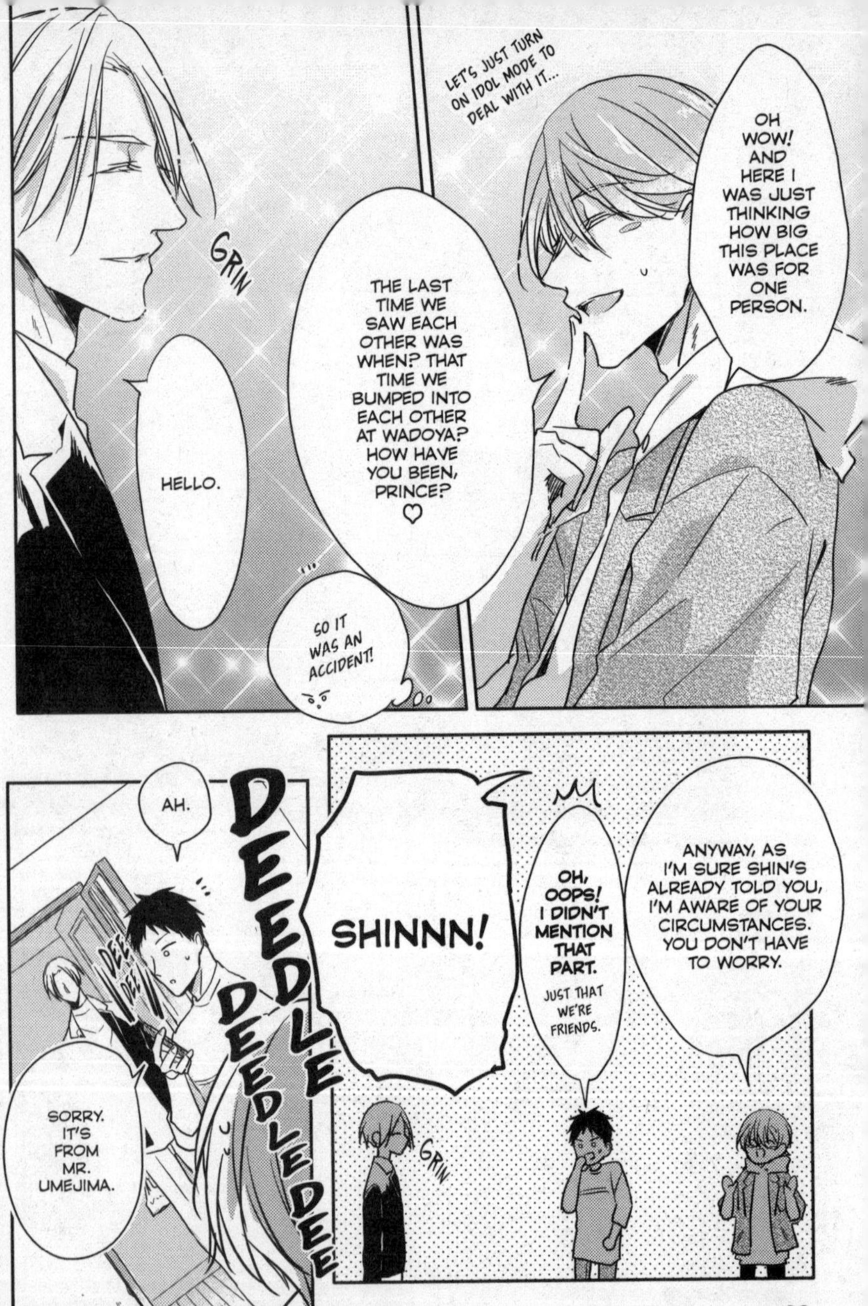
LET'S JUST TURN ON IDOL MODE TO DEAL WITH IT...
OH WOW! AND HERE I WAS JUST THINKING HOW BIG THIS PLACE WAS FOR ONE PERSON.
GRIN
HELLO.
THE LAST TIME WE SAW EACH OTHER WAS WHEN? THAT TIME WE BUMPED INTO EACH OTHER AT WADOYA? HOW HAVE YOU BEEN, PRINCE? ♡
SO IT WAS AN ACCIDENT!
ANYWAY, AS I'M SURE SHIN'S ALREADY TOLD YOU, I'M AWARE OF YOUR CIRCUMSTANCES. YOU DON'T HAVE TO WORRY.
OH, OOPS! I DIDN'T MENTION THAT PART.
JUST THAT WE'RE FRIENDS.
GRIN
SHINNN!
AH.
DEE DEE
DEEDLE DEEDLEDEE
SORRY. IT'S FROM MR. UMEJIMA.

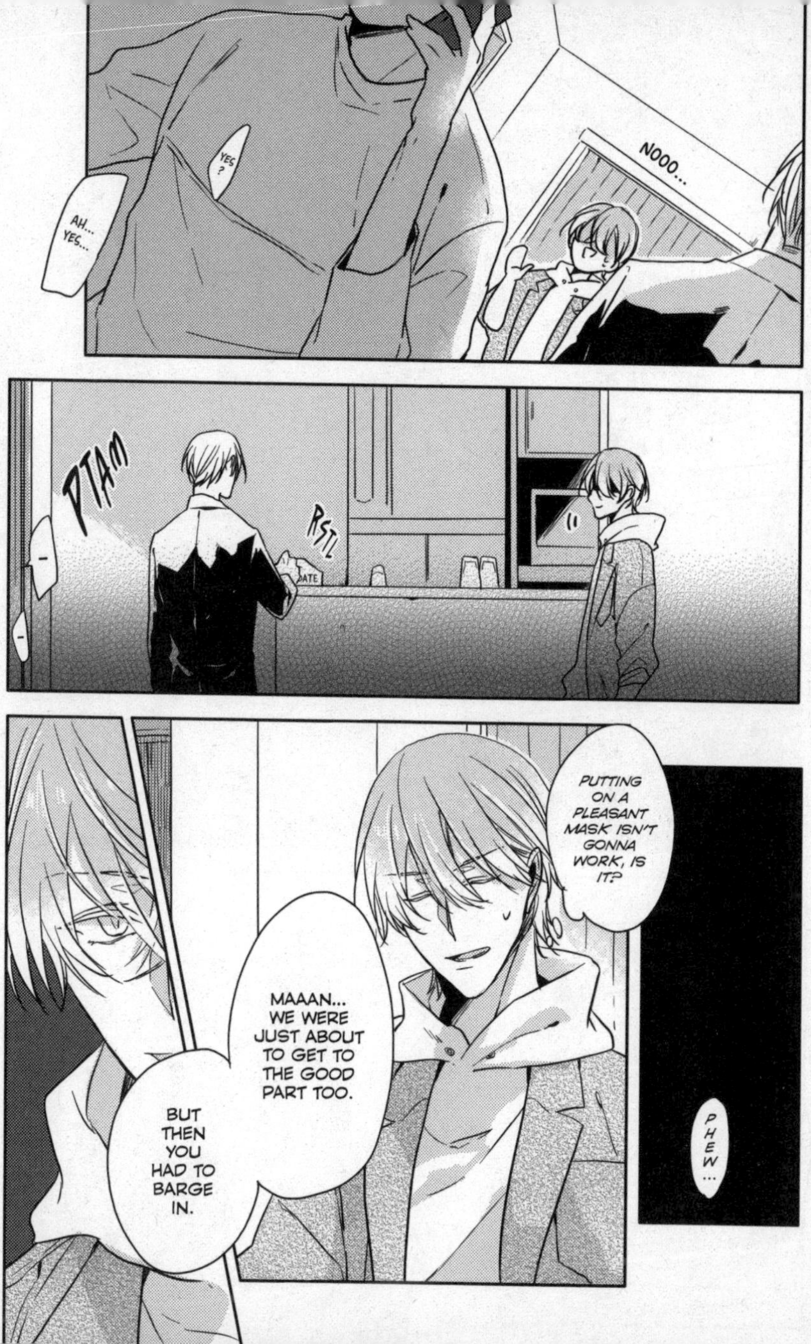
NOOO...
YES?
AH... YES...
RSTL
PTAM
PHEW...
PUTTING ON A PLEASANT MASK ISN'T GONNA WORK, IS IT?
MAAAN... WE WERE JUST ABOUT TO GET TO THE GOOD PART TOO.
BUT THEN YOU HAD TO BARGE IN.

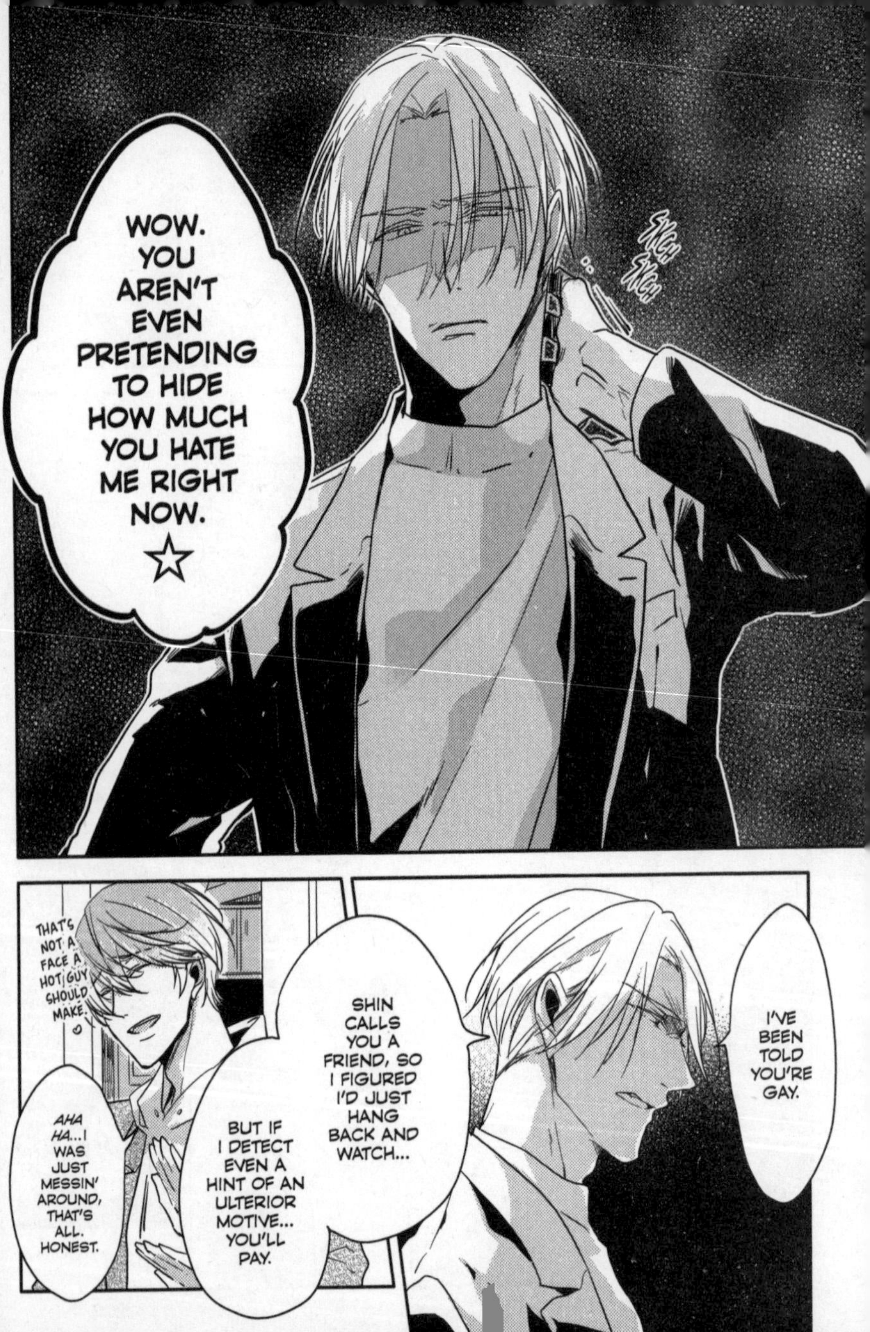
WOW. YOU AREN'T EVEN PRETENDING TO HIDE HOW MUCH YOU HATE ME RIGHT NOW. ☆
I'VE BEEN TOLD YOU'RE GAY.
SHIN CALLS YOU A FRIEND, SO I FIGURED I'D JUST HANG BACK AND WATCH...
BUT IF I DETECT EVEN A HINT OF AN ULTERIOR MOTIVE... YOU'LL PAY.
THAT'S NOT A FACE A HOT GUY SHOULD MAKE.
AHA HA...I WAS JUST MESSIN' AROUND, THAT'S ALL. HONEST.

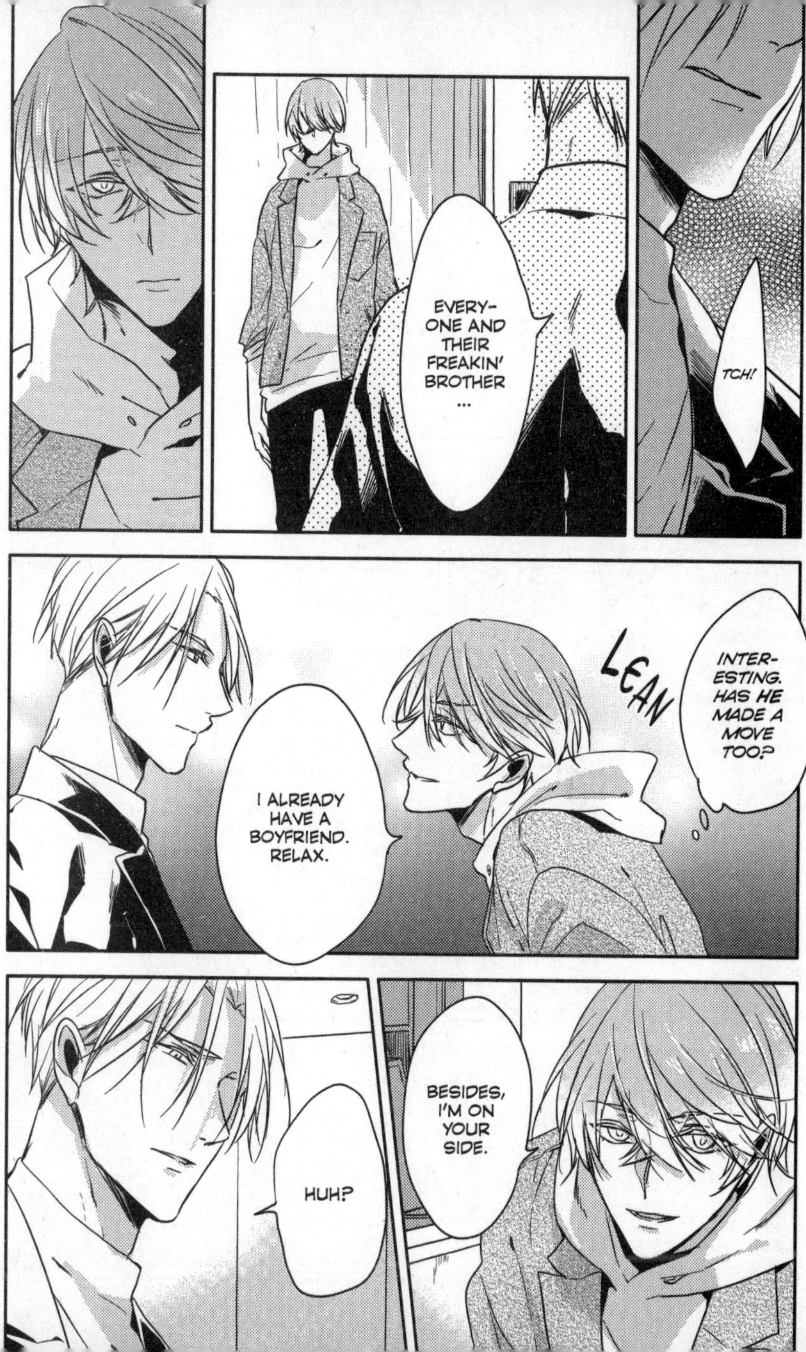
TCH!
EVERY-ONE AND THEIR FREAKIN' BROTHER ...
INTER-ESTING. HAS HE MADE A MOVE TOO?
LEAN
I ALREADY HAVE A BOYFRIEND. RELAX.
BESIDES, I'M ON YOUR SIDE.
HUH?

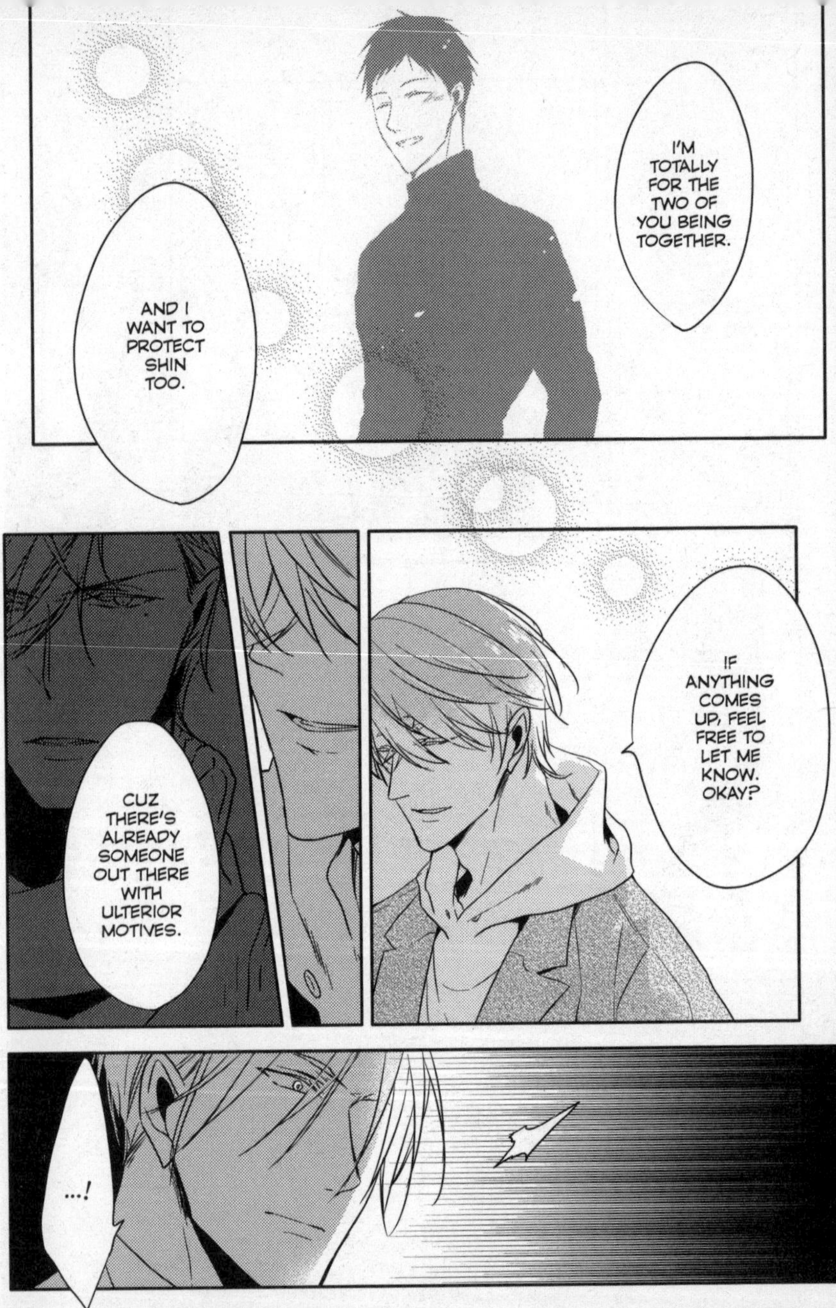
I'M TOTALLY FOR THE TWO OF YOU BEING TOGETHER.
AND I WANT TO PROTECT SHIN TOO.
IF ANYTHING COMES UP, FEEL FREE TO LET ME KNOW. OKAY?
CUZ THERE'S ALREADY SOMEONE OUT THERE WITH ULTERIOR MOTIVES.
...!

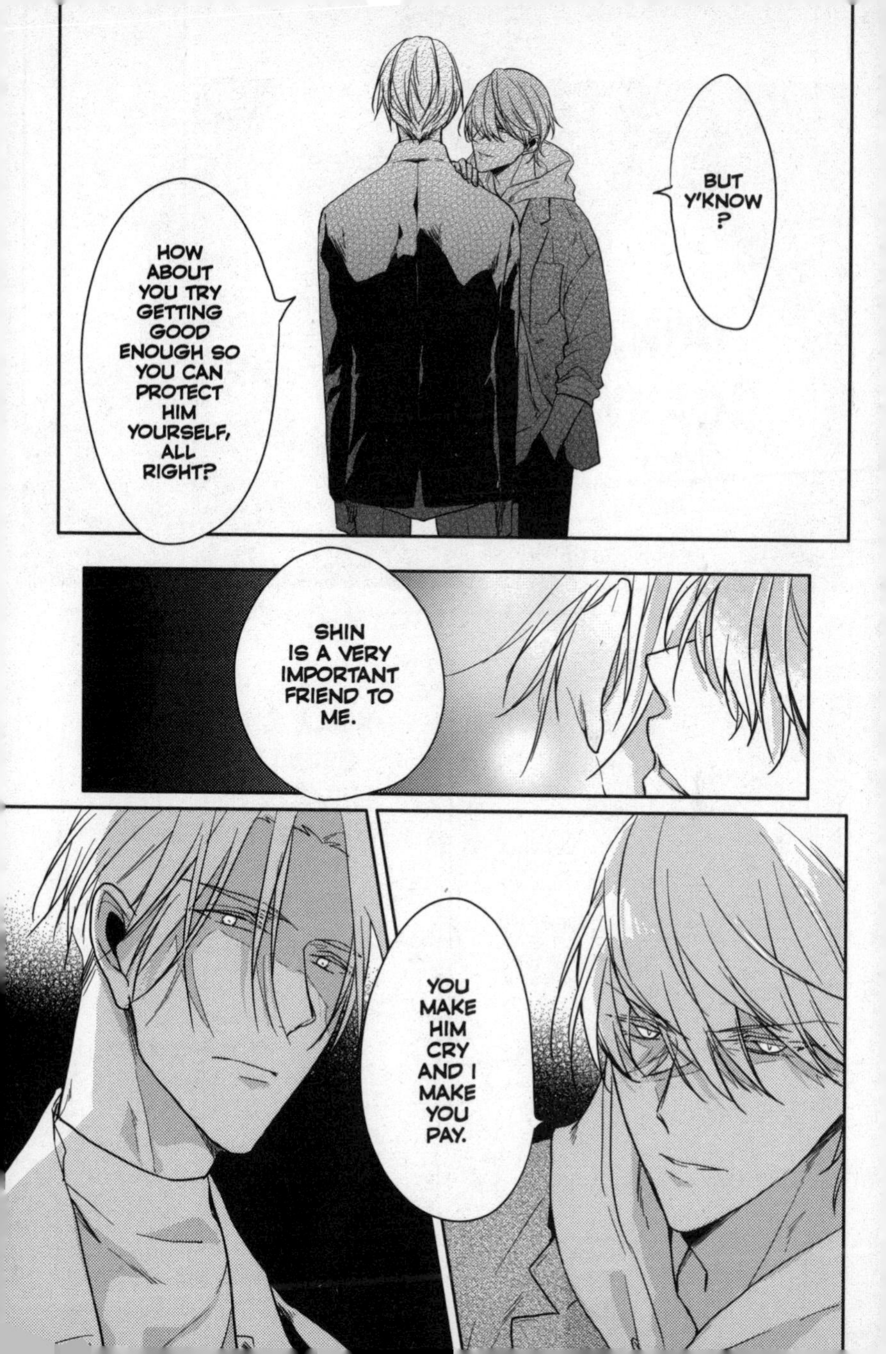
BUT Y'KNOW?
HOW ABOUT YOU TRY GETTING GOOD ENOUGH SO YOU CAN PROTECT HIM YOURSELF, ALL RIGHT?
SHIN IS A VERY IMPORTANT FRIEND TO ME.
YOU MAKE HIM CRY AND I MAKE YOU PAY.

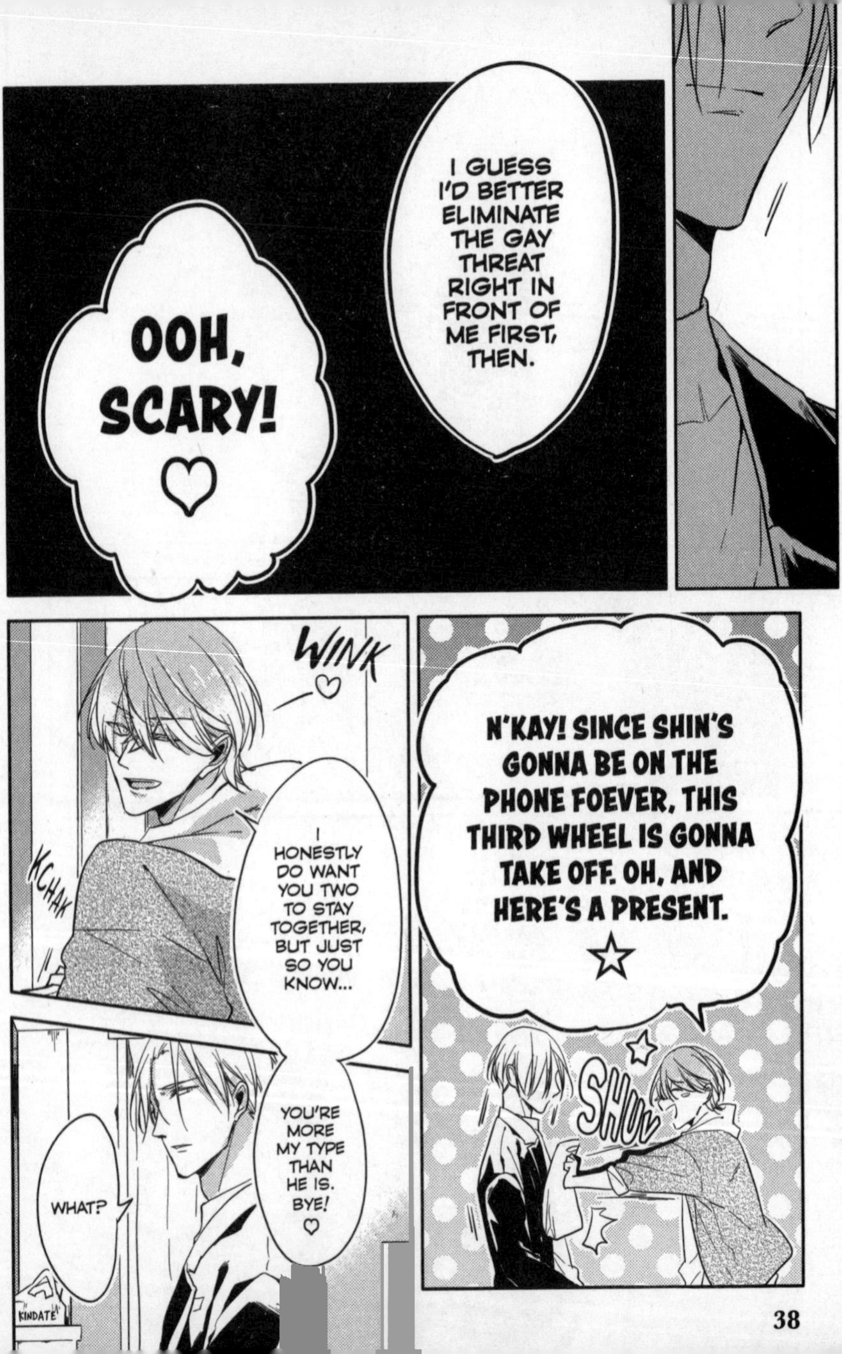

I GUESS I'D BETTER ELIMINATE THE GAY THREAT RIGHT IN FRONT OF ME FIRST, THEN.
OOH, SCARY! ♡
N'KAY! SINCE SHIN'S GONNA BE ON THE PHONE FOEVER, THIS THIRD WHEEL IS GONNA TAKE OFF. OH, AND HERE'S A PRESENT. ☆
SHUV
WINK ♡
KCHAK
I HONESTLY DO WANT YOU TWO TO STAY TOGETHER, BUT JUST SO YOU KNOW...
YOU'RE MORE MY TYPE THAN HE IS. BYE! ♡
WHAT?
KINDATE

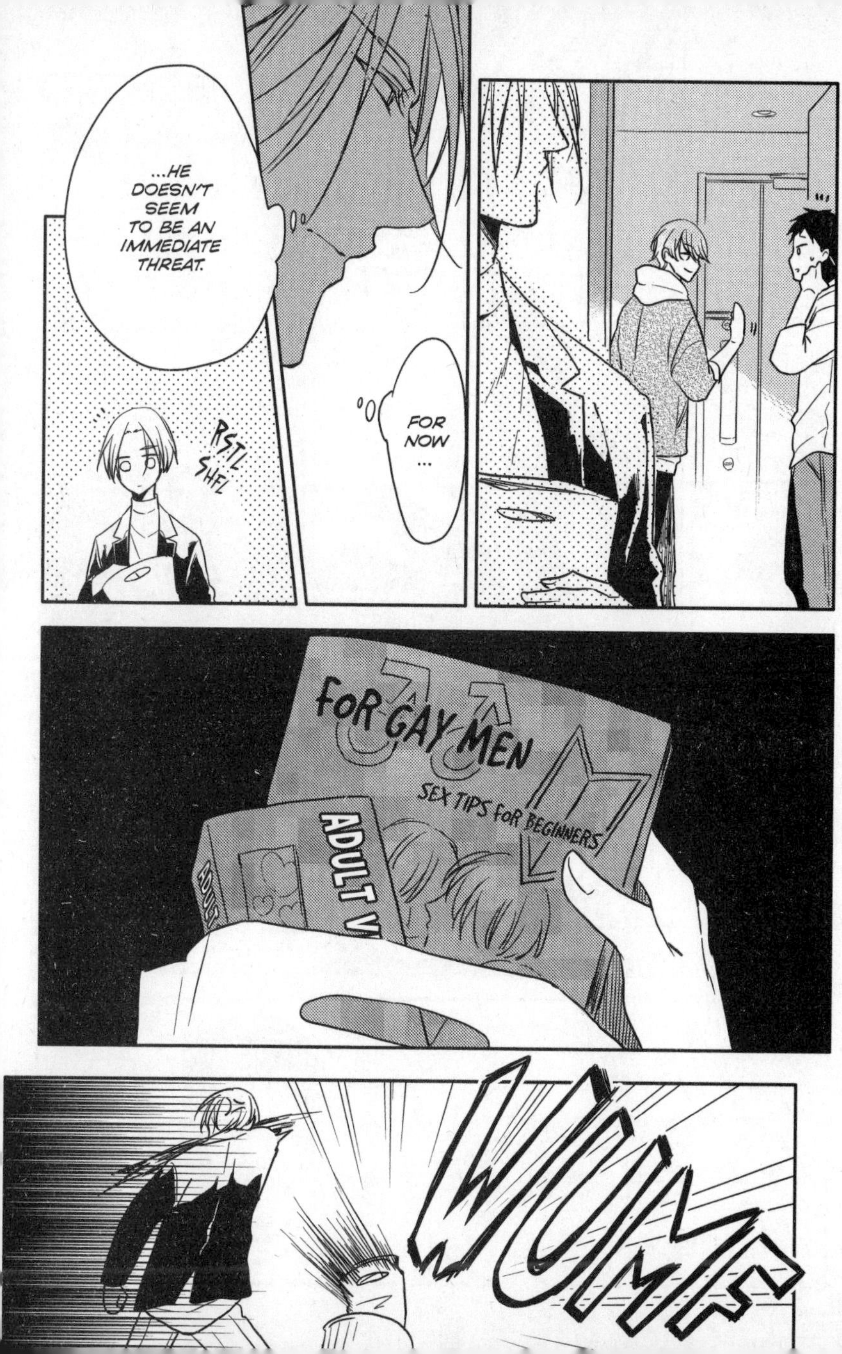
...HE DOESN'T SEEM TO BE AN IMMEDIATE THREAT.
FOR NOW ...
RSTL SHFL
FOR GAY MEN
SEX TIPS FOR BEGINNERS
ADULT V
WOMF

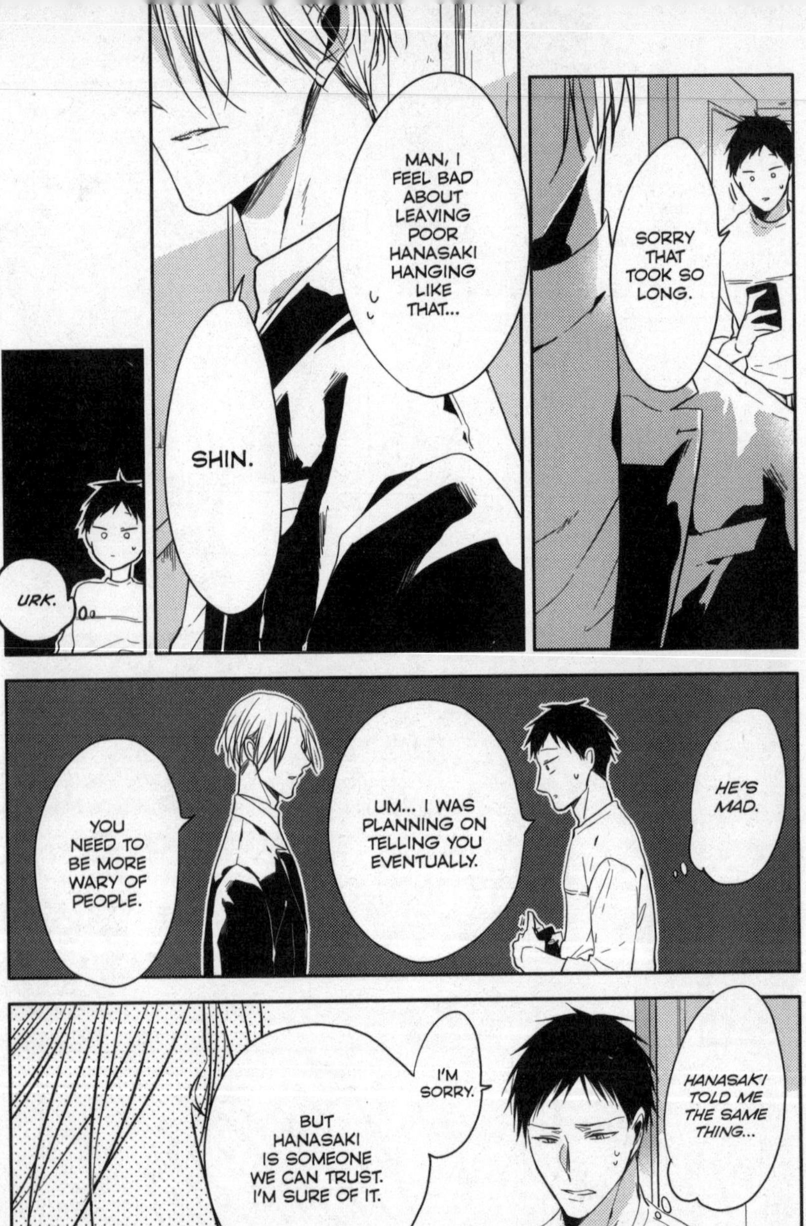
SORRY THAT TOOK SO LONG.
MAN, I FEEL BAD ABOUT LEAVING POOR HANASAKI HANGING LIKE THAT...
SHIN.
URK.
HE'S MAD.
UM... I WAS PLANNING ON TELLING YOU EVENTUALLY.
YOU NEED TO BE MORE WARY OF PEOPLE.
HANASAKI TOLD ME THE SAME THING...
I'M SORRY.
BUT HANASAKI IS SOMEONE WE CAN TRUST. I'M SURE OF IT.

AND THAT'S WHY YOU WENT TO HIM FOR ADVICE ON SEX?

HUH ?!

SO YOU REALLY DID ASK HIM FOR ADVICE.

UM! I-I, UH... WELL...

I'M SORRY.

I DON'T FORGIVE YOU.

I KNOW... WAIT, HUH?

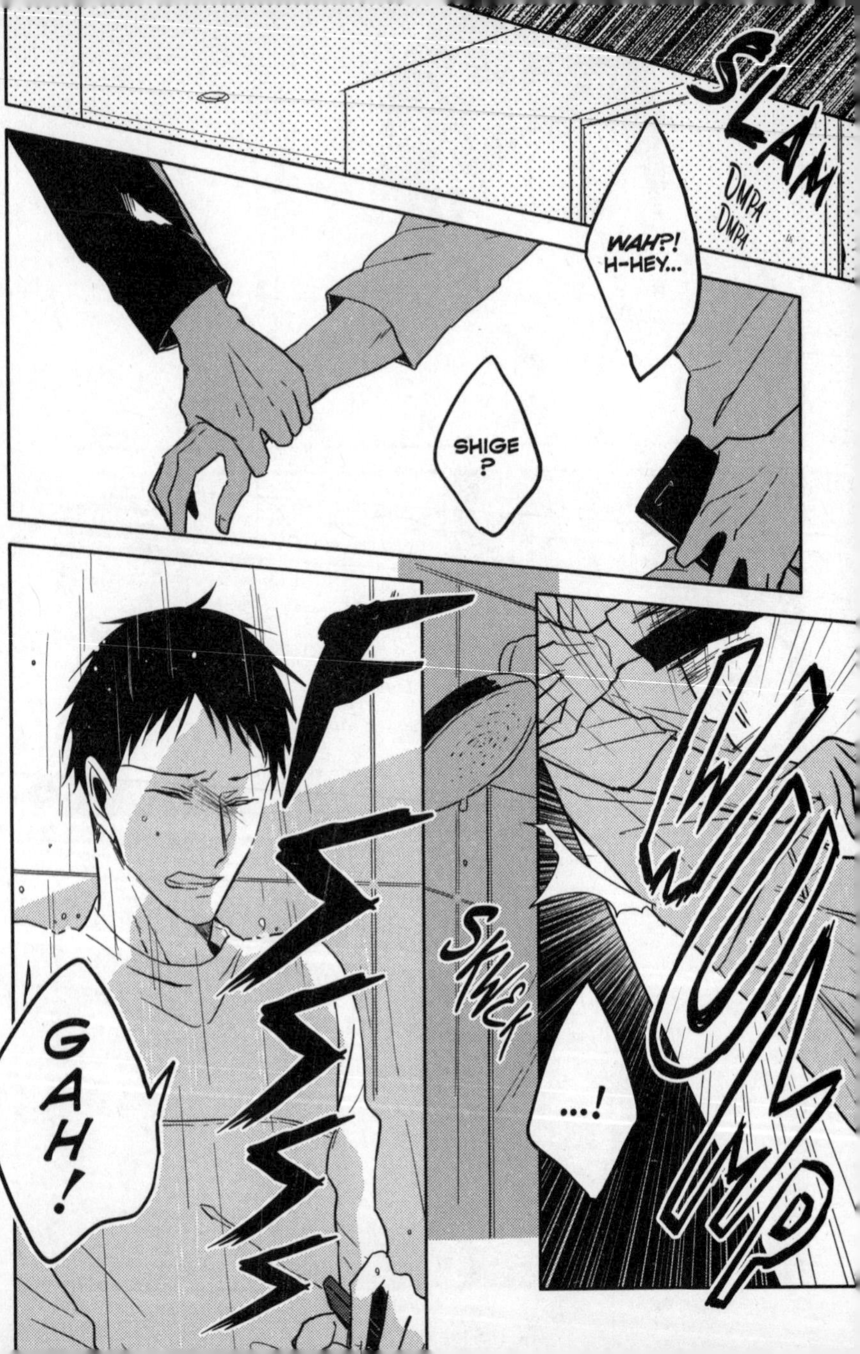
SLAM
DMPA DMPA
WAH?! H-HEY...
SHIGE?
WUMP
...!
SKWEK
GAH!

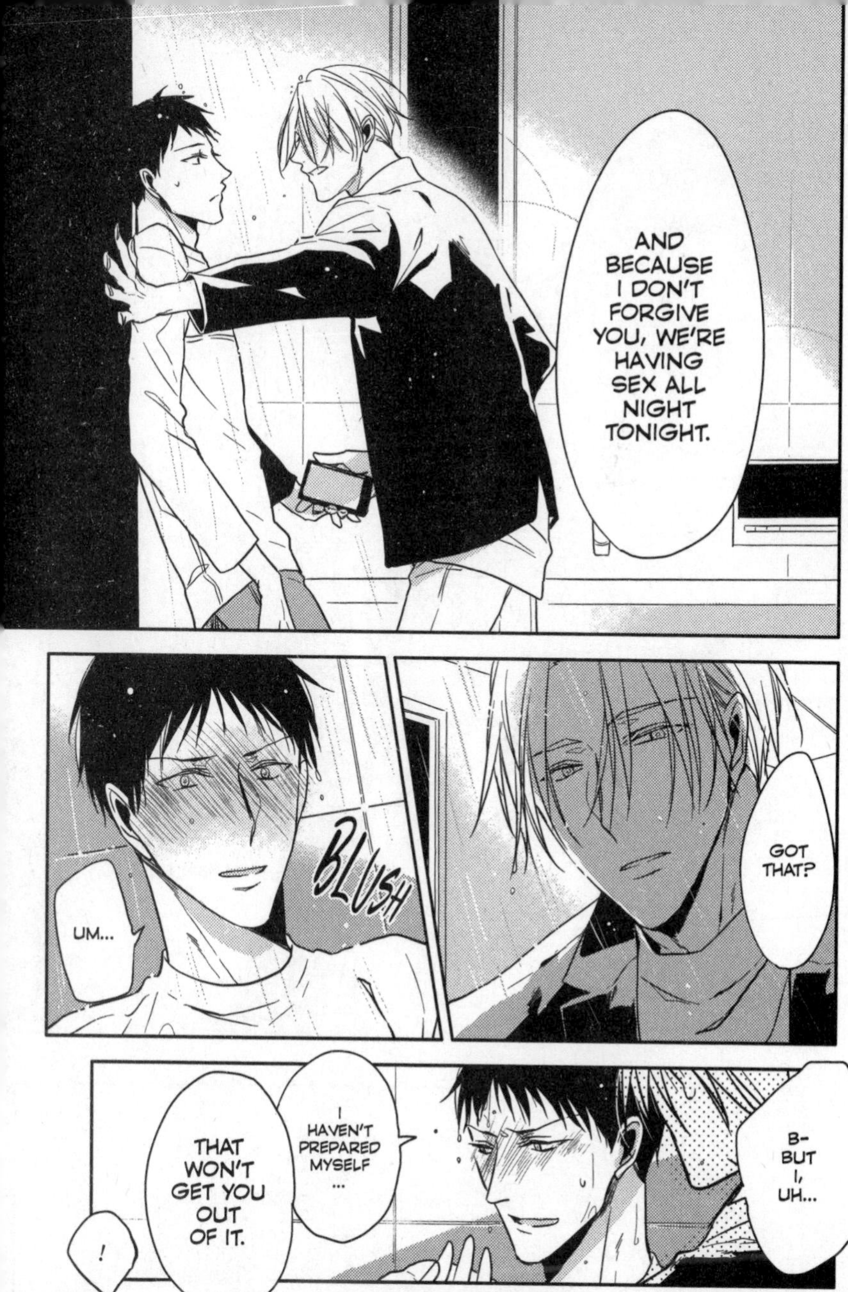
AND BECAUSE I DON'T FORGIVE YOU, WE'RE HAVING SEX ALL NIGHT TONIGHT.
GOT THAT?
BLUSH
UM...
B-BUT I, UH...
I HAVEN'T PREPARED MYSELF ...
THAT WON'T GET YOU OUT OF IT.
!

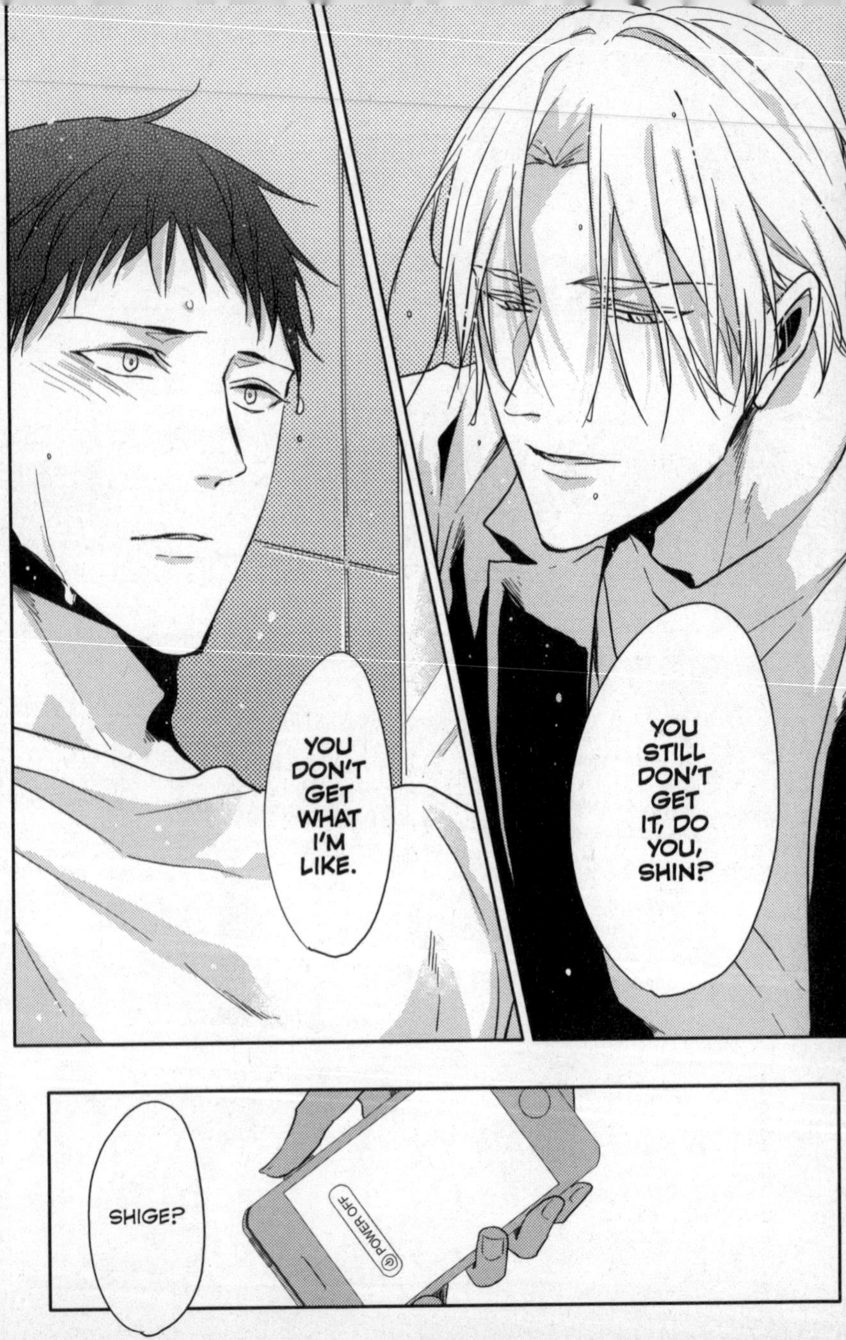
YOU STILL DON'T GET IT, DO YOU, SHIN?
YOU DON'T GET WHAT I'M LIKE.
POWER OFF
SHIGE?

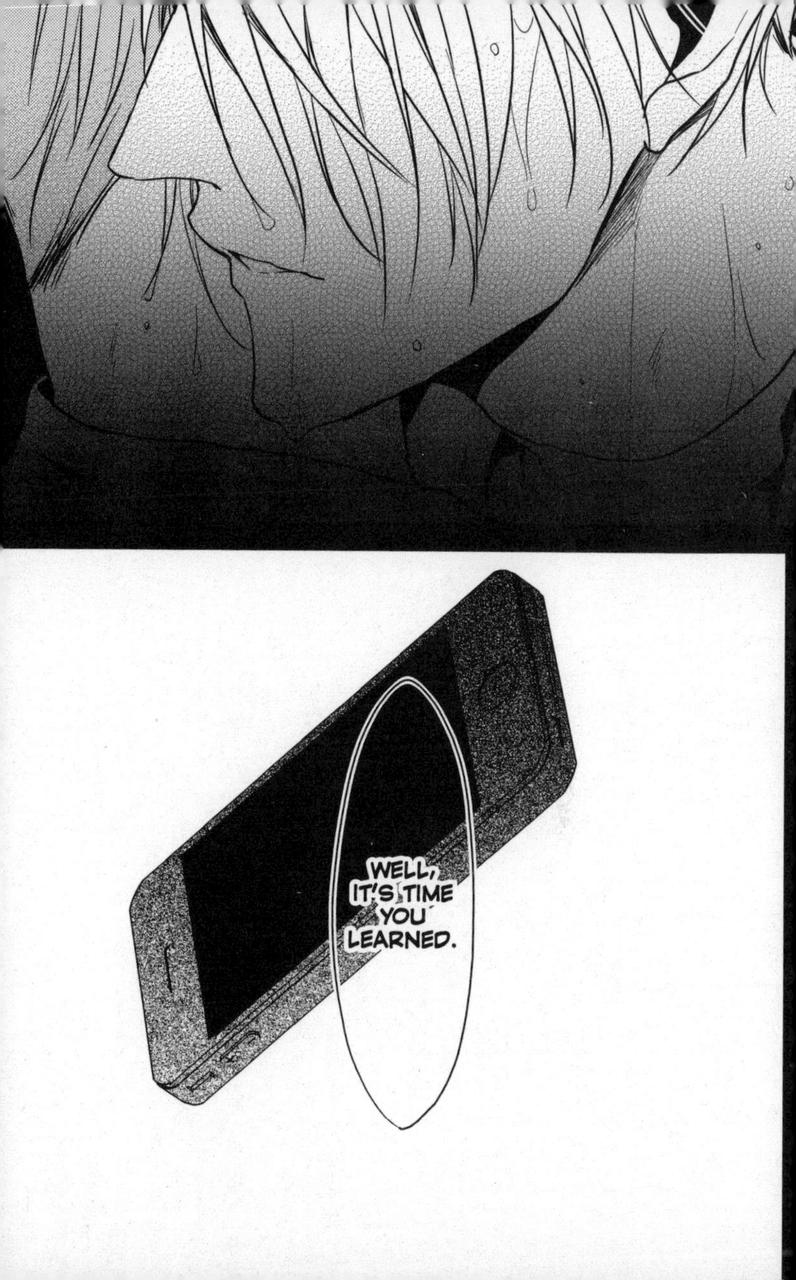
WELL, IT'S TIME YOU LEARNED.

Black
or White

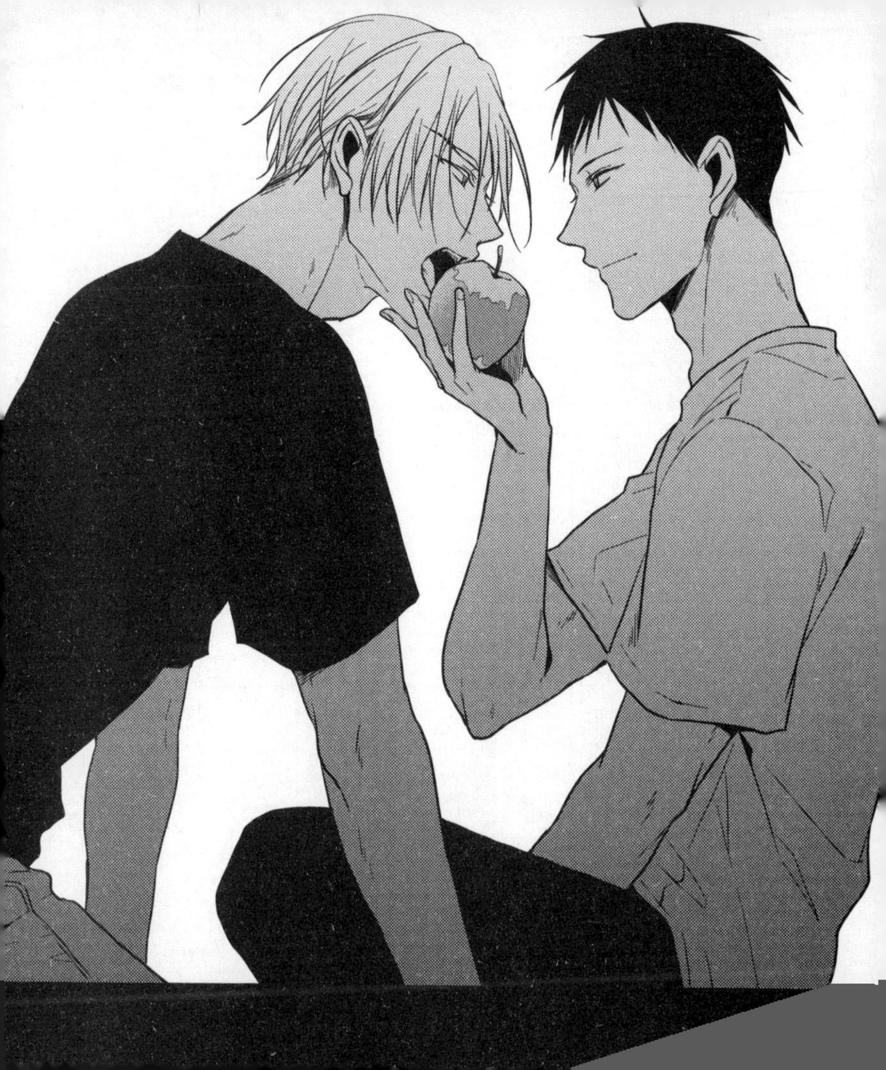

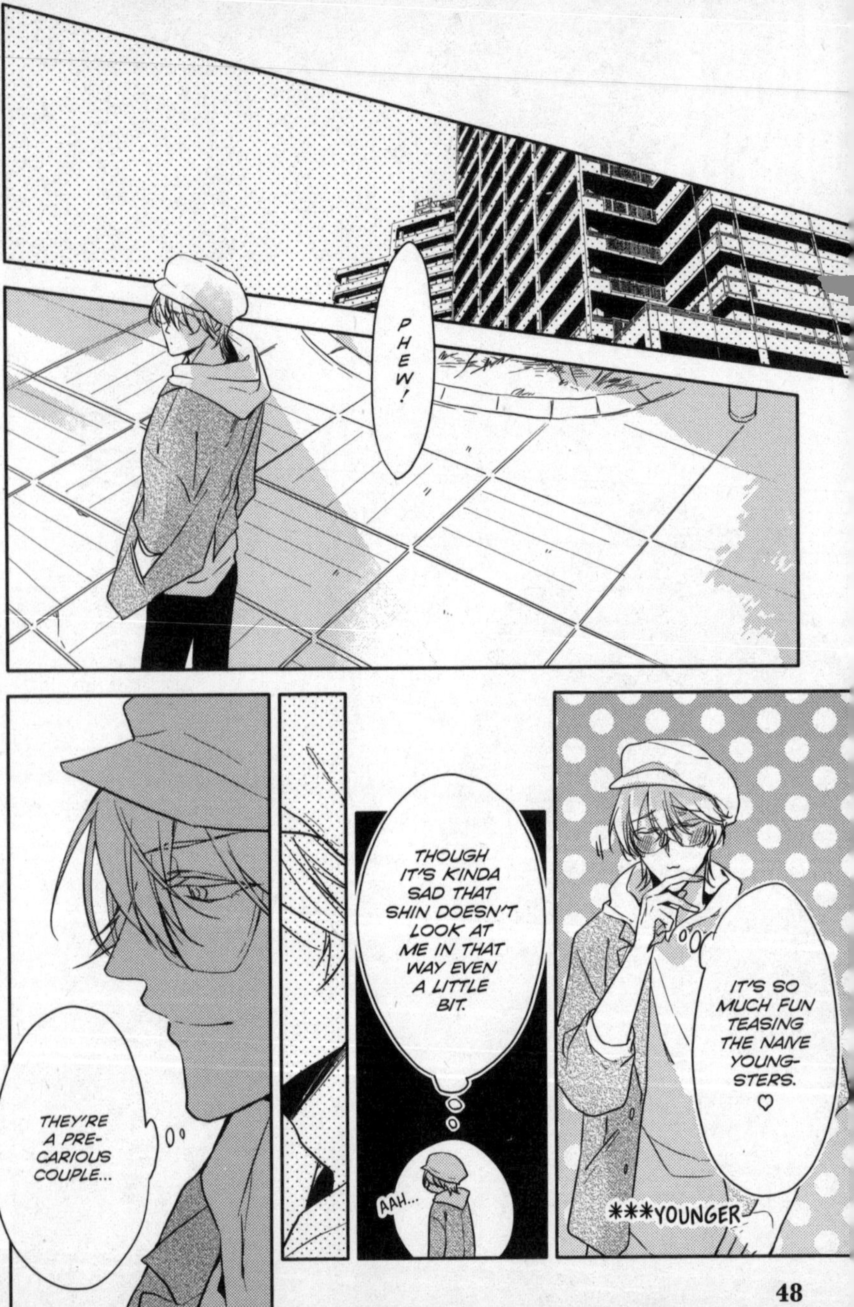
PHEW!
IT'S SO MUCH FUN TEASING THE NAIVE YOUNG-STERS. ♡
***YOUNGER
THOUGH IT'S KINDA SAD THAT SHIN DOESN'T LOOK AT ME IN THAT WAY EVEN A LITTLE BIT.
AAH...
THEY'RE A PRE-CARIOUS COUPLE...

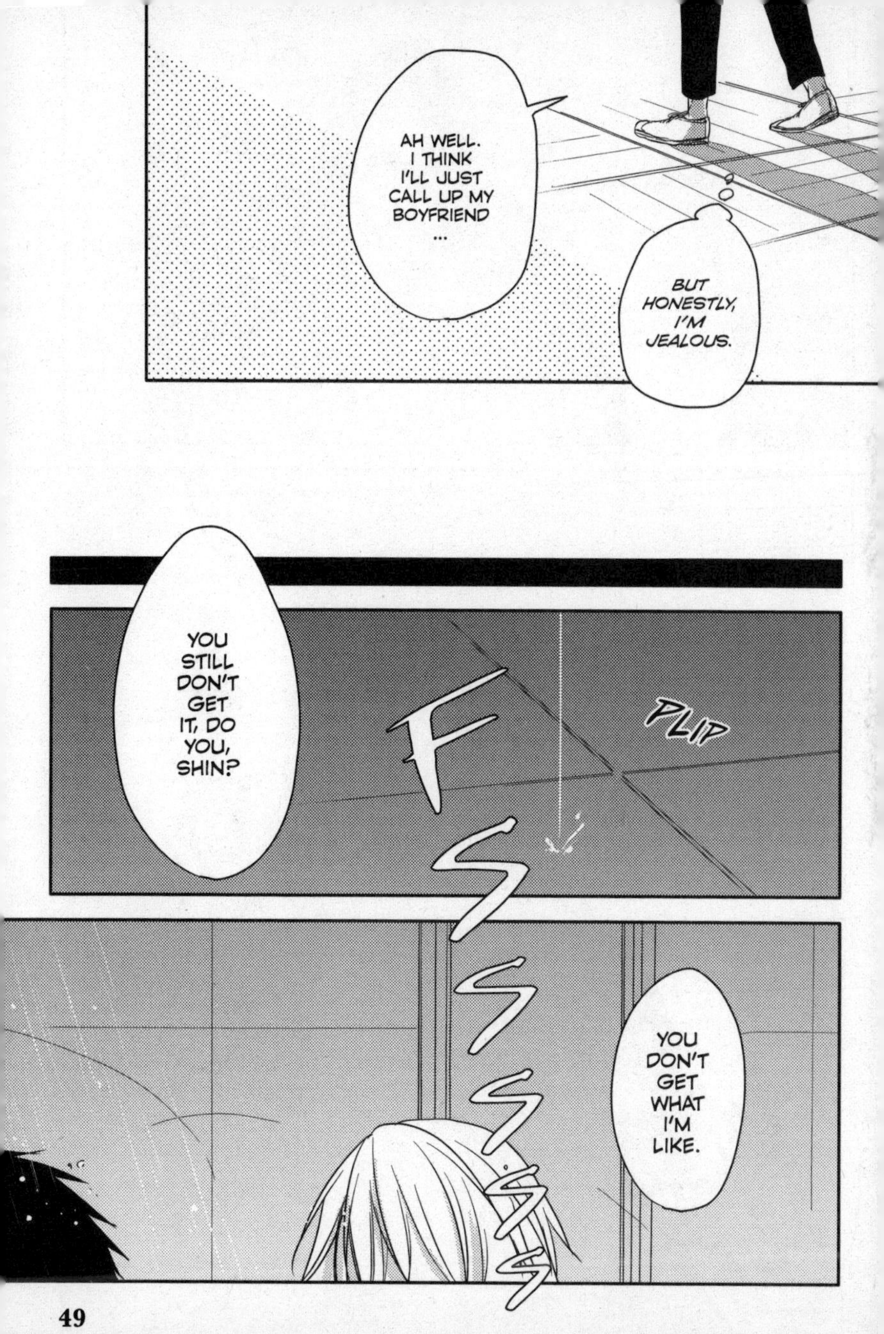
AH WELL. I THINK I'LL JUST CALL UP MY BOYFRIEND ...
BUT HONESTLY, I'M JEALOUS.
YOU STILL DON'T GET IT, DO YOU, SHIN?
PLIP
FSSSSSS
YOU DON'T GET WHAT I'M LIKE.

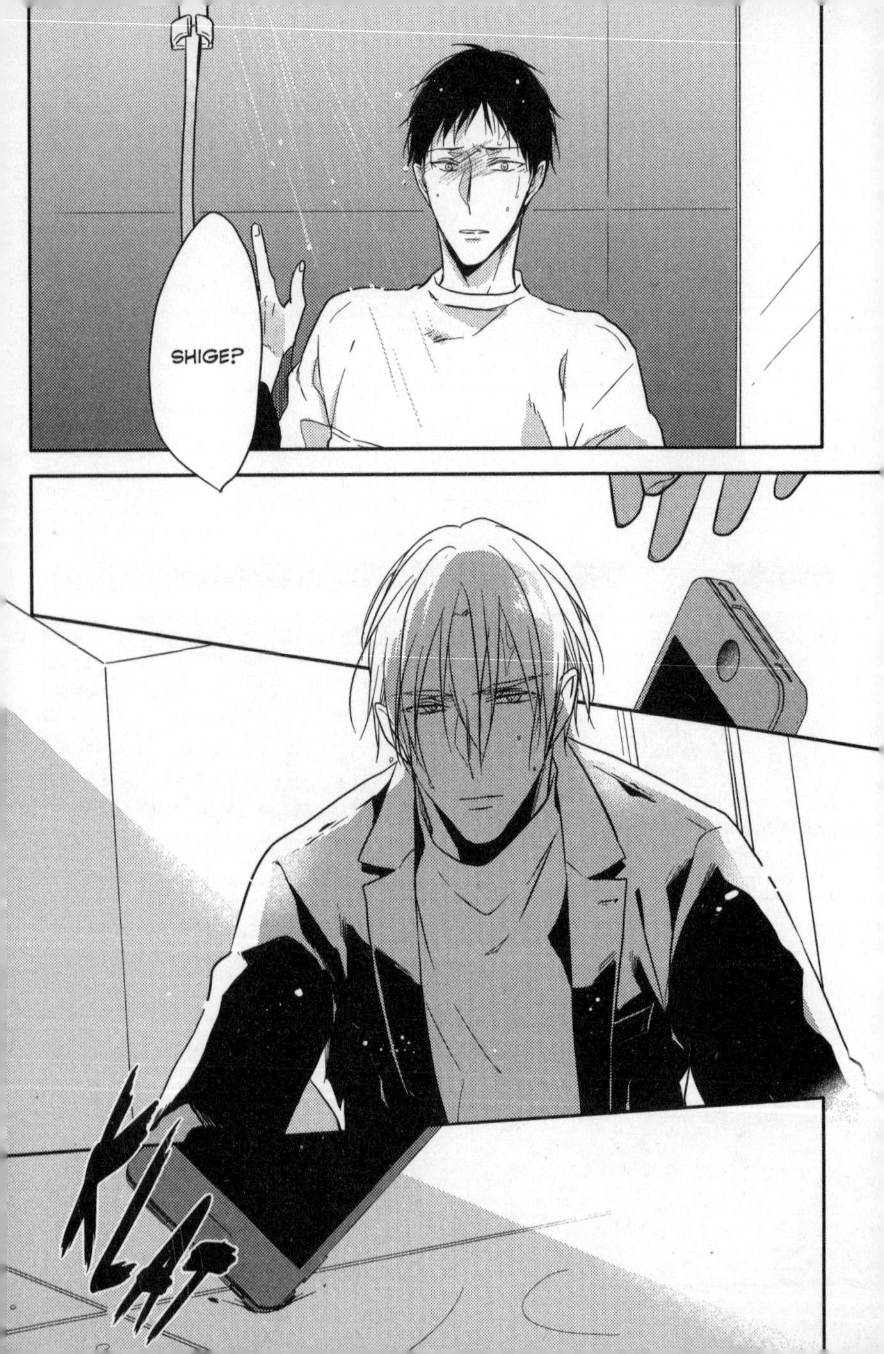
SHIGE?
KLAP

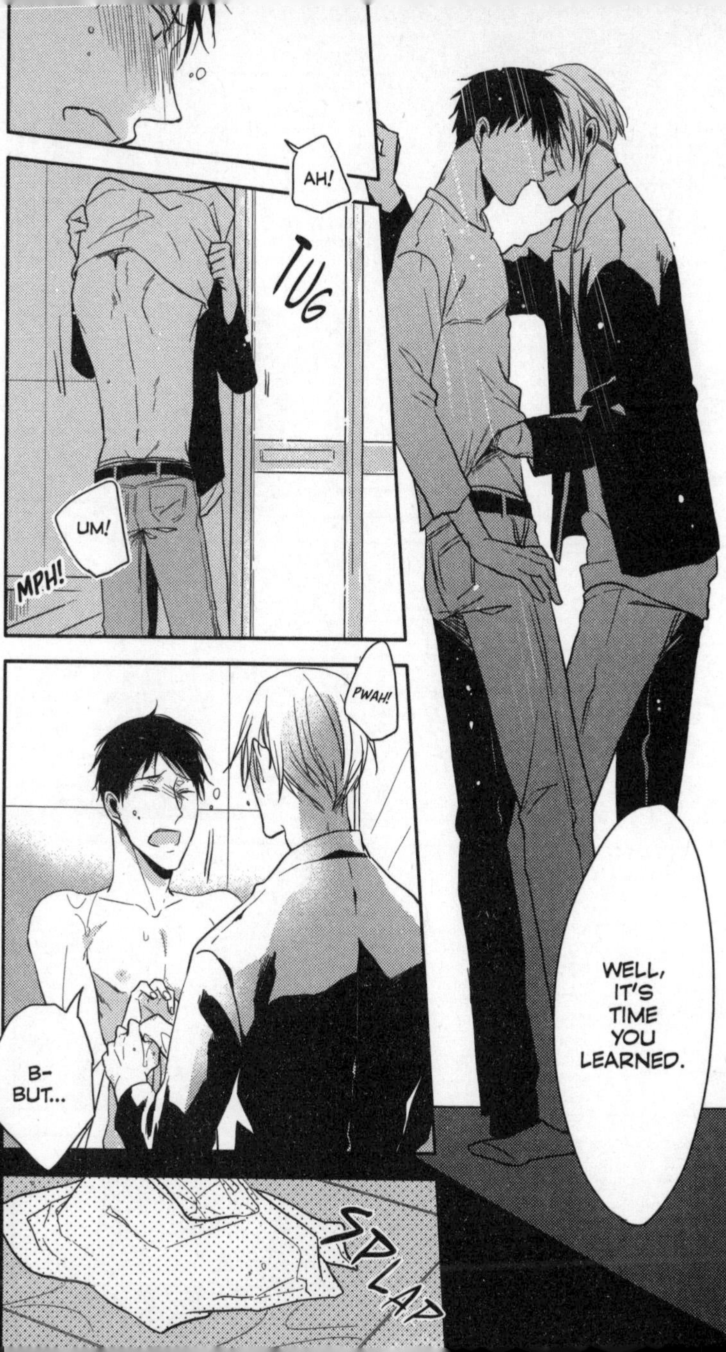
WELL, IT'S TIME YOU LEARNED.
AH!
TUG
UM!
MPH!
PWAH!
B-BUT...
SPLAP

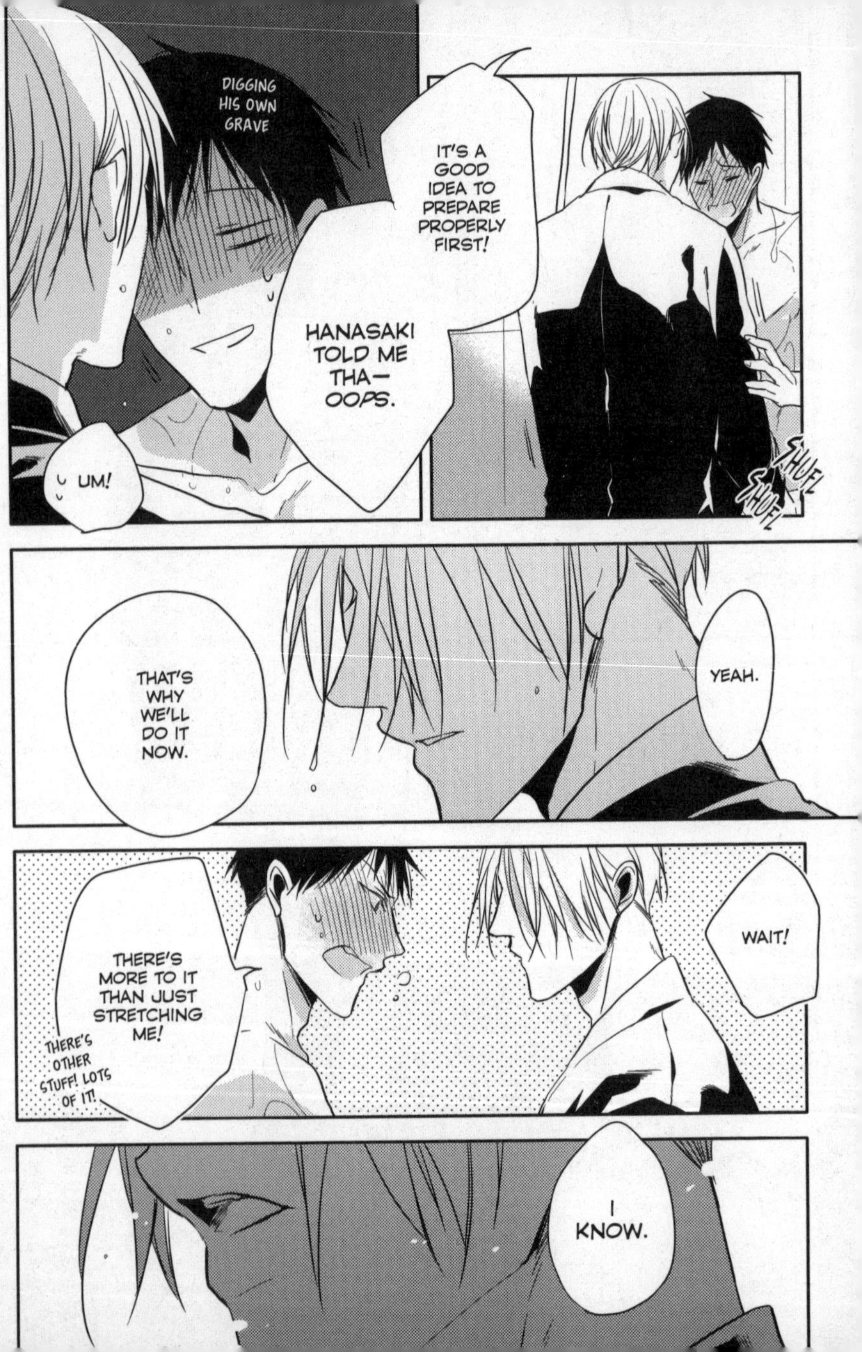
IT'S A GOOD IDEA TO PREPARE PROPERLY FIRST!
SHUFL SHUFL
HANASAKI TOLD ME THA— OOPS.
DIGGING HIS OWN GRAVE
UM!
YEAH.
THAT'S WHY WE'LL DO IT NOW.
WAIT!
THERE'S MORE TO IT THAN JUST STRETCHING ME!
THERE'S OTHER STUFF! LOTS OF IT!
I KNOW.

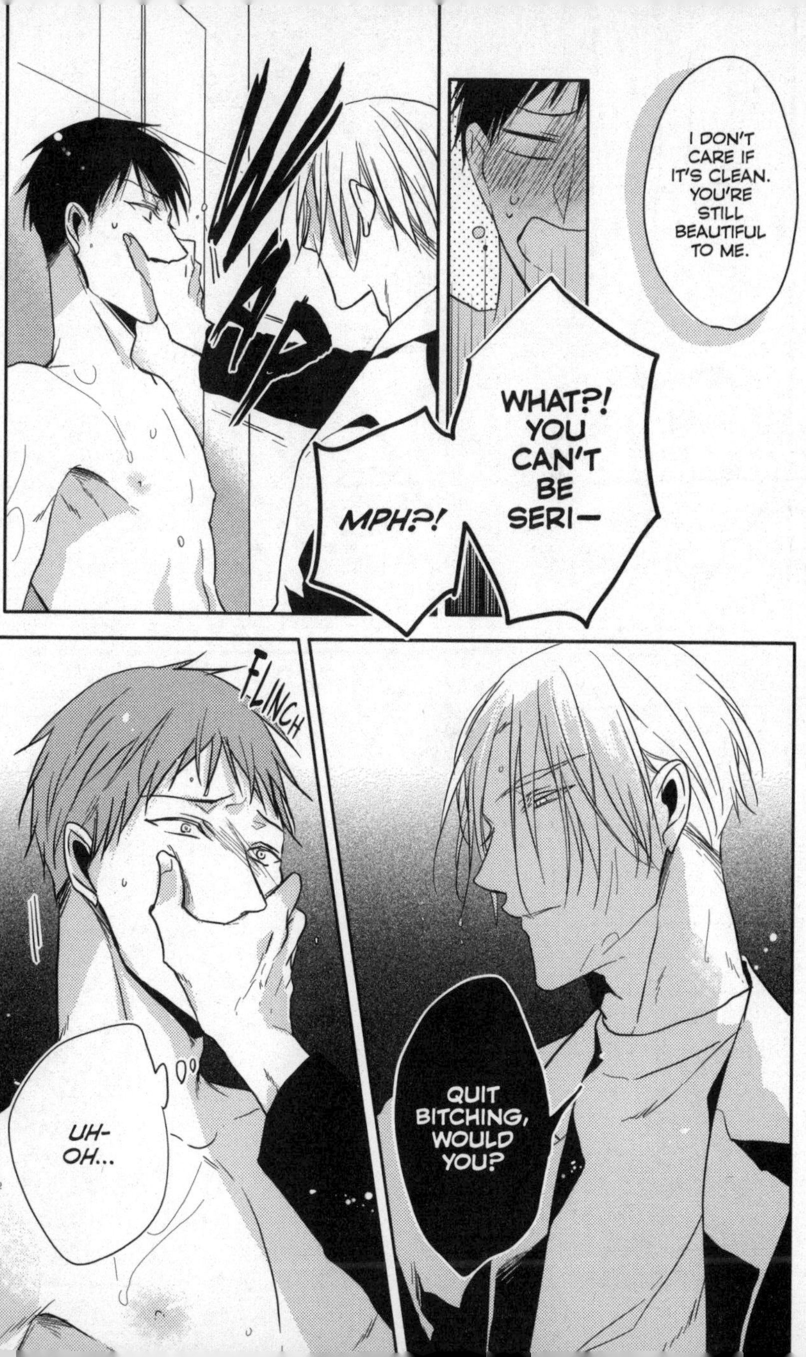
I DON'T CARE IF IT'S CLEAN. YOU'RE STILL BEAUTIFUL TO ME.
WHAT?! YOU CAN'T BE SERI—
MPH?!
QUIT BITCHING, WOULD YOU?
FLINCH
UH-OH...

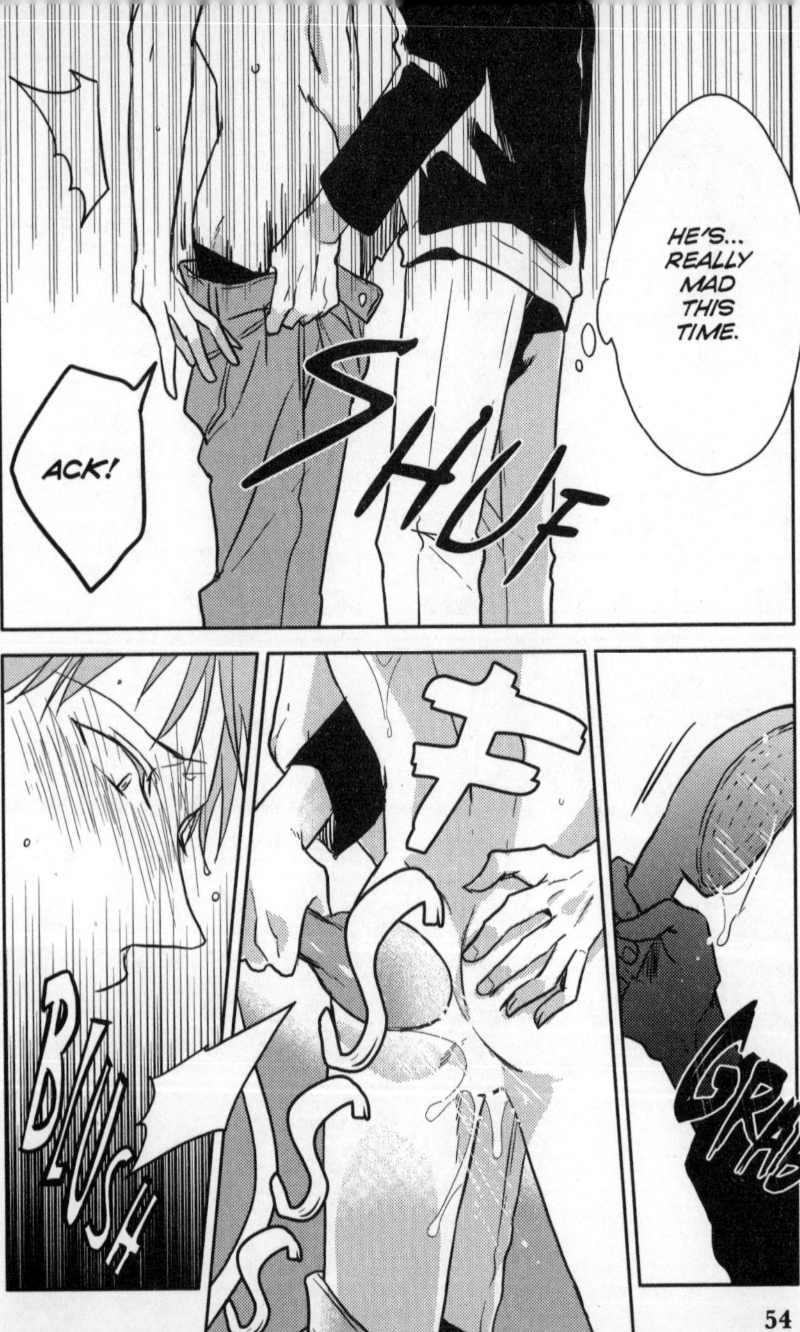
HE'S... REALLY MAD THIS TIME.
SHUF
ACK!
GRAB
BLUSH

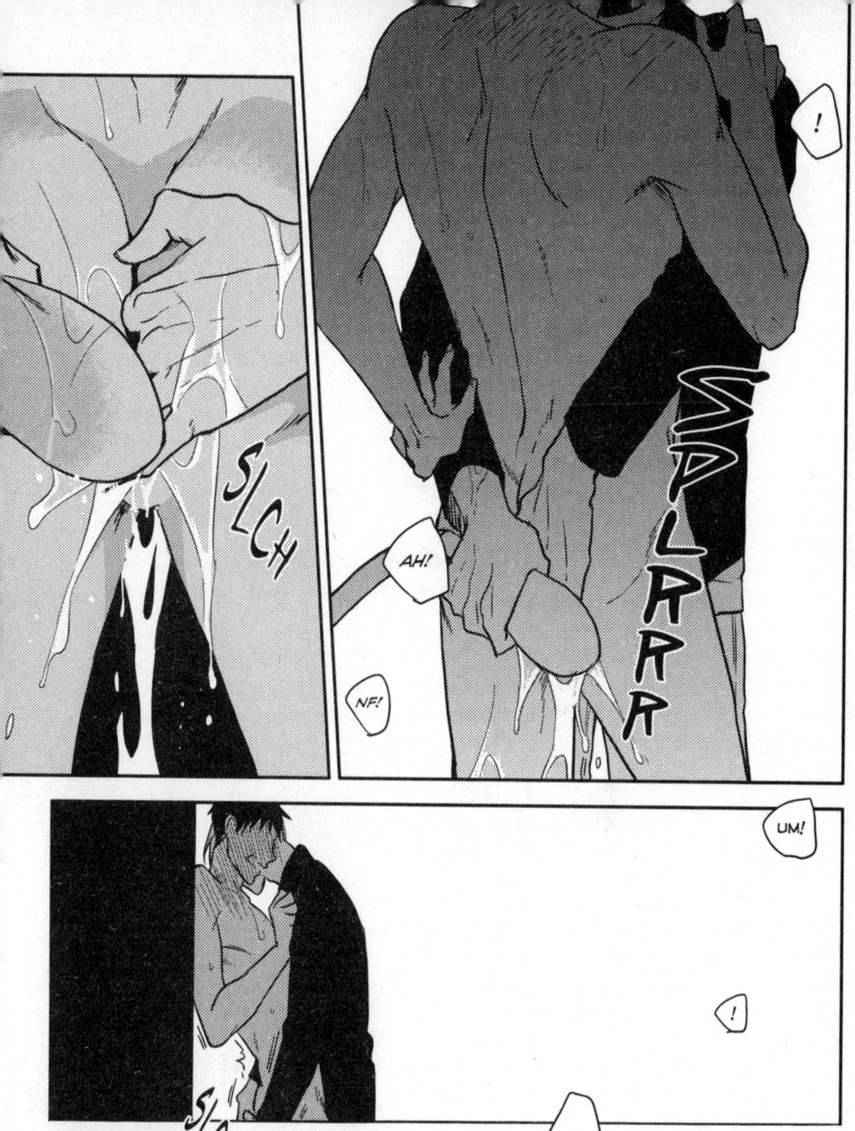
!
SPLRRR
AH!
NF!
SLCH
UM!
!
SHIGE ...
SLCH
SLCH
SLCH
!

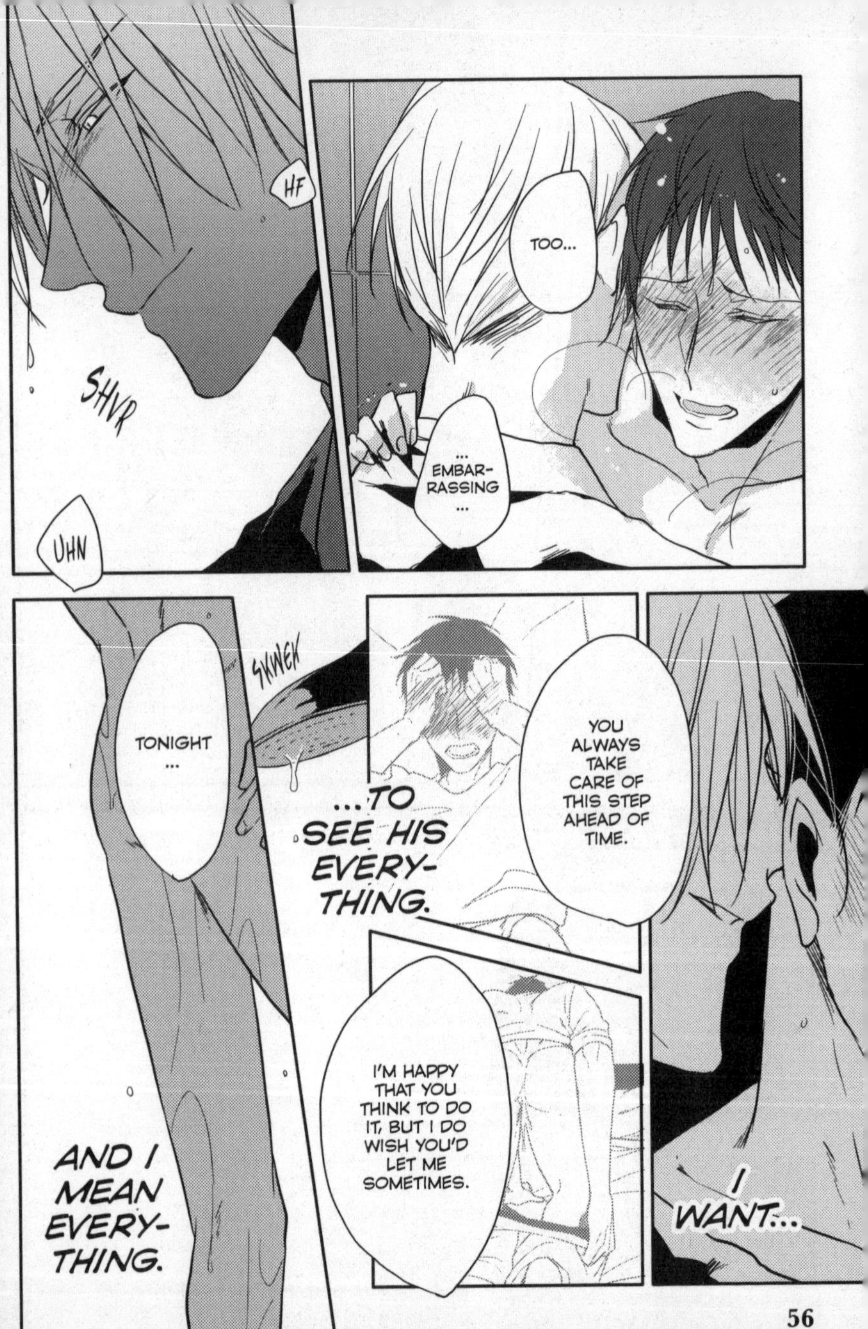
TOO...
...EMBARRASSING...
HF
SHVR
UHN
I WANT...
YOU ALWAYS TAKE CARE OF THIS STEP AHEAD OF TIME.
...TO SEE HIS EVERYTHING.
I'M HAPPY THAT YOU THINK TO DO IT, BUT I DO WISH YOU'D LET ME SOMETIMES.
TONIGHT...
SKWEK
AND I MEAN EVERYTHING.

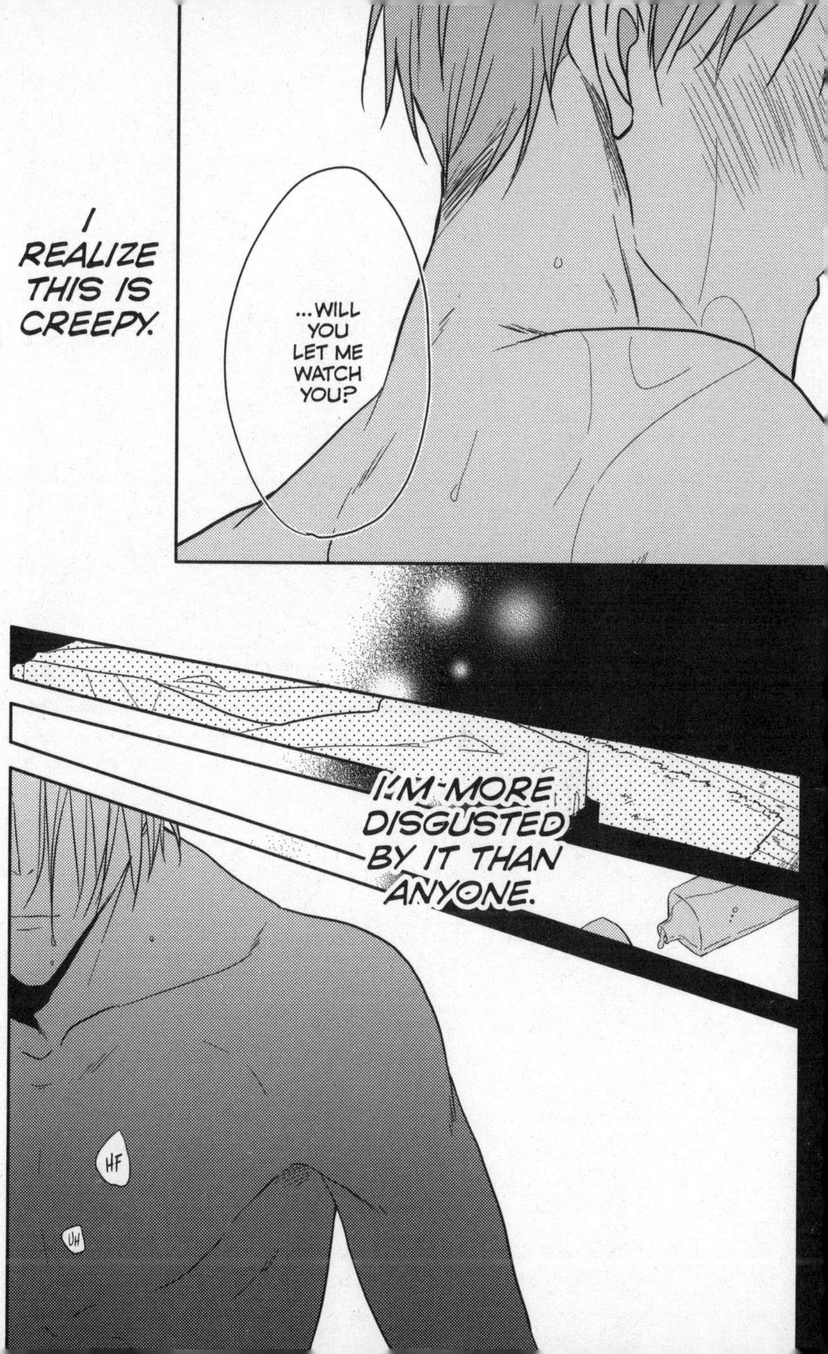
...WILL YOU LET ME WATCH YOU?
I REALIZE THIS IS CREEPY.
I'M MORE DISGUSTED BY IT THAN ANYONE.
HF
UH

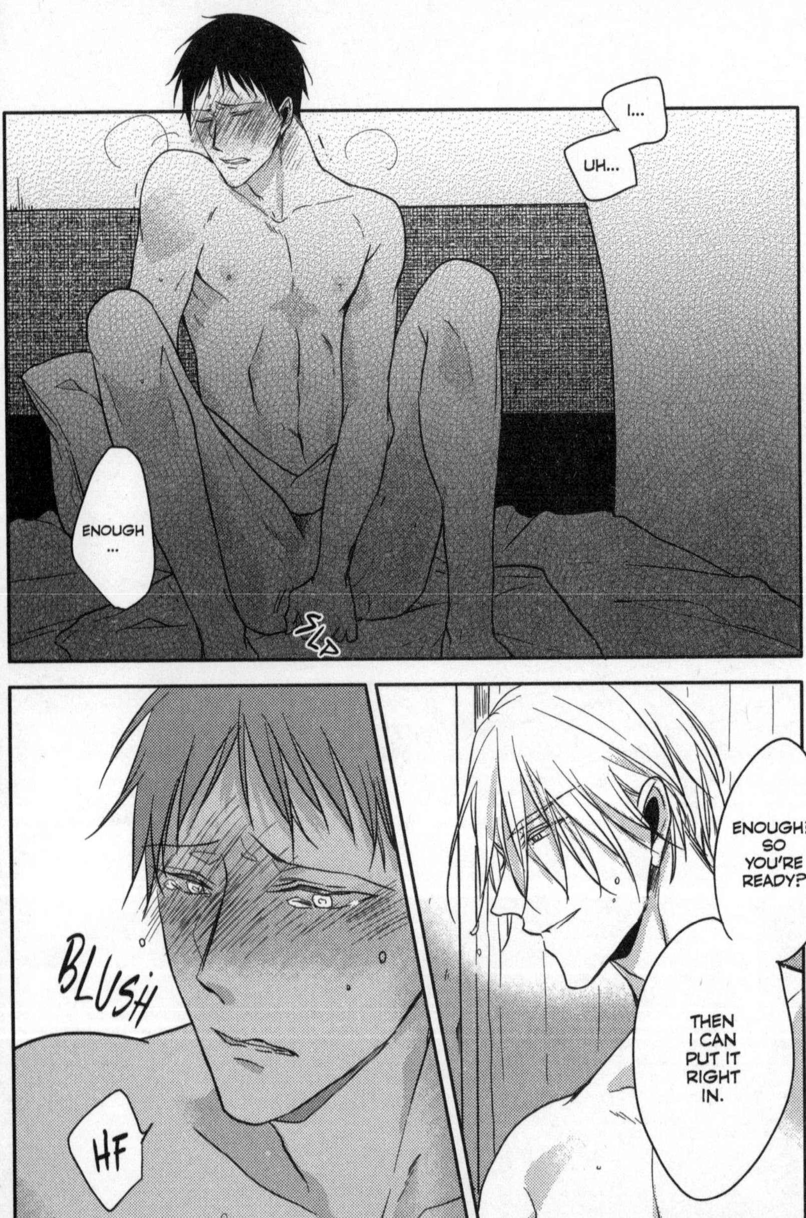
I...
UH...
ENOUGH ...
SLP
ENOUGH? SO YOU'RE READY?
THEN I CAN PUT IT RIGHT IN.
BLUSH
HF

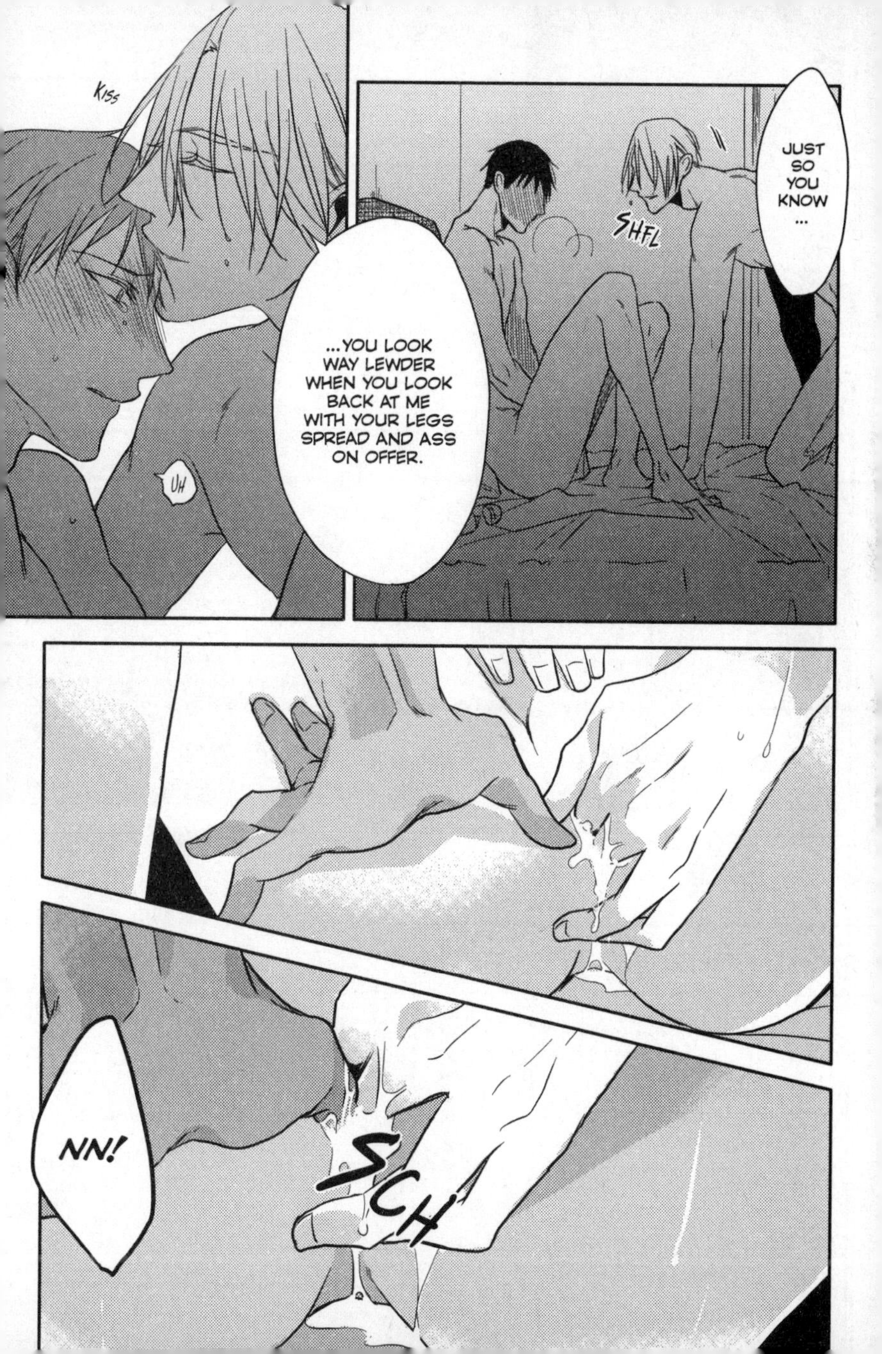

JUST SO YOU KNOW ...
SHFL
...YOU LOOK WAY LEWDER WHEN YOU LOOK BACK AT ME WITH YOUR LEGS SPREAD AND ASS ON OFFER.
KISS
UH
NN!
SCH

SHAKE

SHAKE

SCH

SCH

SCH

SCH

TWCH

DOES IT HURT?

NN.

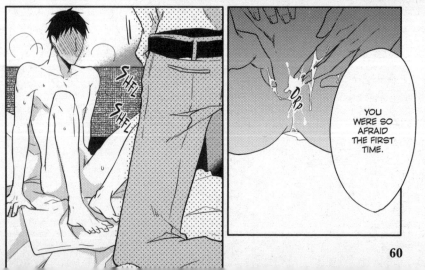

SHFL

SHFL

DRP

YOU WERE SO AFRAID THE FIRST TIME.

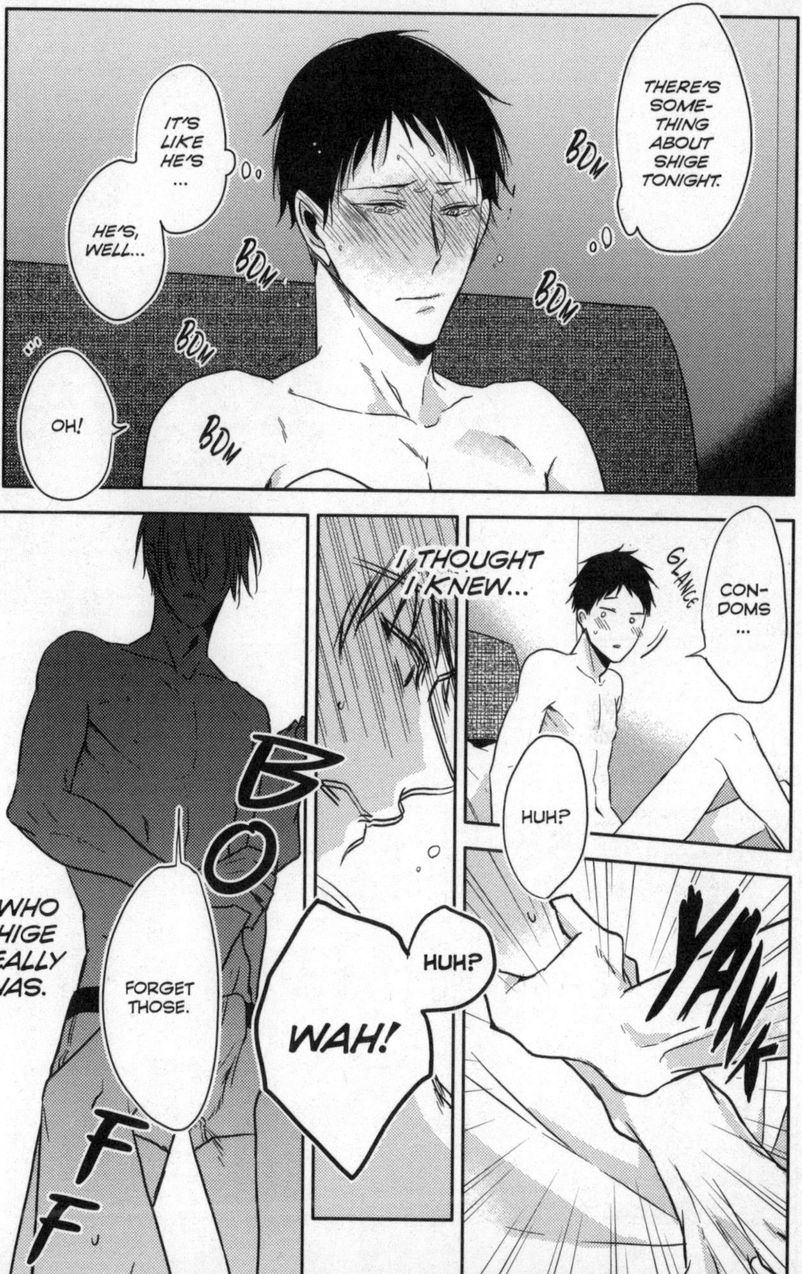
THERE'S SOME-THING ABOUT SHIGE TONIGHT.
BDM
BDM
IT'S LIKE HE'S ...
HE'S, WELL...
BDM
BDM
BDM
OH!
GLANCE
CON-DOMS ...
HUH?
YANK
HUH?
WAH!
I THOUGHT I KNEW...
...WHO SHIGE REALLY WAS.
FORGET THOSE.
BOFF

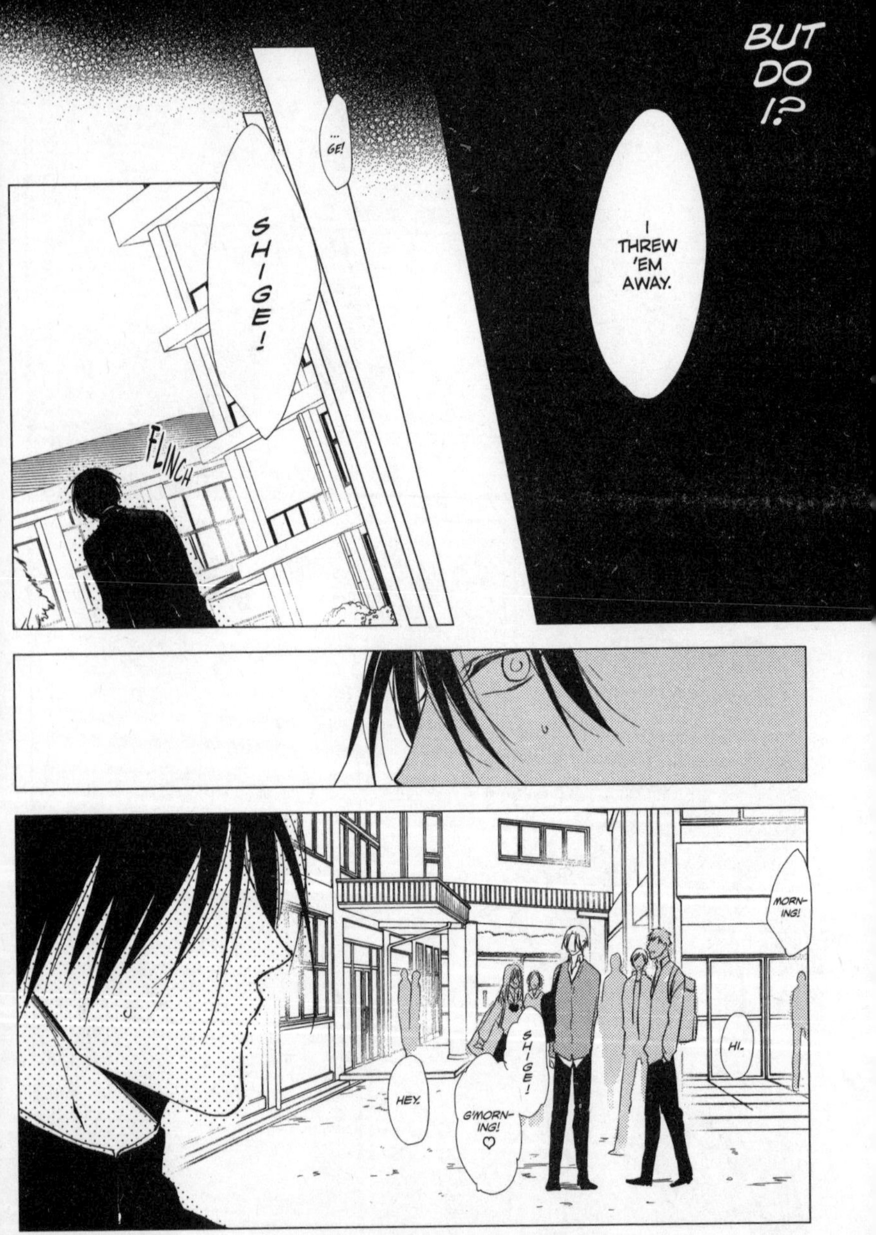
BUT DO I!?
I THREW 'EM AWAY.
...GE!
SHIGE!
FLINCH
MORNING!
HI.
SHIGE!
G'MORNING! ♡
HEY.

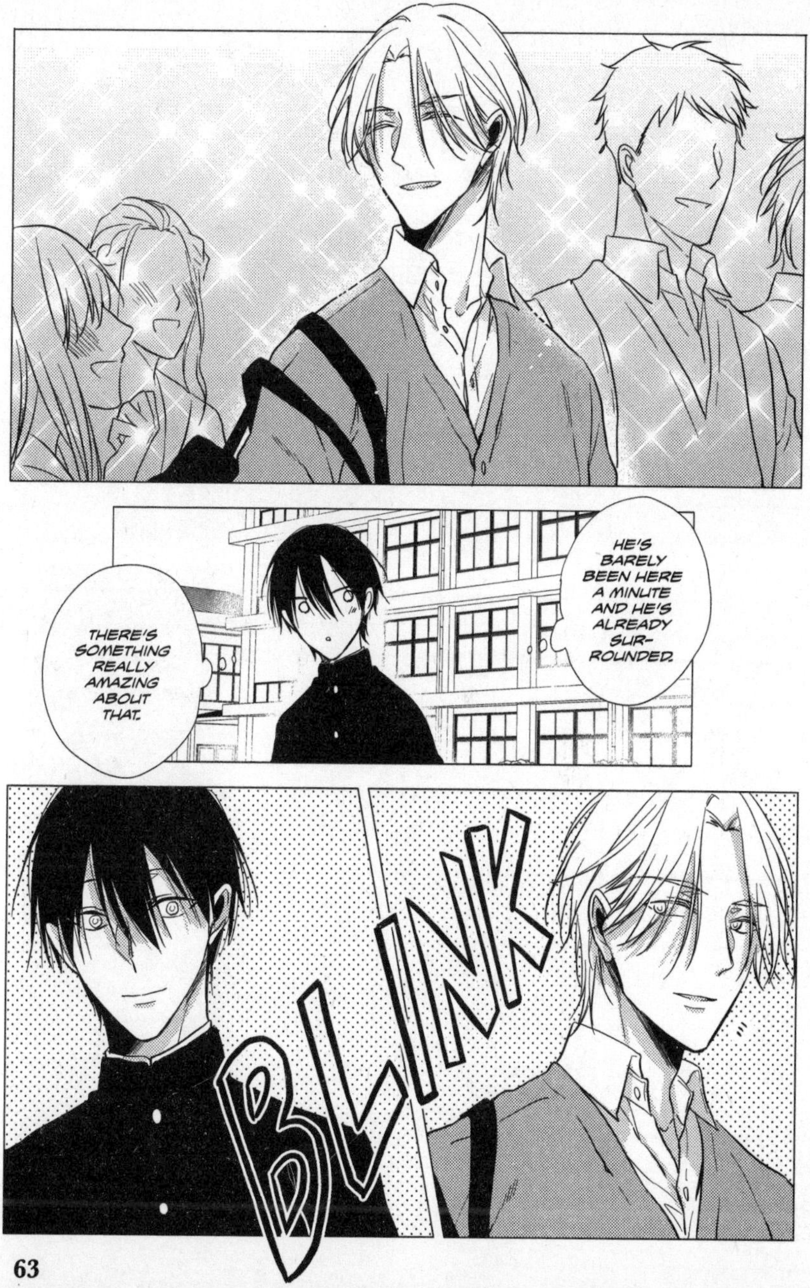
HE'S BARELY BEEN HERE A MINUTE AND HE'S ALREADY SUR-ROUNDED.
THERE'S SOMETHING REALLY AMAZING ABOUT THAT.
BLINK

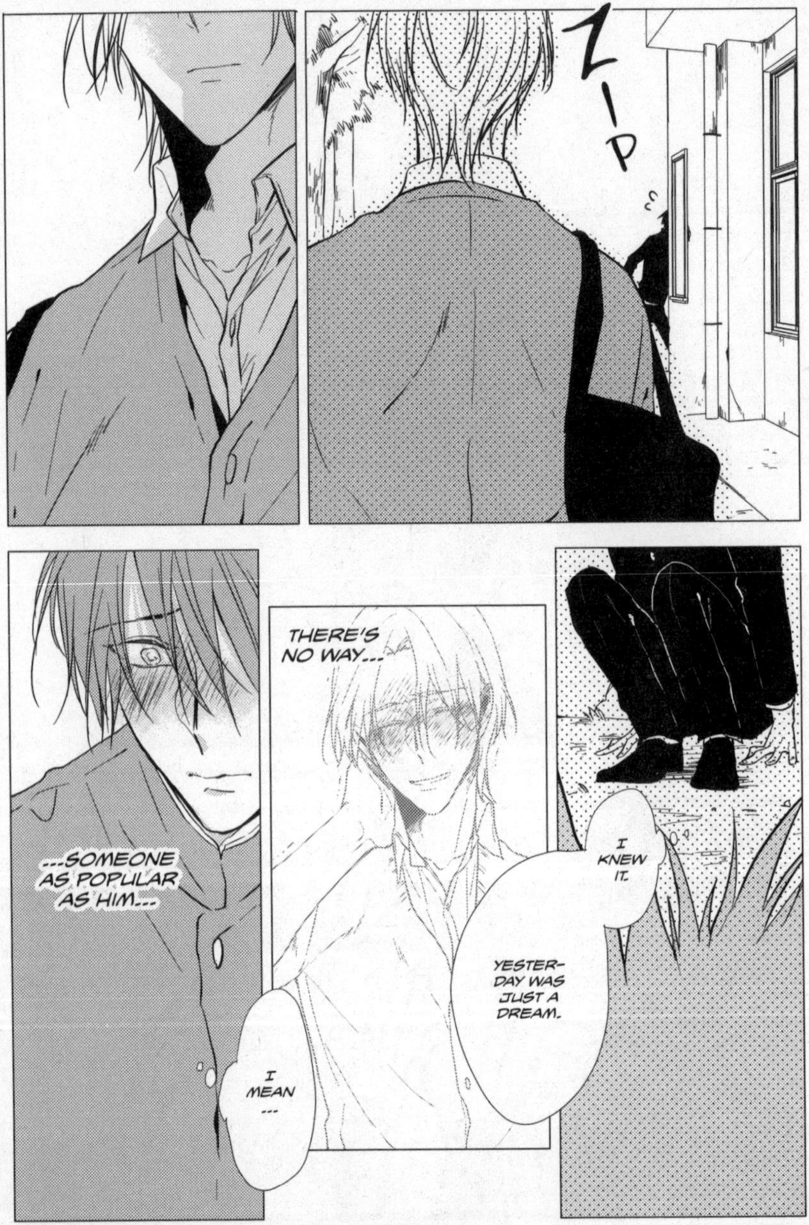
ZIP
I KNEW IT.
YESTERDAY WAS JUST A DREAM.
I MEAN...
THERE'S NO WAY...
...SOMEONE AS POPULAR AS HIM...

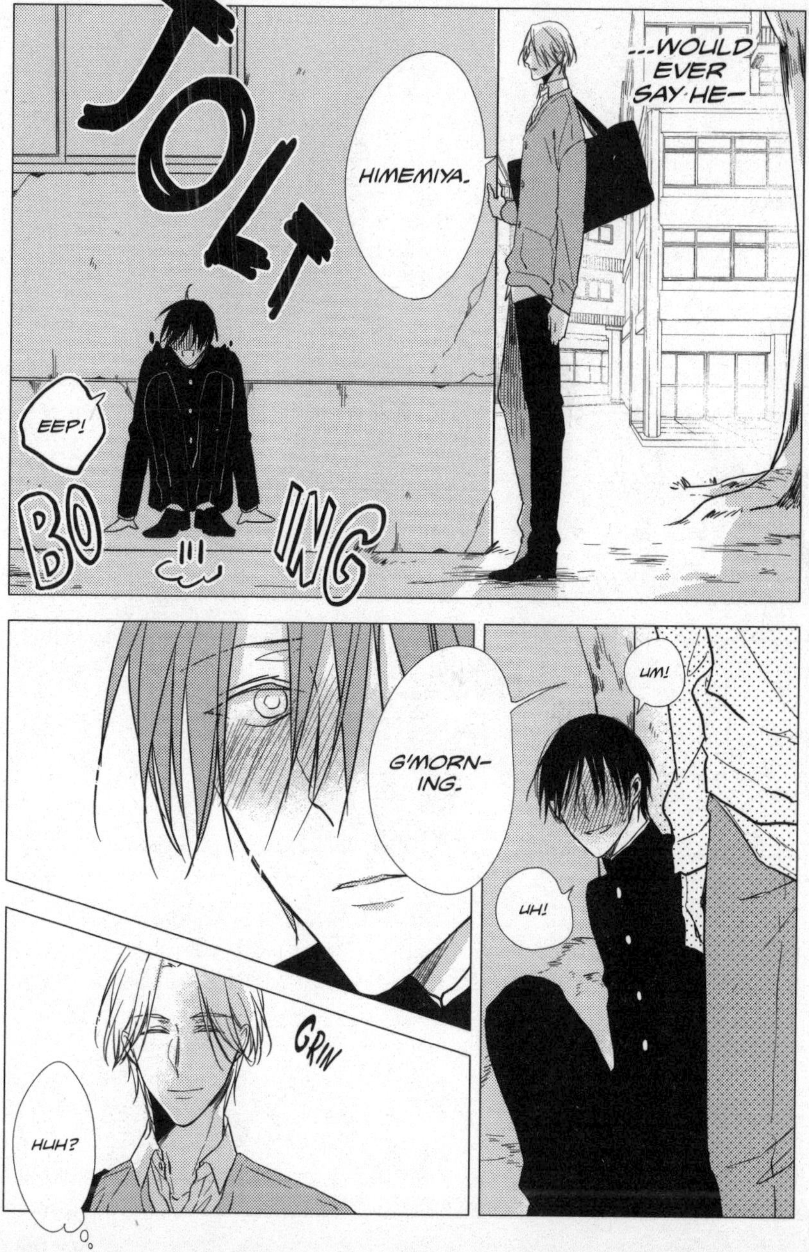
---WOULD EVER SAY HE—
HIMEMIYA.
JOLT
EEP!
BOING
UM!
UH!
G'MORN-ING.
GRIN
HUH?

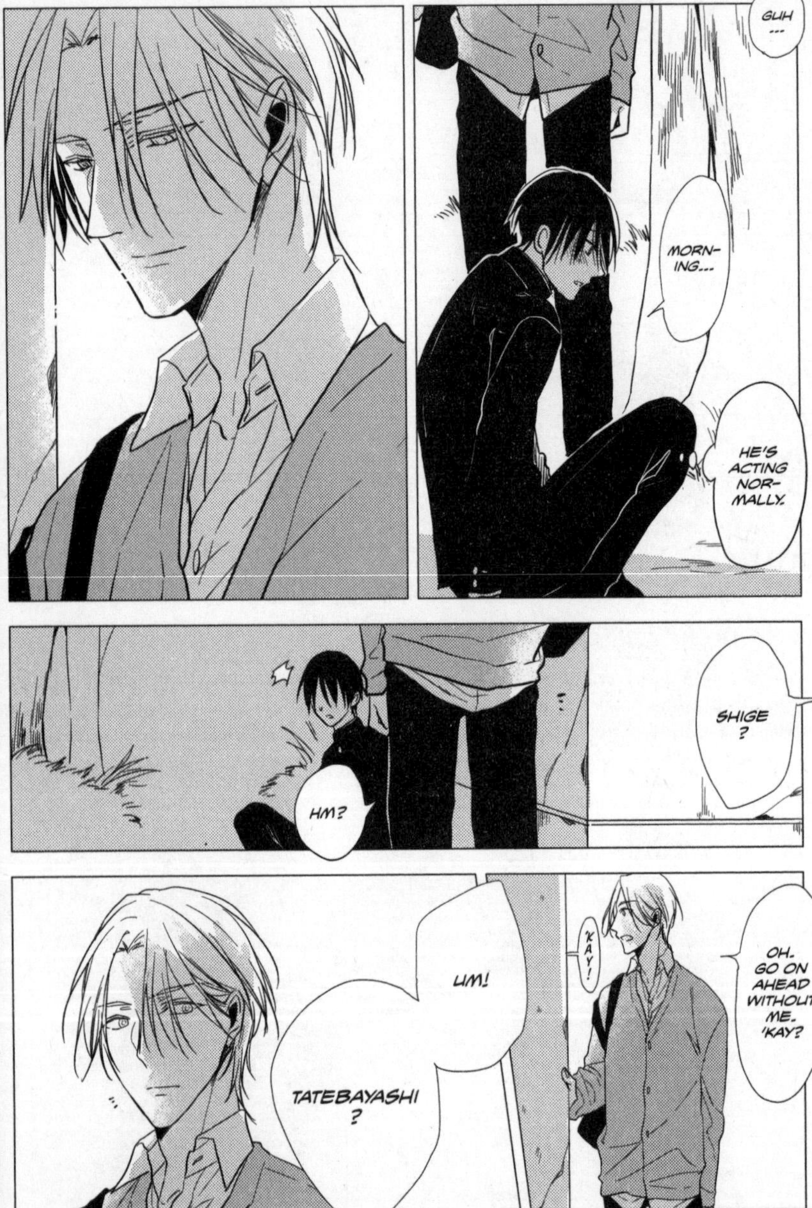
GUH ---
MORNING---
HE'S ACTING NORMALLY.
SHIGE?
HM?
OH. GO ON AHEAD WITHOUT ME. 'KAY?
'KAY!
UM!
TATEBAYASHI?

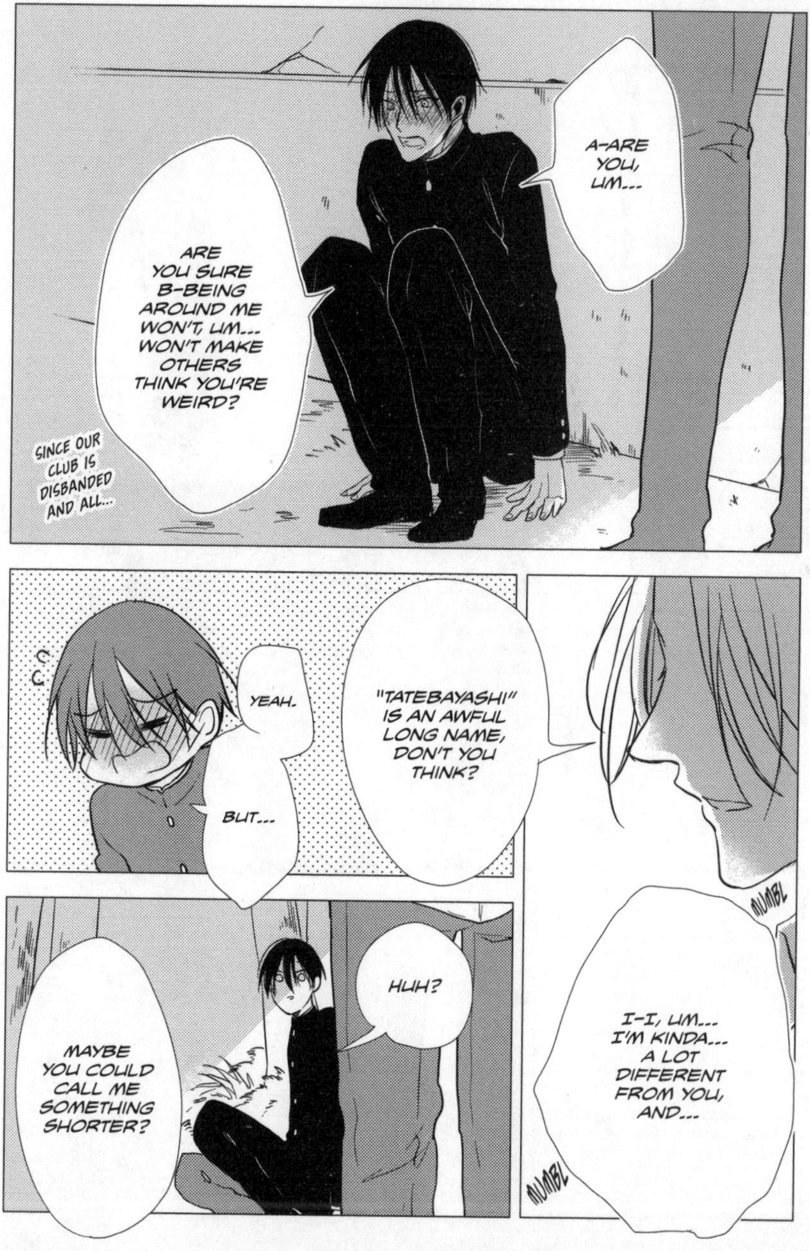
A-ARE YOU, UM...
ARE YOU SURE B-BEING AROUND ME WON'T, UM... WON'T MAKE OTHERS THINK YOU'RE WEIRD?
SINCE OUR CLUB IS DISBANDED AND ALL...
"TATEBAYASHI" IS AN AWFUL LONG NAME, DON'T YOU THINK?
MUMBL
I-I, UM... I'M KINDA... A LOT DIFFERENT FROM YOU, AND...
MUMBL
YEAH.
BUT...
HUH?
MAYBE YOU COULD CALL ME SOMETHING SHORTER?

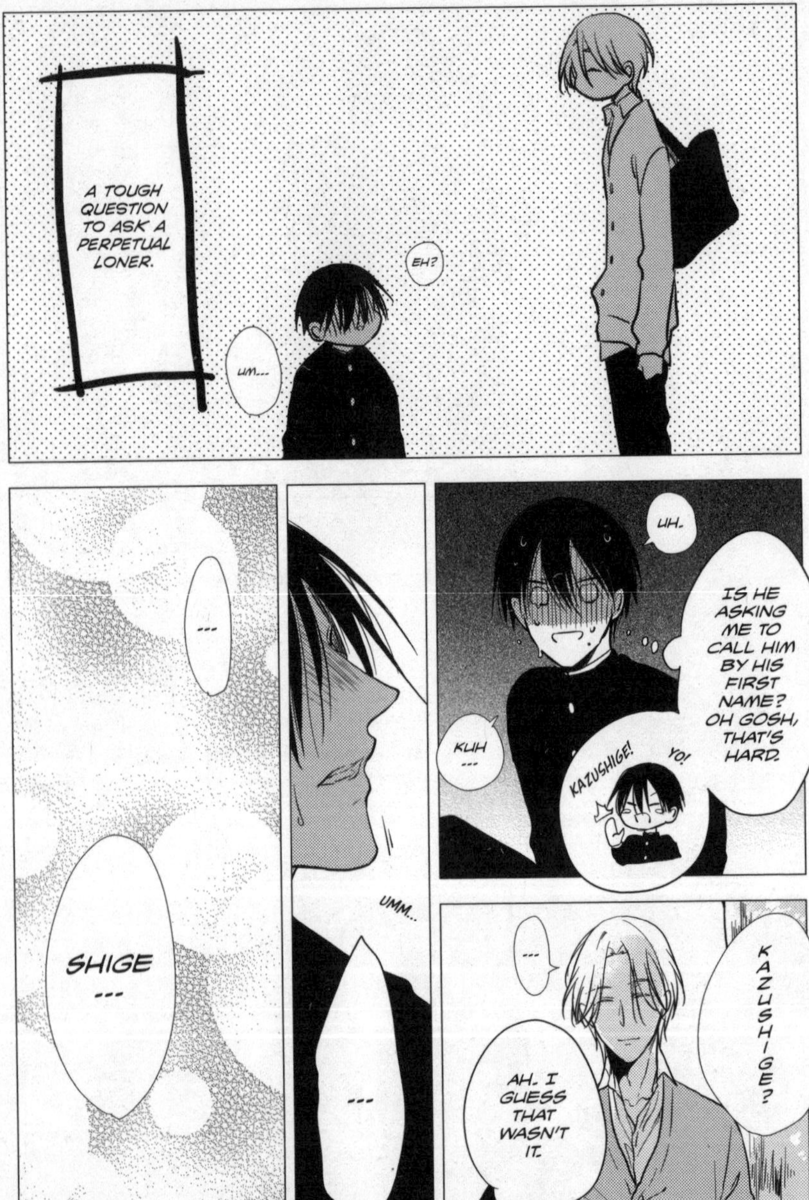
EH?
A TOUGH QUESTION TO ASK A PERPETUAL LONER.
UM...
UH.
IS HE ASKING ME TO CALL HIM BY HIS FIRST NAME? OH GOSH, THAT'S HARD.
KAZUSHIGE!
YO!
KUH ...
KAZUSHIGE?
AH. I GUESS THAT WASN'T IT.
...
UMM..
...
...
SHIGE ...

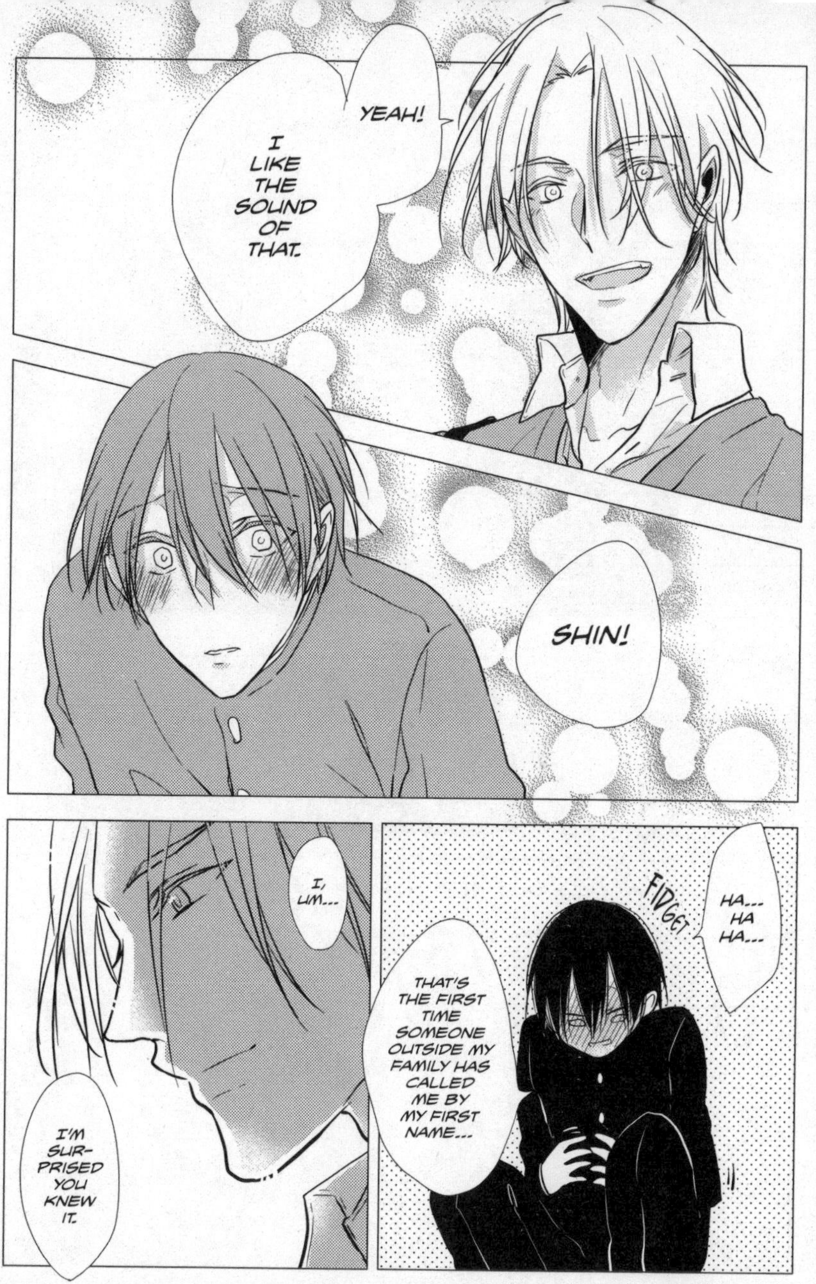
YEAH! I LIKE THE SOUND OF THAT.
SHIN!
HA... HA HA...
FIDGET
THAT'S THE FIRST TIME SOMEONE OUTSIDE MY FAMILY HAS CALLED ME BY MY FIRST NAME...
I, UM...
I'M SURPRISED YOU KNEW IT.

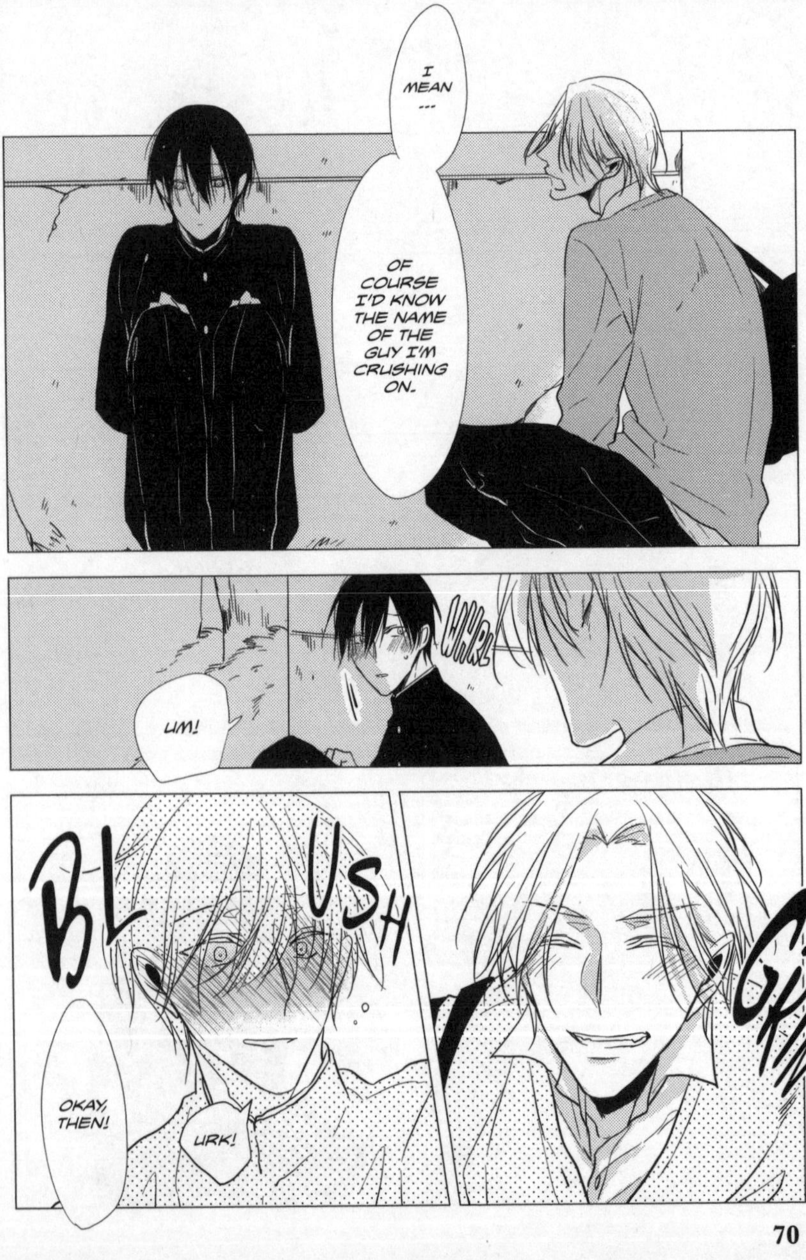
I MEAN ---
OF COURSE I'D KNOW THE NAME OF THE GUY I'M CRUSHING ON.
WHRL
UM!
GRIN
BLUSH
URK!
OKAY, THEN!

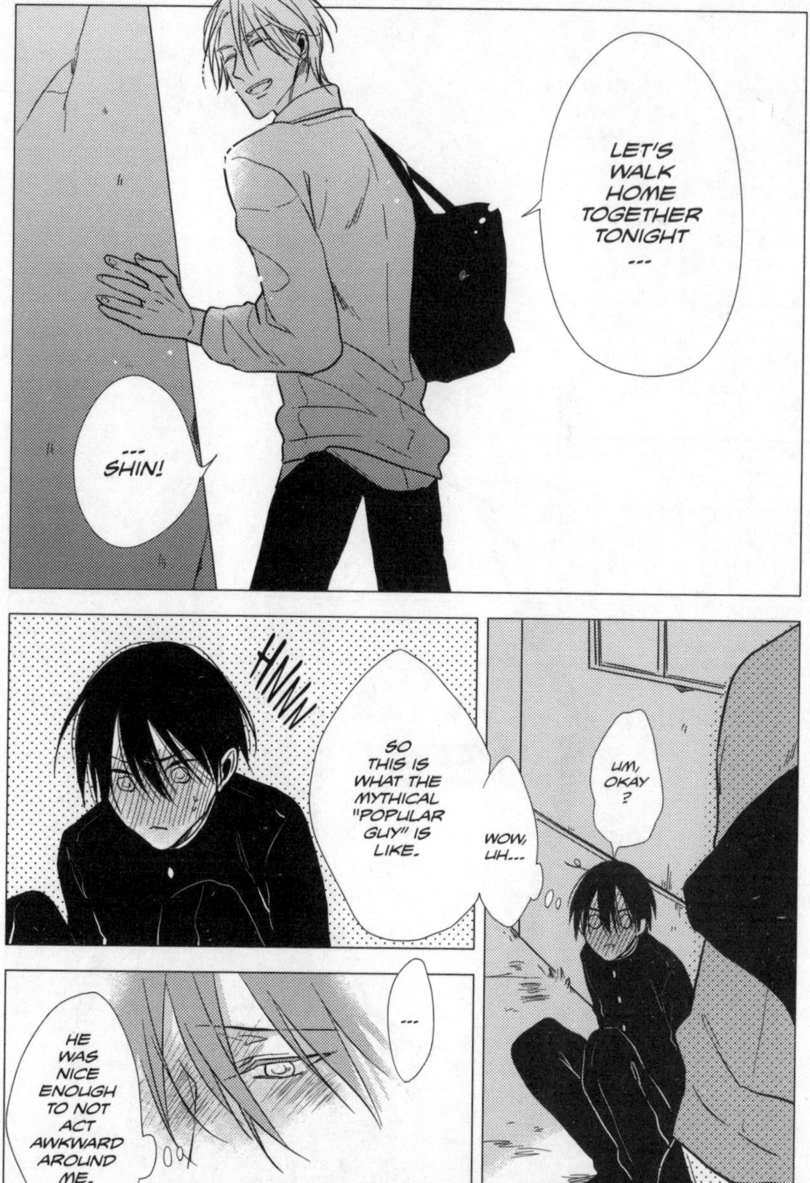
LET'S WALK HOME TOGETHER TONIGHT ...
...SHIN!
UM, OKAY?
WOW, UH...
SO THIS IS WHAT THE MYTHICAL "POPULAR GUY" IS LIKE.
HNNN
...
HE WAS NICE ENOUGH TO NOT ACT AWKWARD AROUND ME.

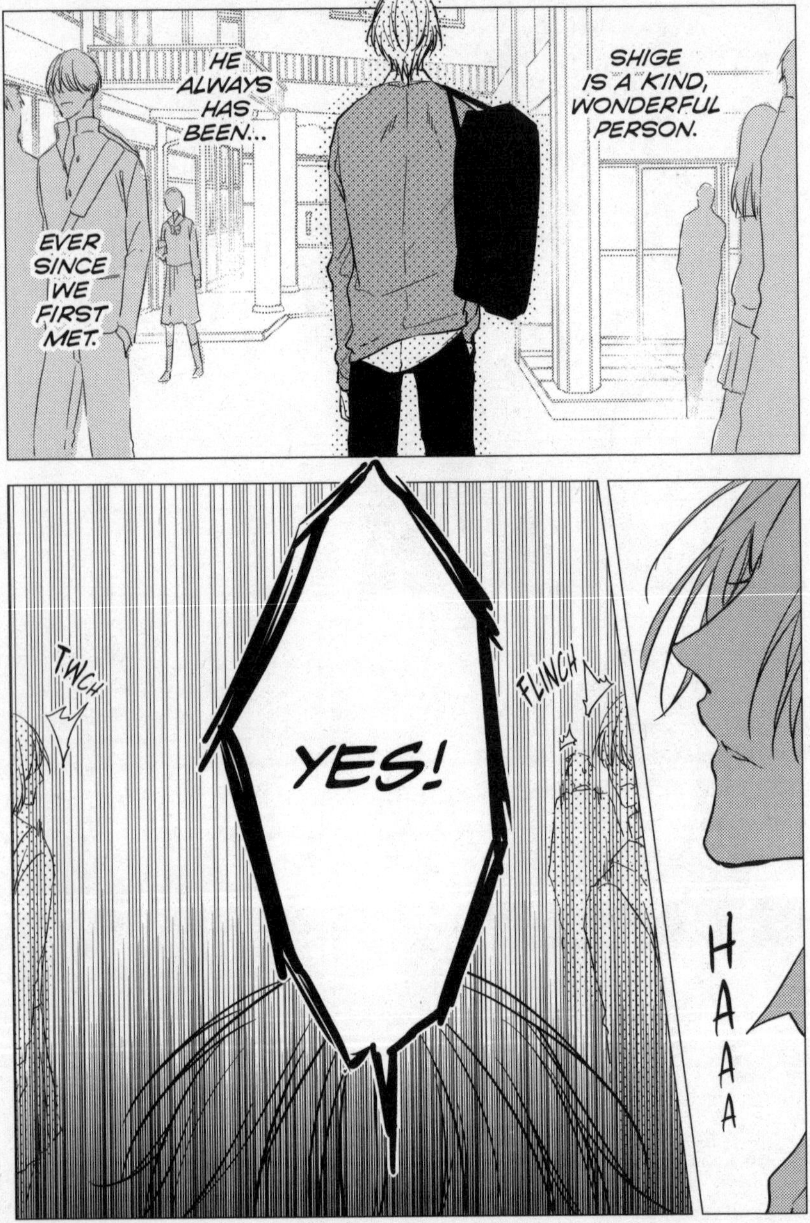
SHIGE IS A KIND, WONDERFUL PERSON.
HE ALWAYS HAS BEEN...
EVER SINCE WE FIRST MET.
HAAA
FLINCH
YES!
TWCH

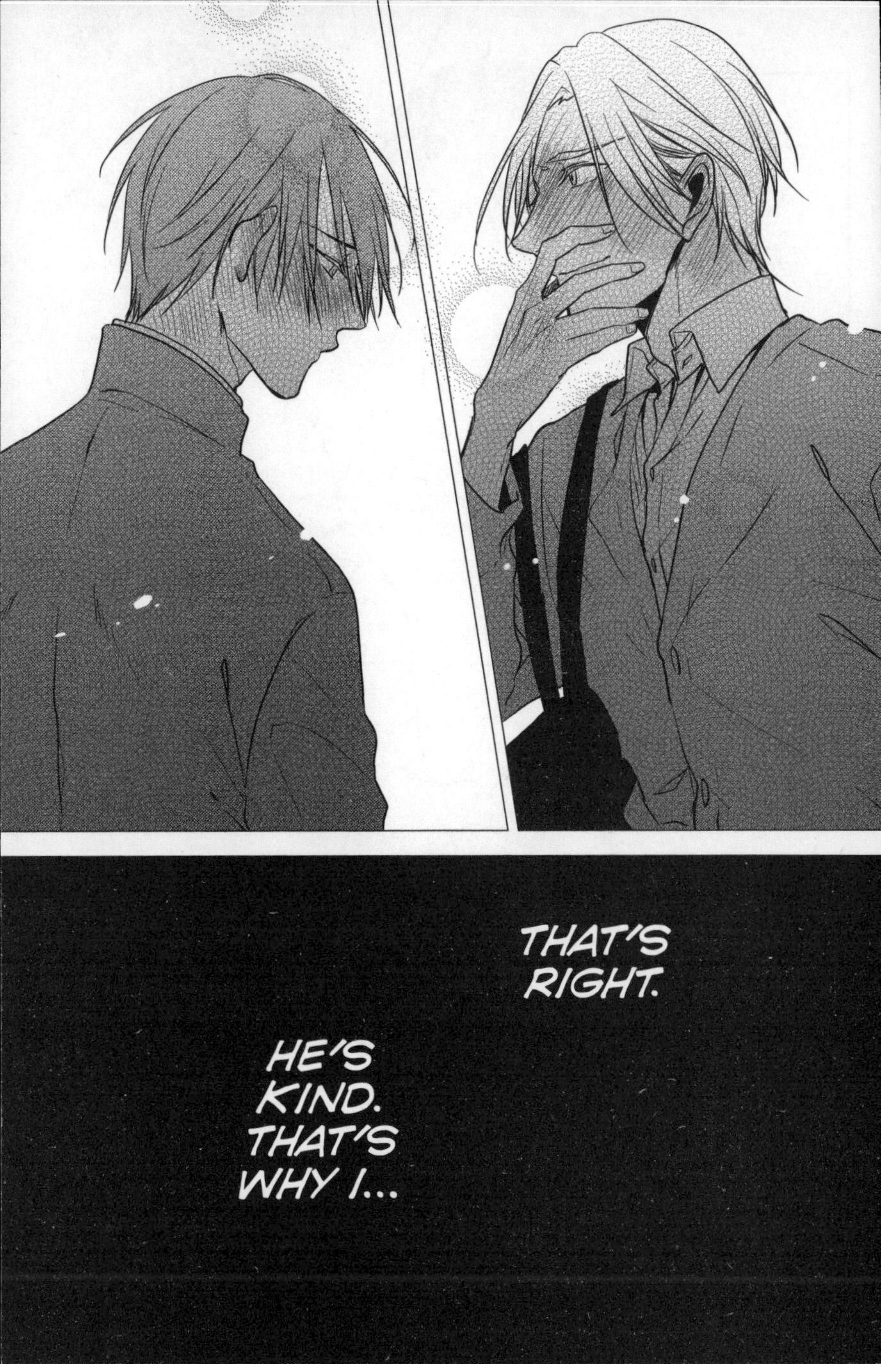
THAT'S RIGHT.
HE'S KIND. THAT'S WHY I...

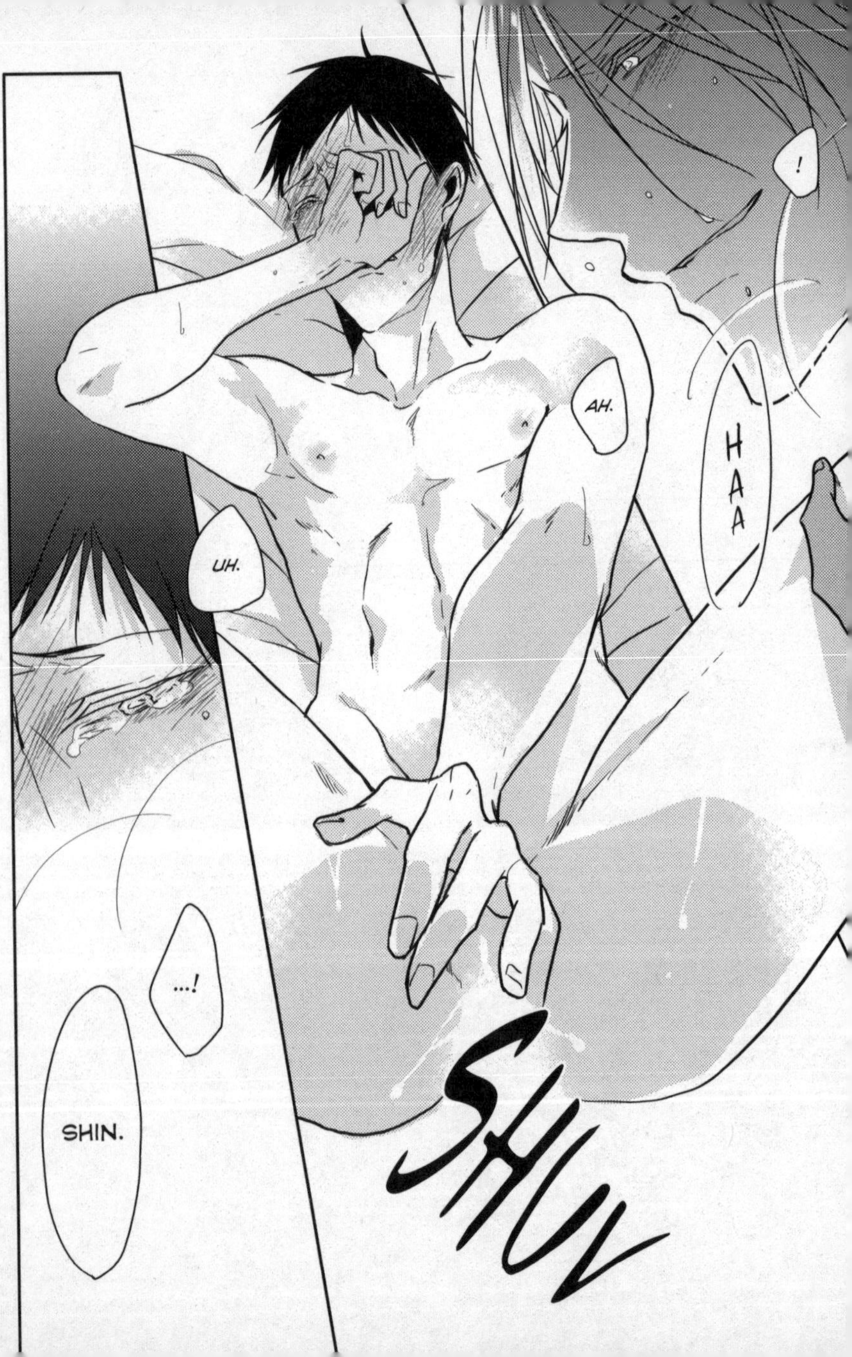
!
HAA
AH.
UH.
SHUV
...!
SHIN.

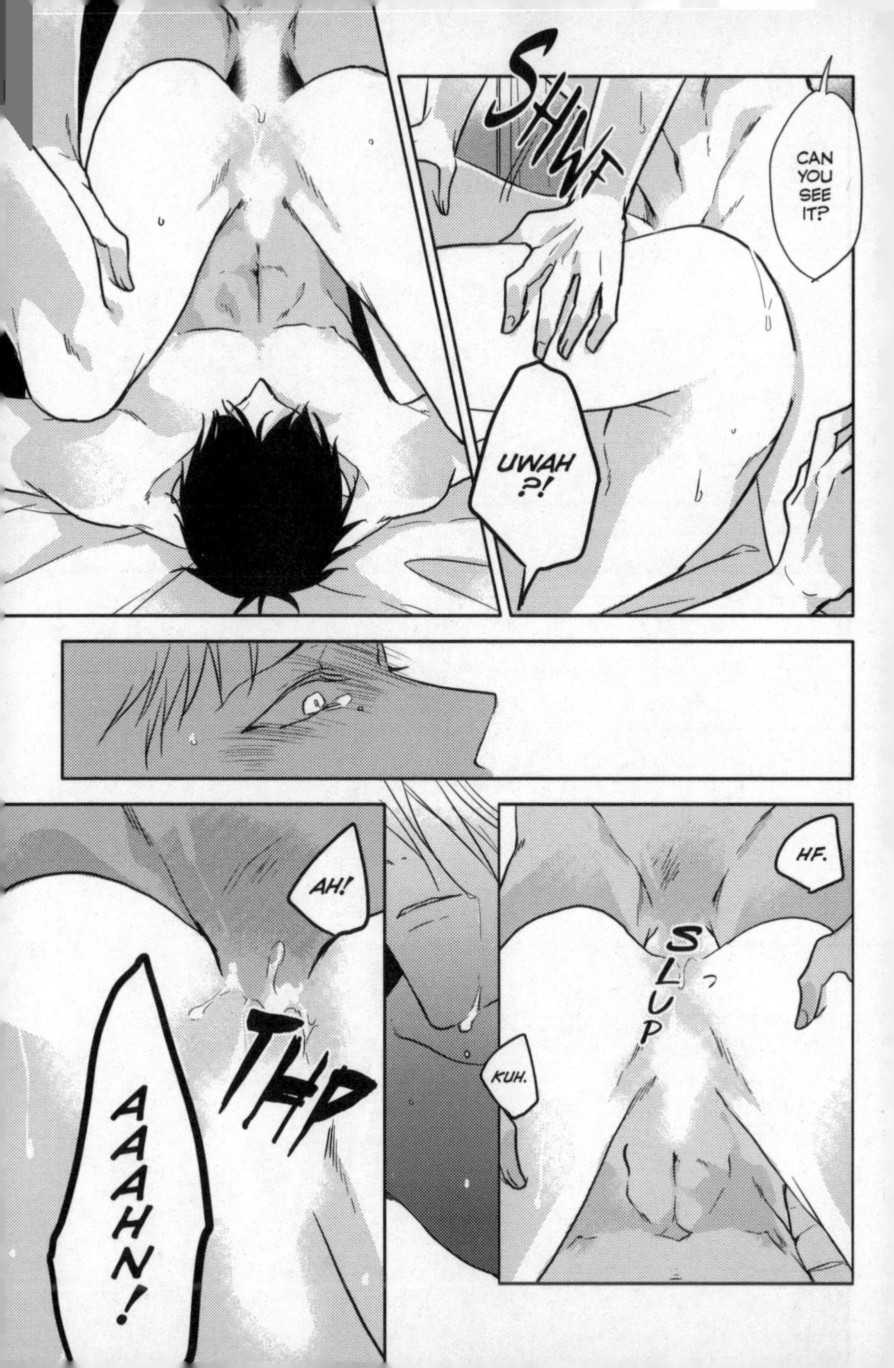
CAN YOU SEE IT?
SHWF
UWAH ?!
HF.
SLUP
KUH.
AH!
THP
AAAAHN!

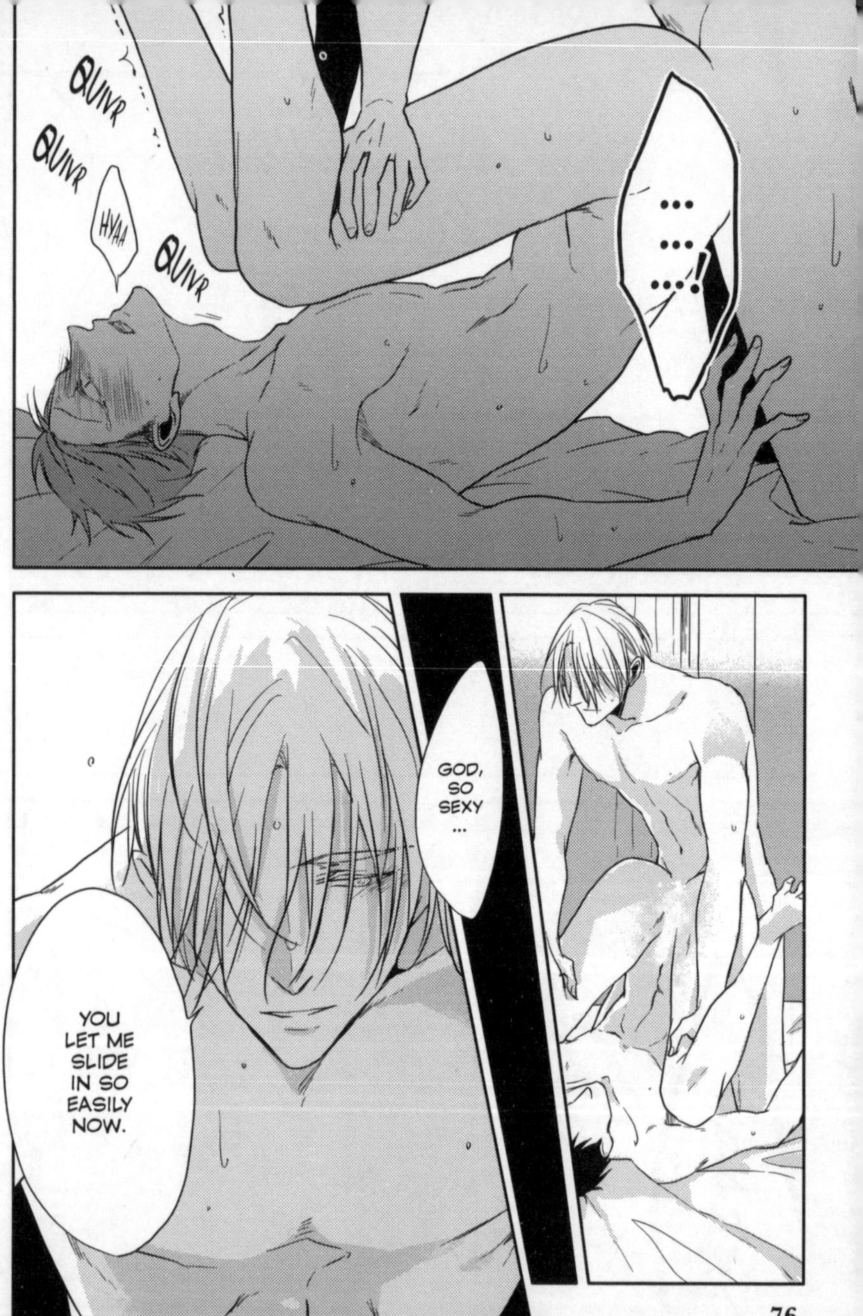
...
...
...!
QUIVR
QUIVR
HYAA
QUIVR
GOD, SO SEXY ...
YOU LET ME SLIDE IN SO EASILY NOW.

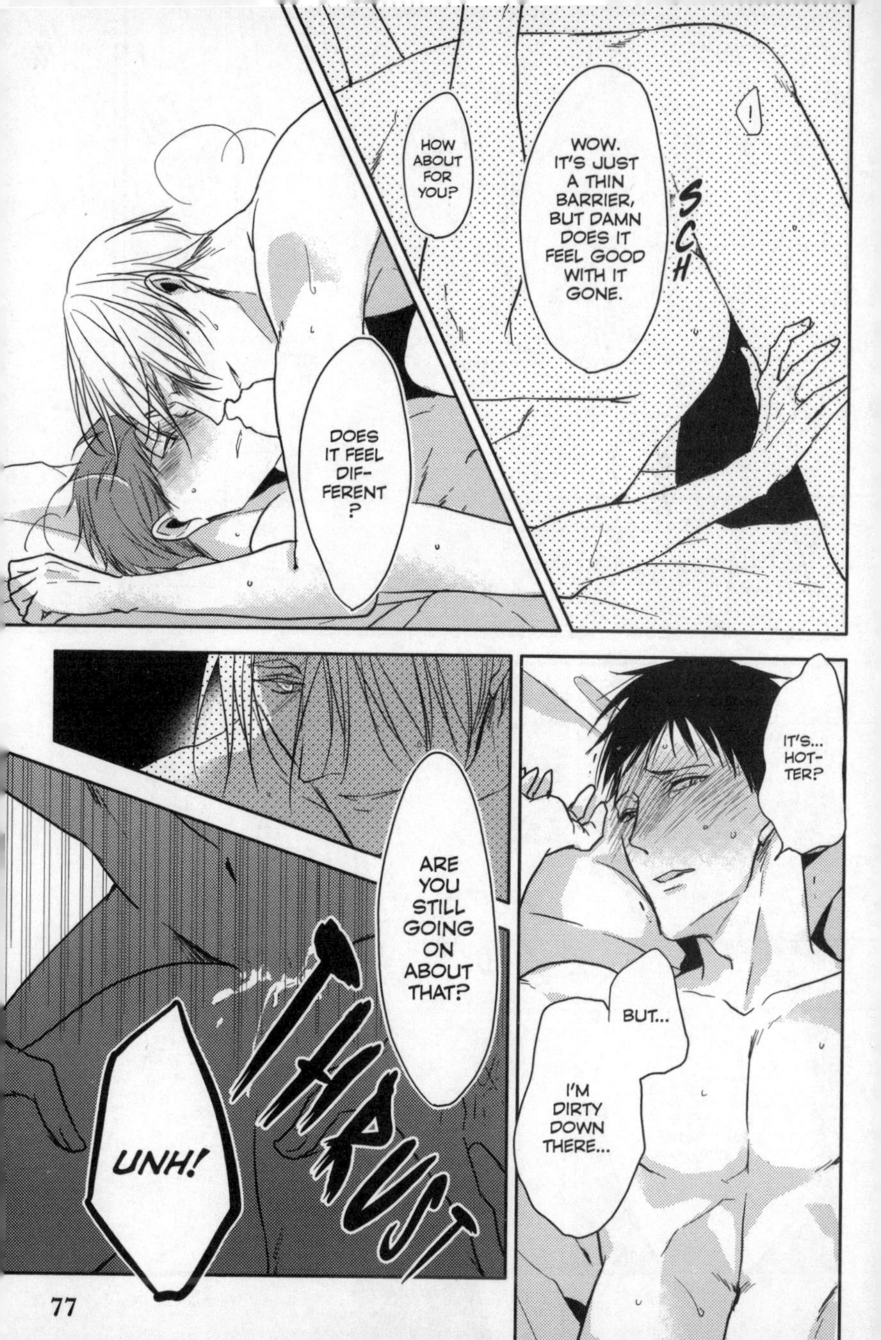
!
SCH
WOW. IT'S JUST A THIN BARRIER, BUT DAMN DOES IT FEEL GOOD WITH IT GONE.
HOW ABOUT FOR YOU?
DOES IT FEEL DIF-FERENT?
IT'S... HOT-TER?
BUT...
I'M DIRTY DOWN THERE...
ARE YOU STILL GOING ON ABOUT THAT?
THRUST
UNH!

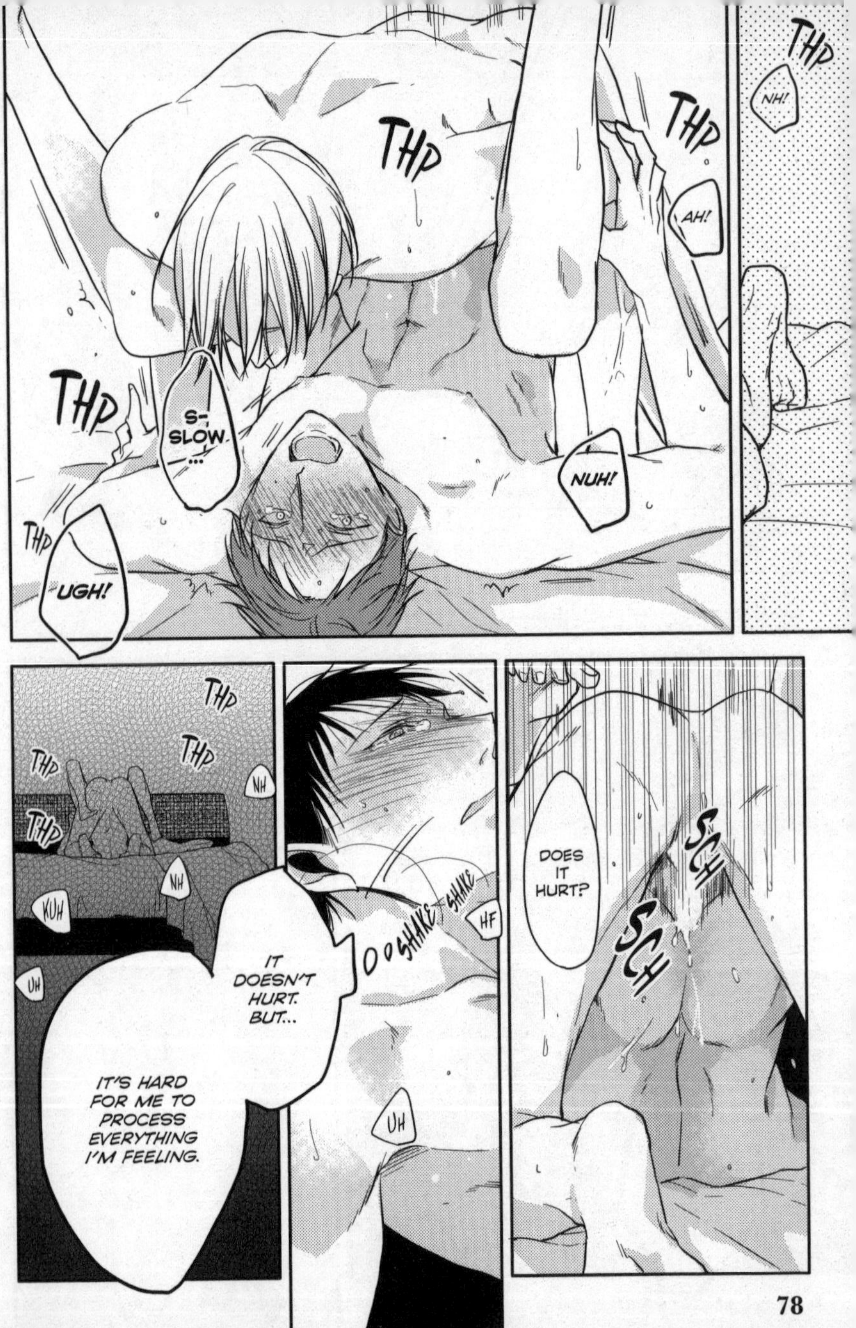
THP
NH!
THP
AH!
THP
NUH!
S-SLOW...
THP
THP
UGH!
DOES IT HURT?
SCH
SCH
HF
SHAKE
SHAKE
DOSHAKE
IT DOESN'T HURT. BUT...
UH
THP
THP
NH
THP
THP
NH
KUH
UH
IT'S HARD FOR ME TO PROCESS EVERYTHING I'M FEELING.

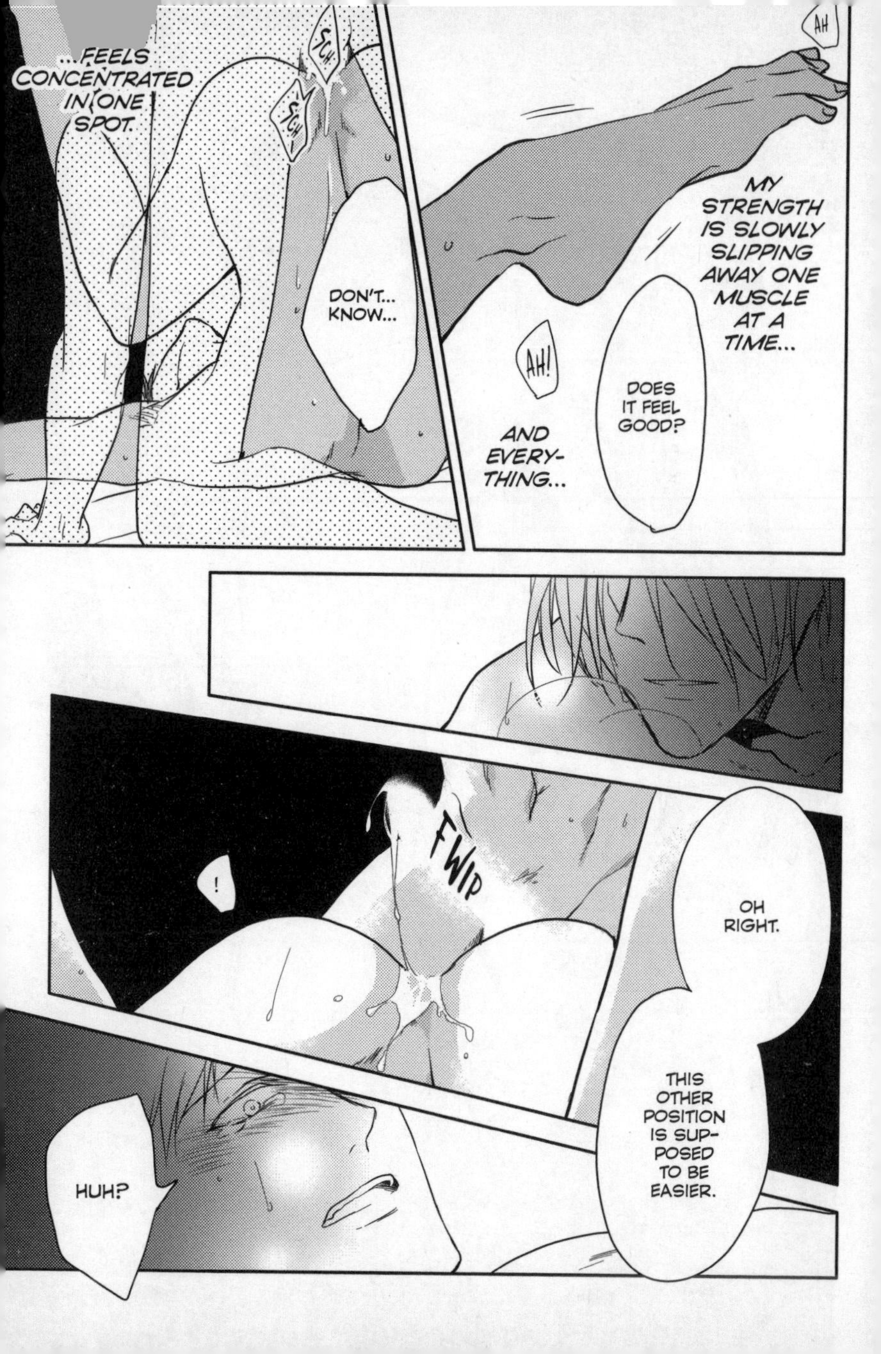
AH
MY STRENGTH IS SLOWLY SLIPPING AWAY ONE MUSCLE AT A TIME...
DOES IT FEEL GOOD?
AH!
AND EVERY-THING...
SCH
SCH
...FEELS CONCENTRATED IN ONE SPOT.
DON'T... KNOW...
FWIP
!
OH RIGHT.
THIS OTHER POSITION IS SUP-POSED TO BE EASIER.
HUH?

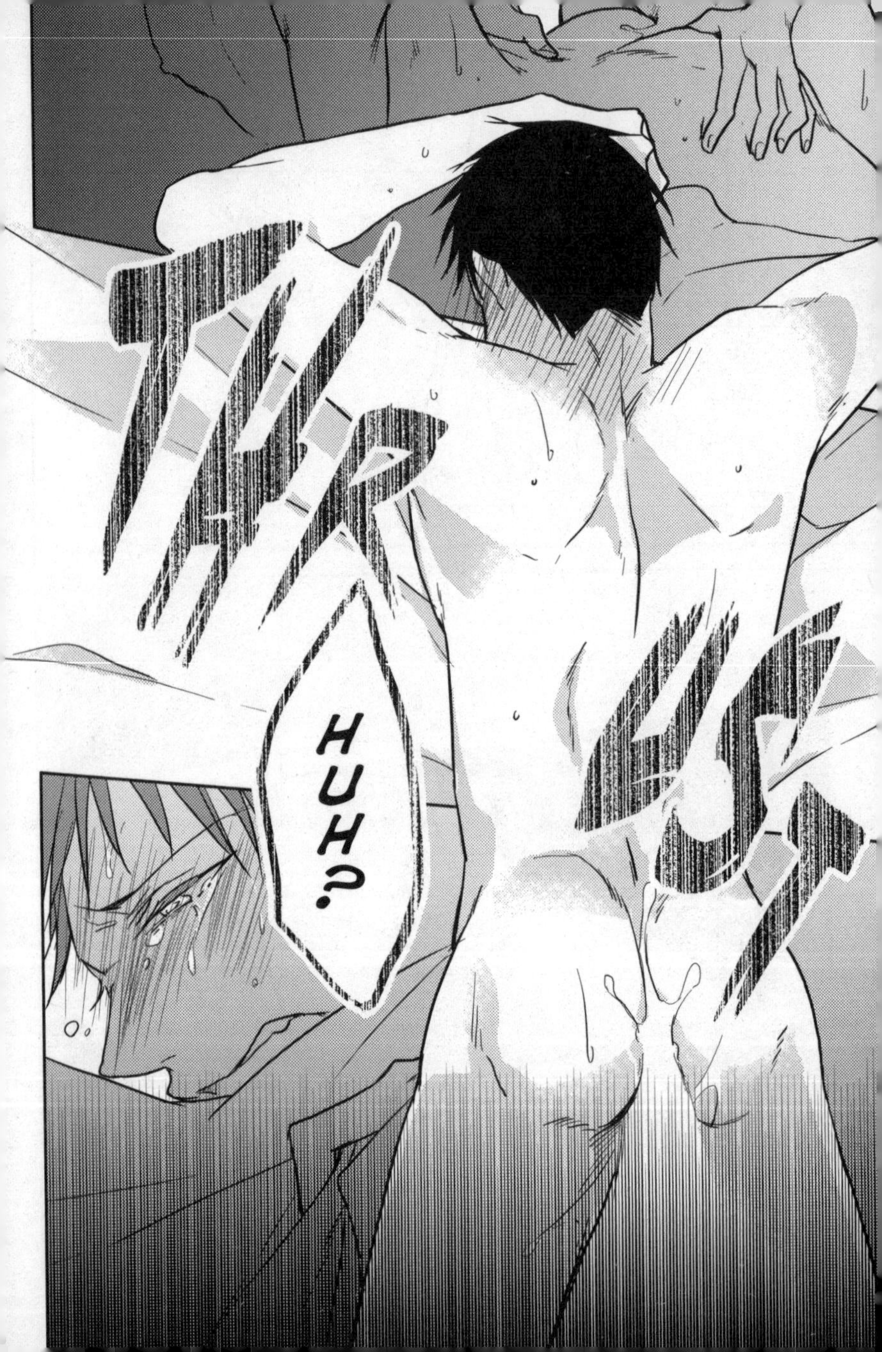
THRUST
HUH?

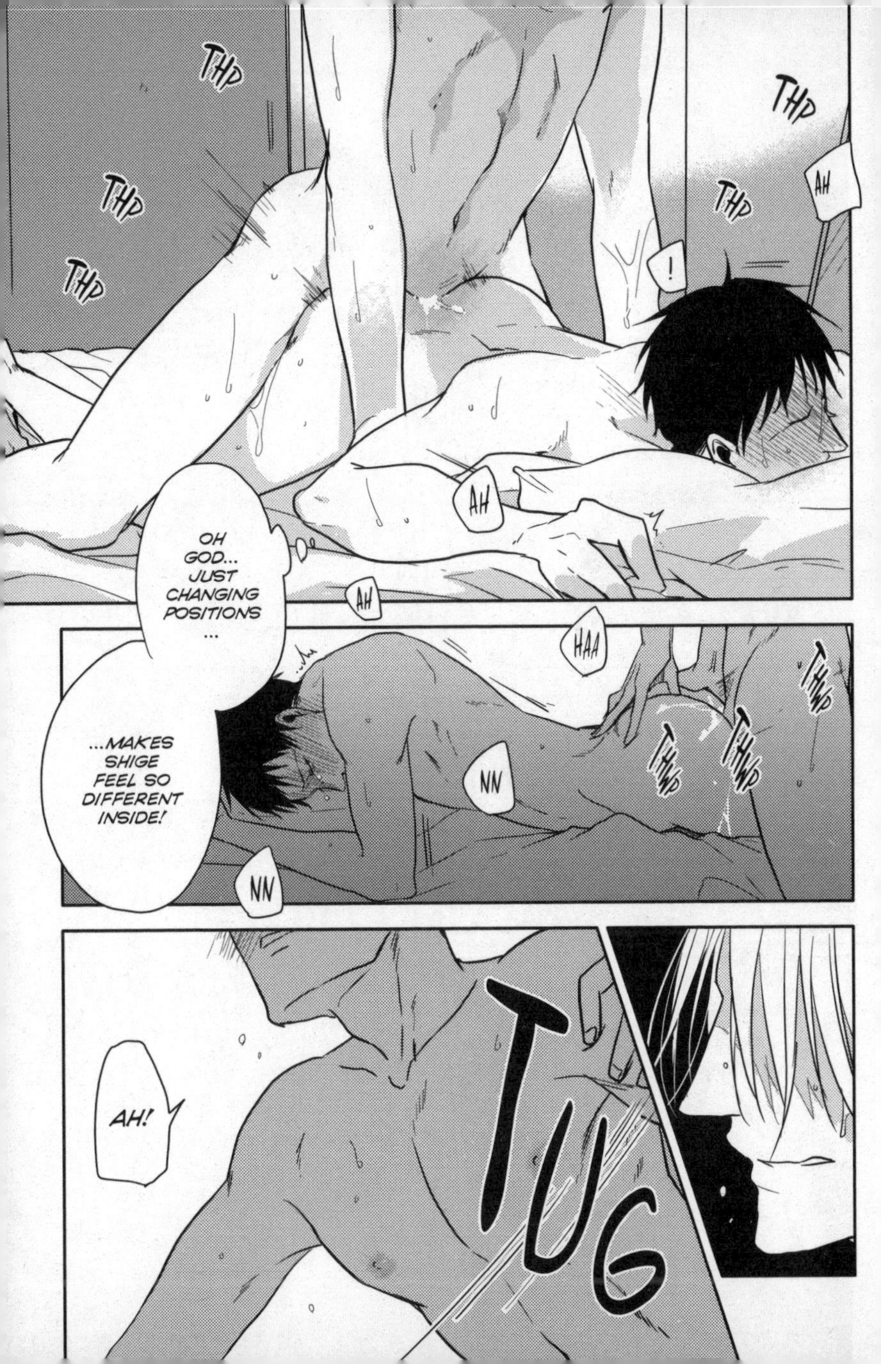
THP
AH
THP
!
THP
THP
THP
AH
OH GOD... JUST CHANGING POSITIONS ...
AH
HAA
THWP
THWP
THWP
...MAKES SHIGE FEEL SO DIFFERENT INSIDE!
NN
NN
TUG
AH!

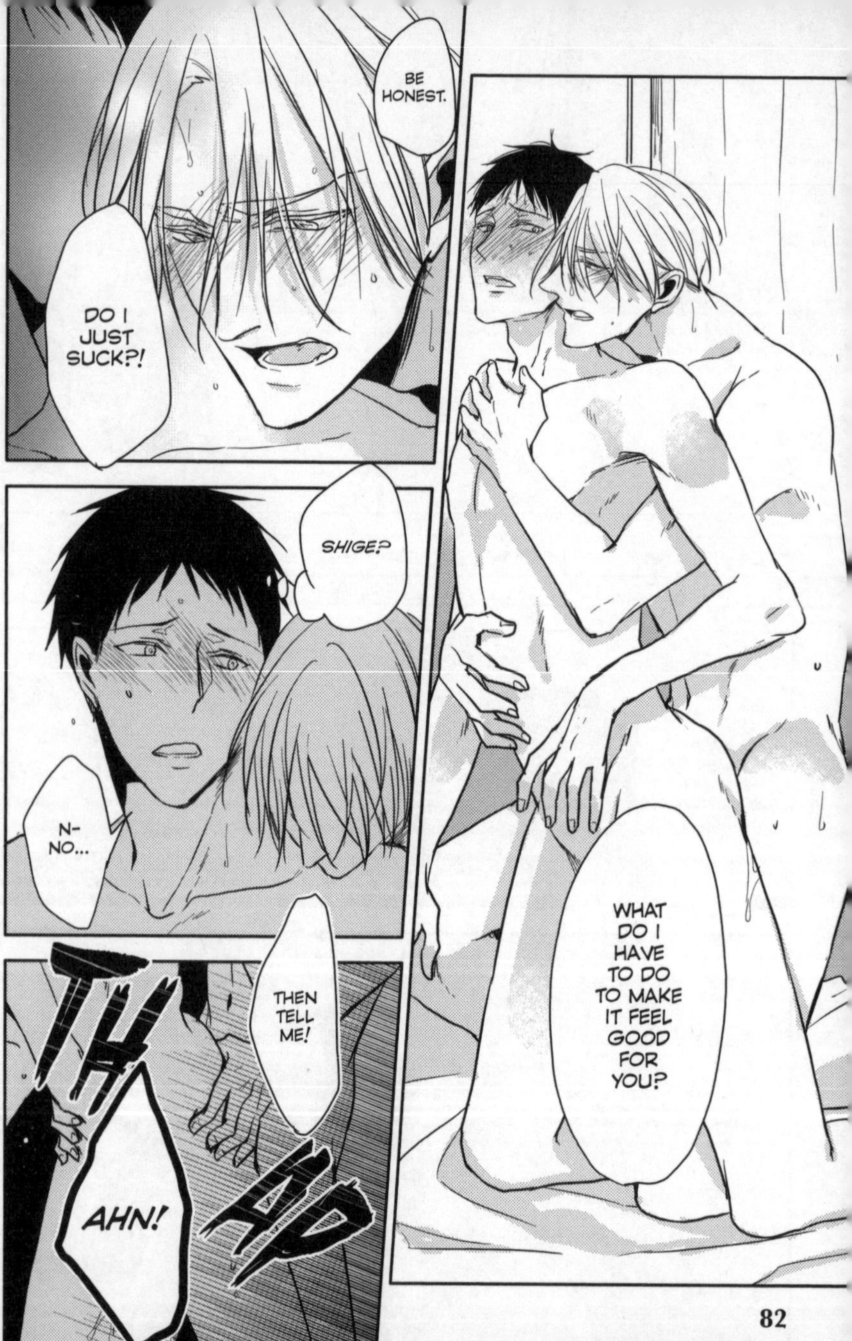
WHAT DO I HAVE TO DO TO MAKE IT FEEL GOOD FOR YOU?
BE HONEST.
DO I JUST SUCK?!
SHIGE?
N-NO...
THEN TELL ME!
THAP
AHN!

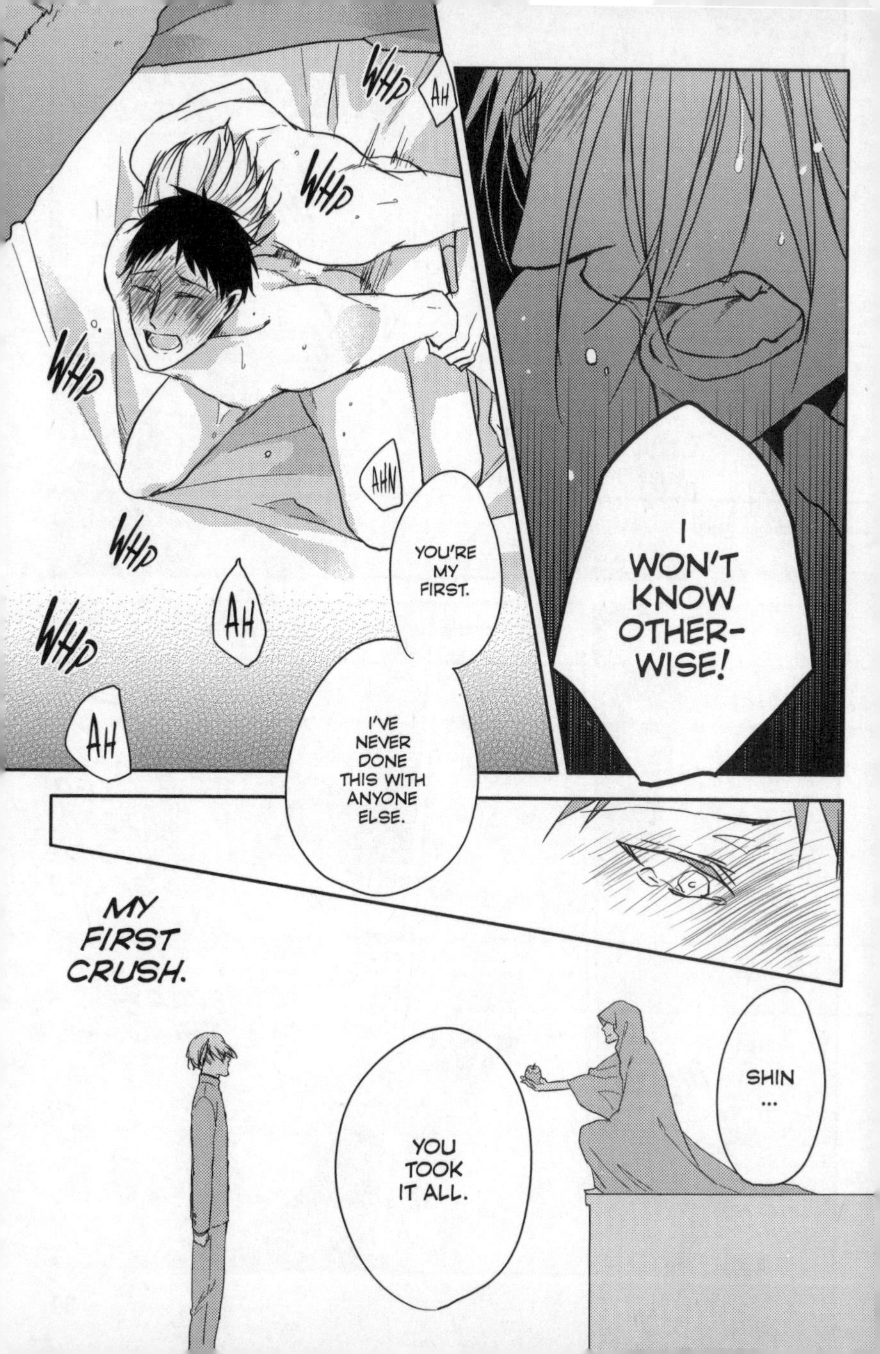
I WON'T KNOW OTHER-WISE!
AH
WHP
WHP
WHP
AHN
YOU'RE MY FIRST.
I'VE NEVER DONE THIS WITH ANYONE ELSE.
WHP
AH
WHP
AH
SHIN ...
YOU TOOK IT ALL.
MY FIRST CRUSH.

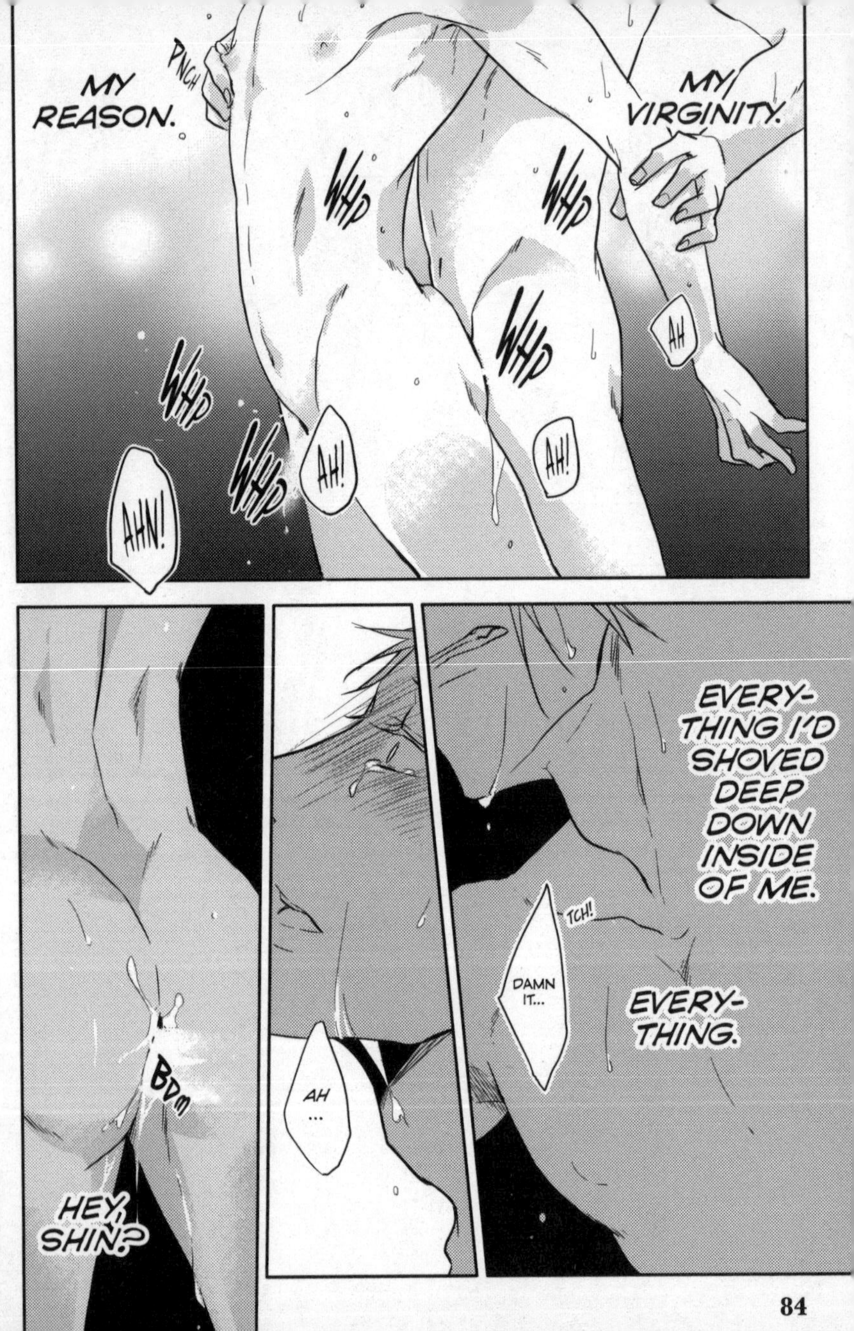
MY VIRGINITY.
PNCH
MY REASON.
WHP
WHP
WHP
AH
AH!
AH!
WHP
WHP
AHN!
EVERY-THING I'D SHOVED DEEP DOWN INSIDE OF ME.
TCH!
DAMN IT...
EVERY-THING.
AH...
BDM
HEY, SHIN?

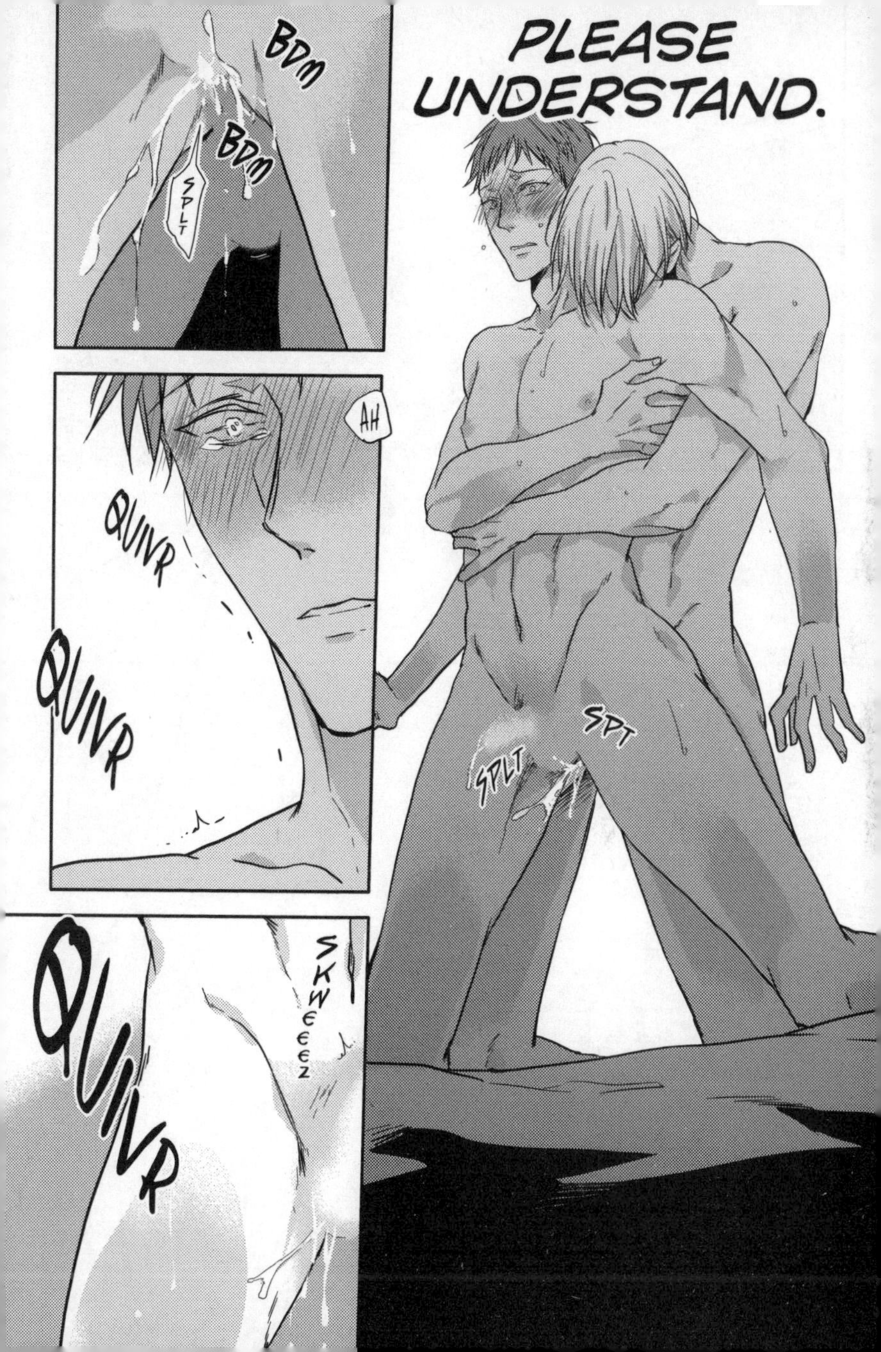

PLEASE UNDERSTAND.
SPT
SPLT
BDM
BDM
SPLT
AH
QUIVR
QUIVR
SKWEEEZ
QUIVR

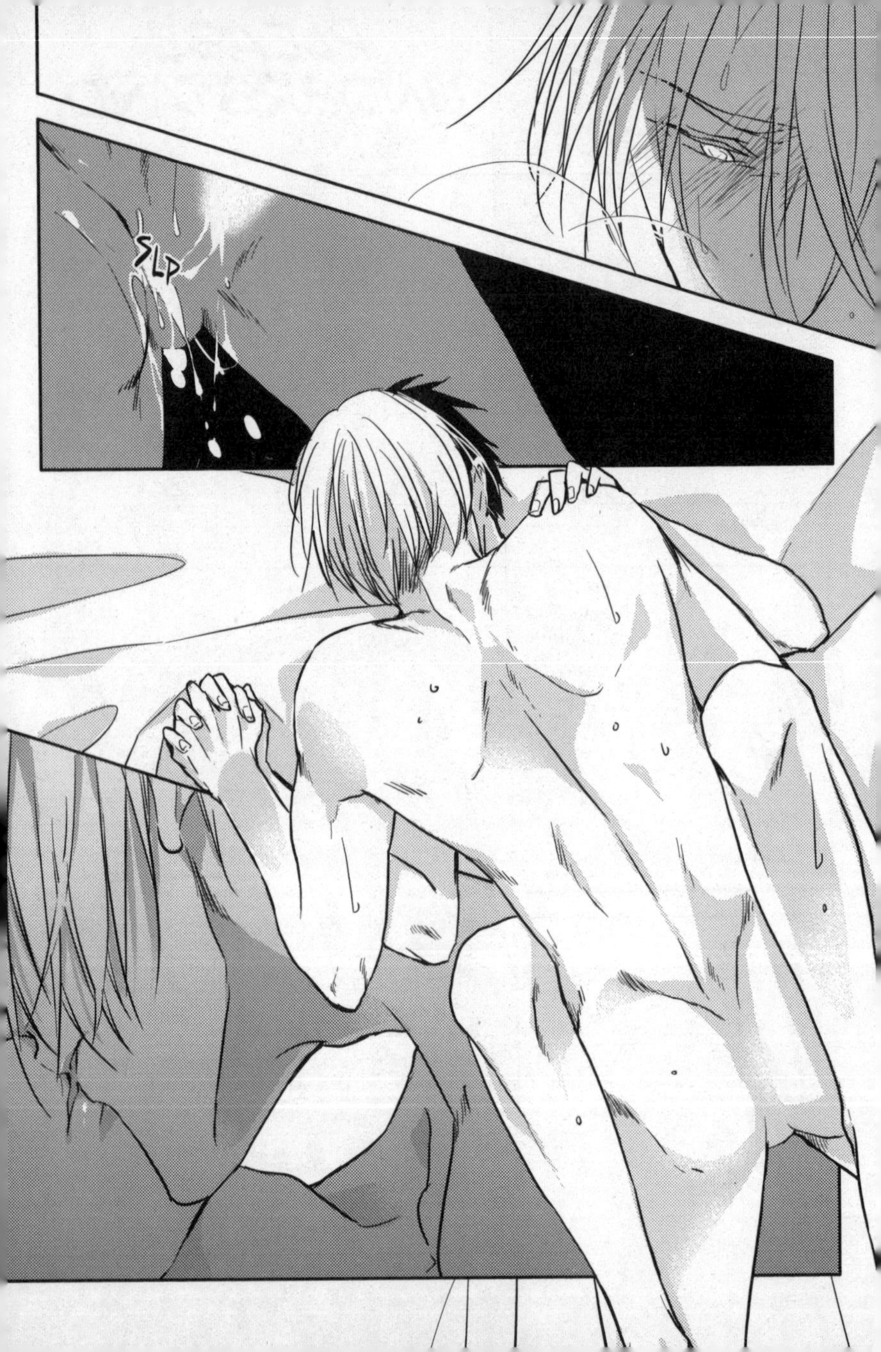
SLP

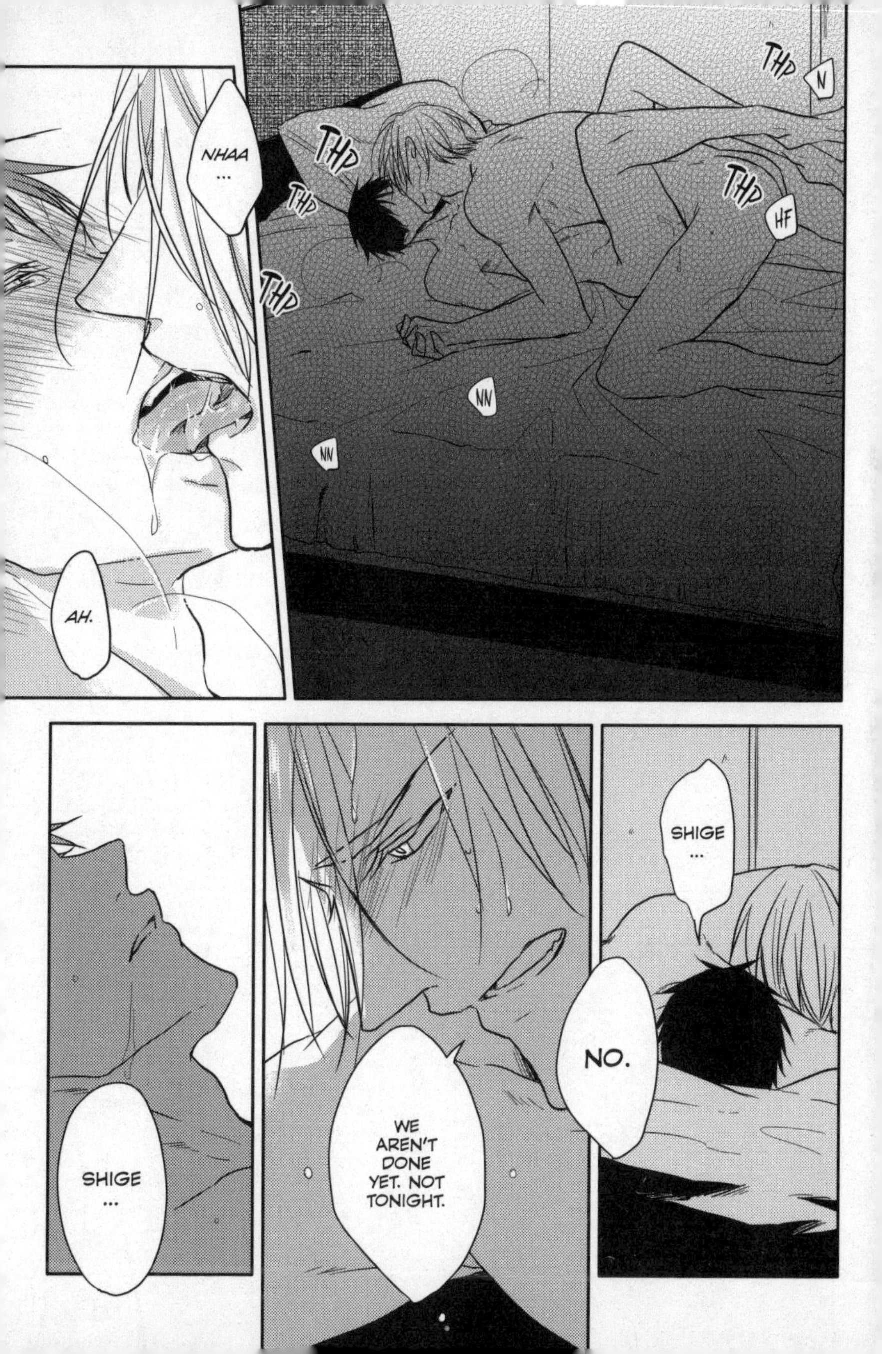
THP
N
THP
THP
THP
HF
THP
NN
NN
NHAA ...
AH.
SHIGE ...
NO.
WE AREN'T DONE YET. NOT TONIGHT.
SHIGE ...

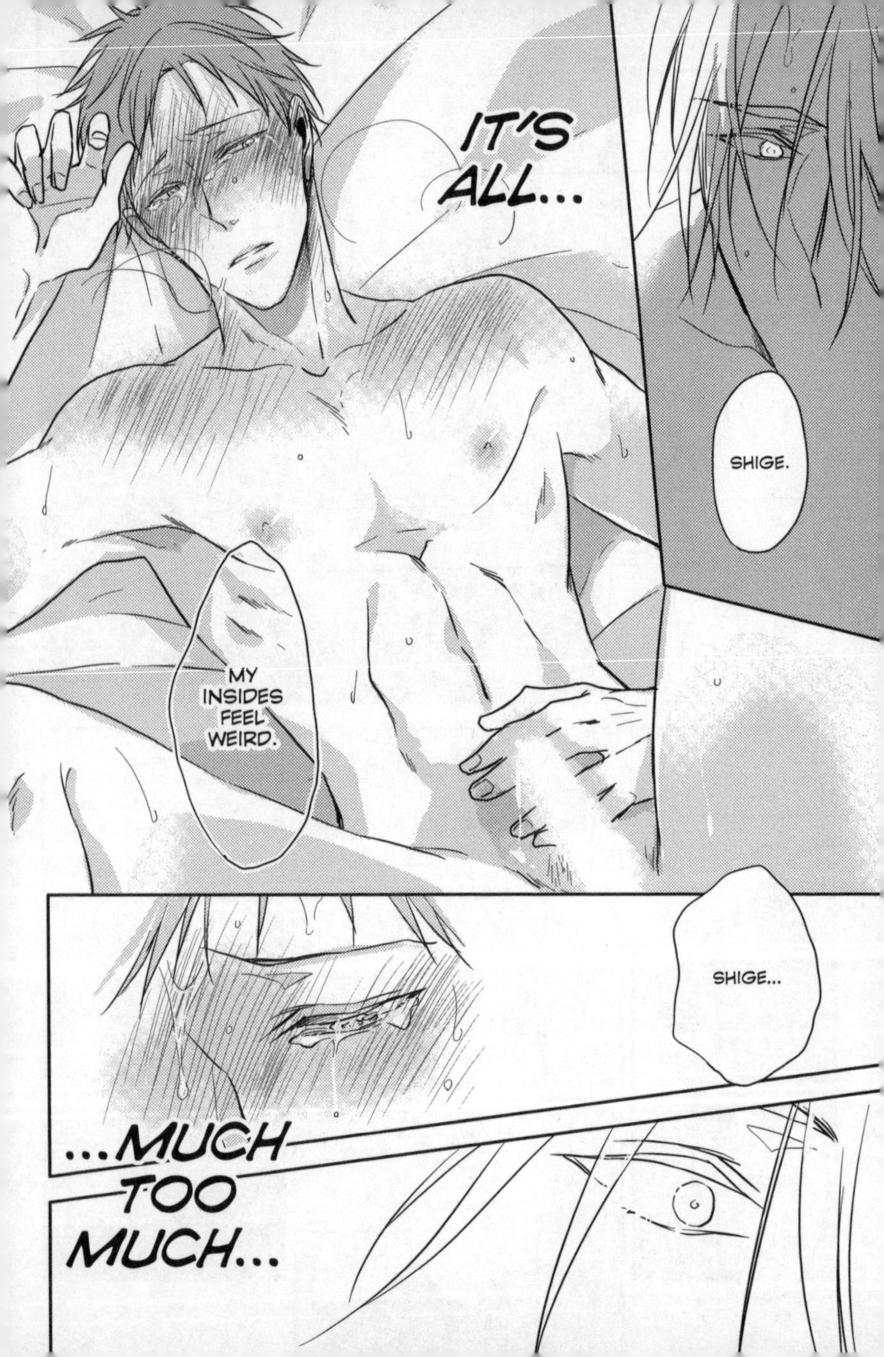
SHIGE.
IT'S ALL...
MY INSIDES FEEL WEIRD.
SHIGE...
...MUCH TOO MUCH...

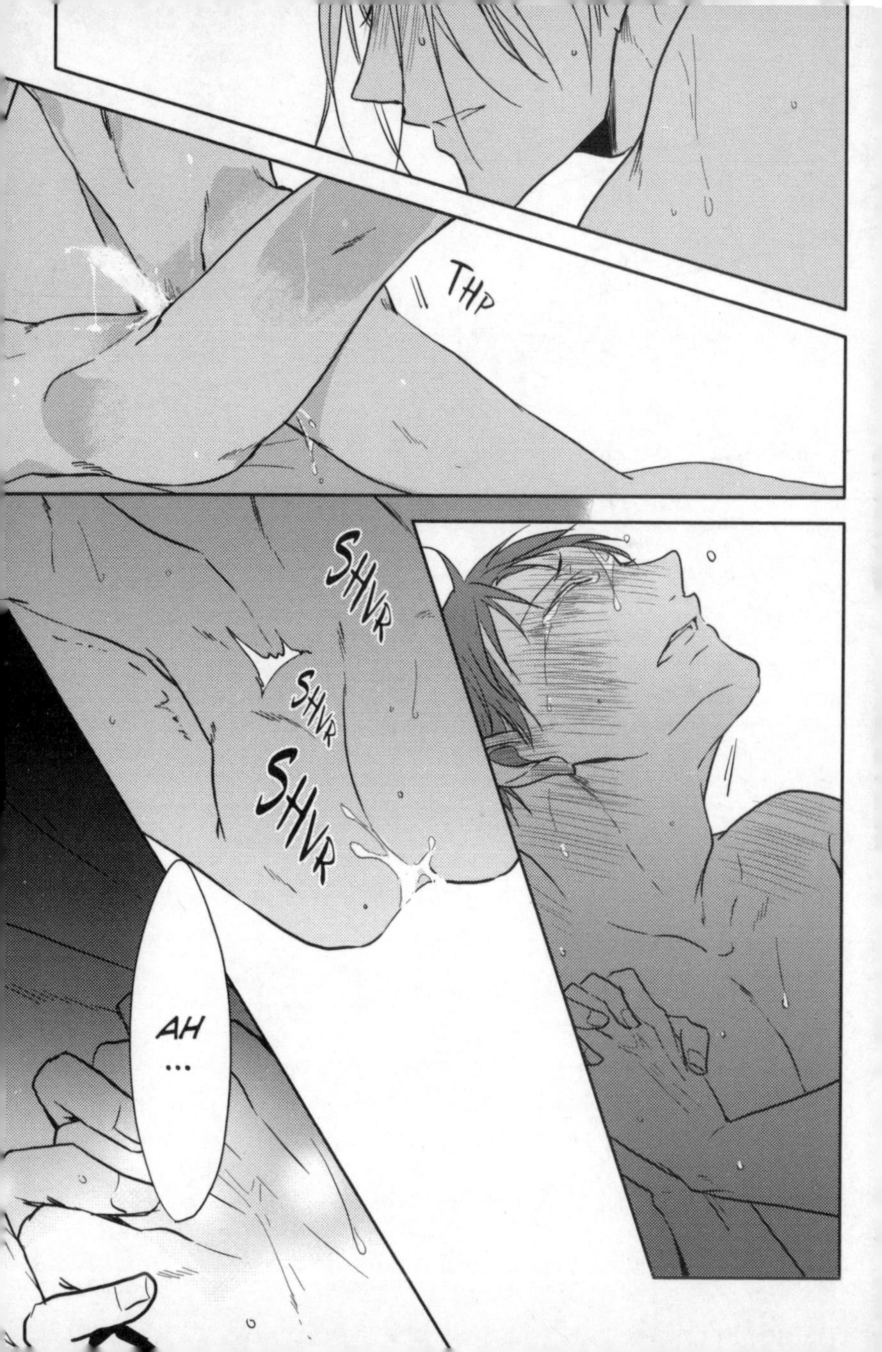
THP
SHVR
SHVR
SHVR
AH ...

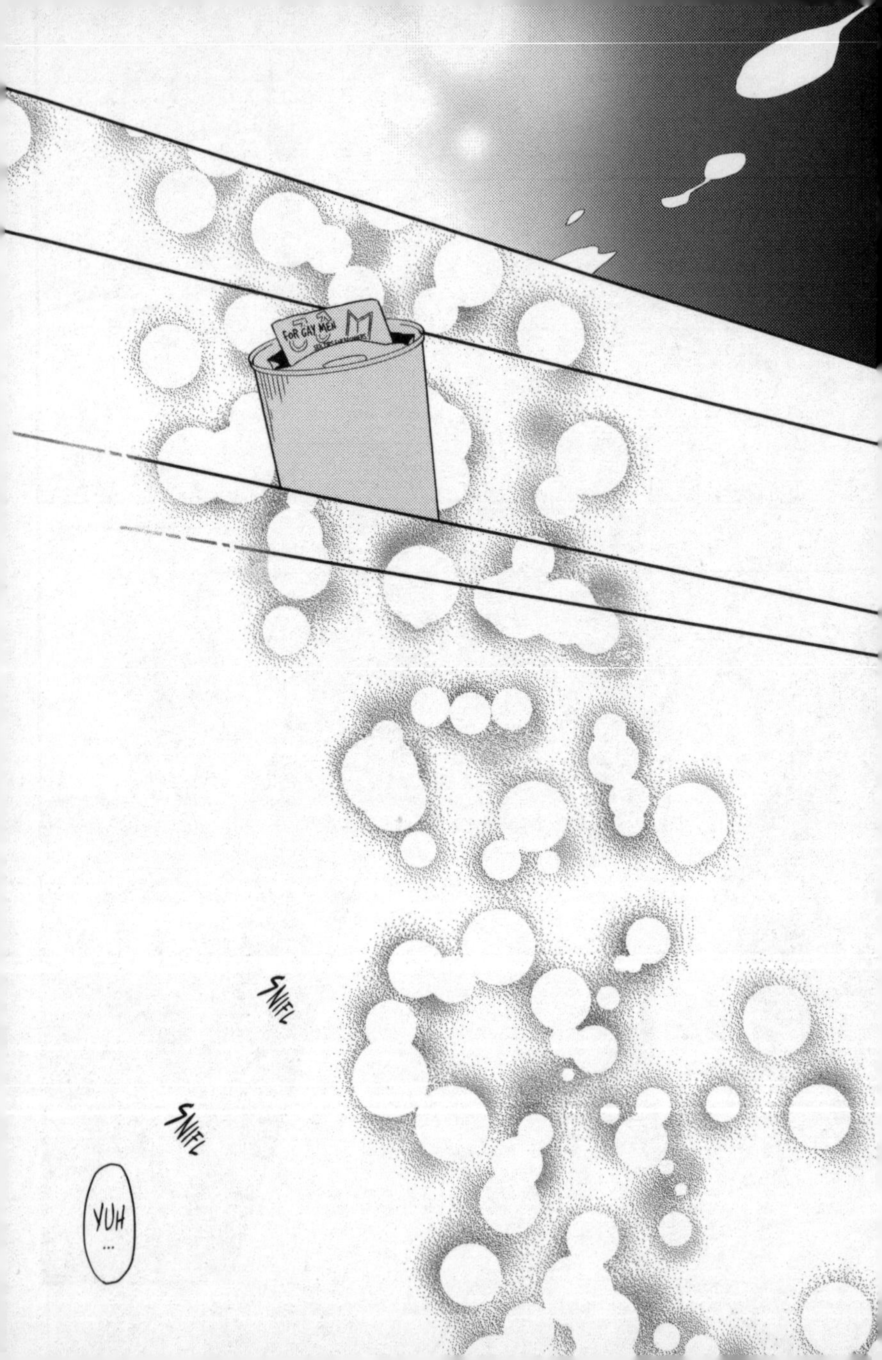
FOR GAY MEN
SNIFL
SNIFL
YUH
...

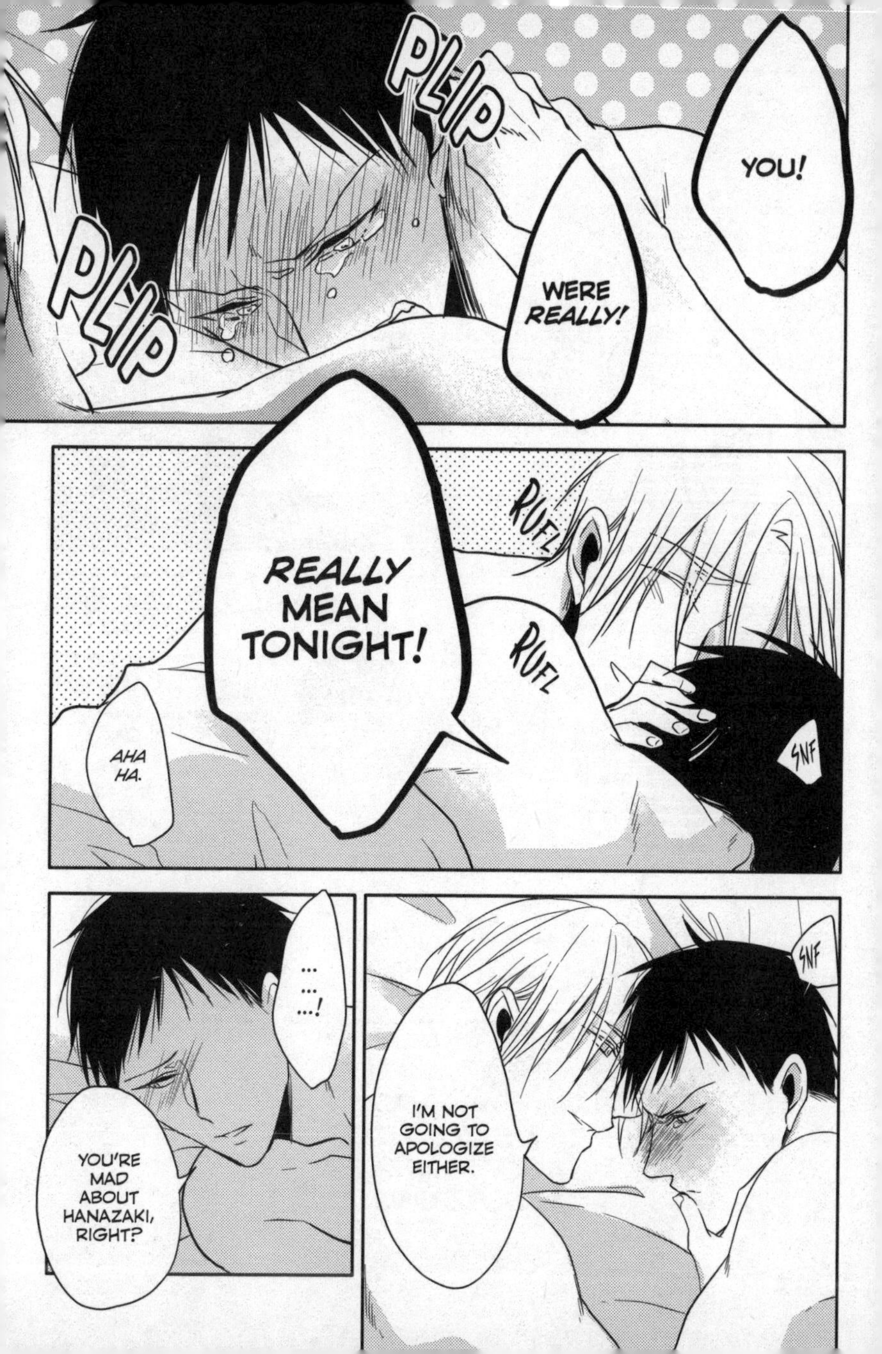
YOU!
WERE REALLY!
PLIP PLIP
PLIP
REALLY MEAN TONIGHT!
RUFL
RUFL
SNF
AHA HA.
SNF
I'M NOT GOING TO APOLOGIZE EITHER.
...
...
...!
YOU'RE MAD ABOUT HANAZAKI, RIGHT?

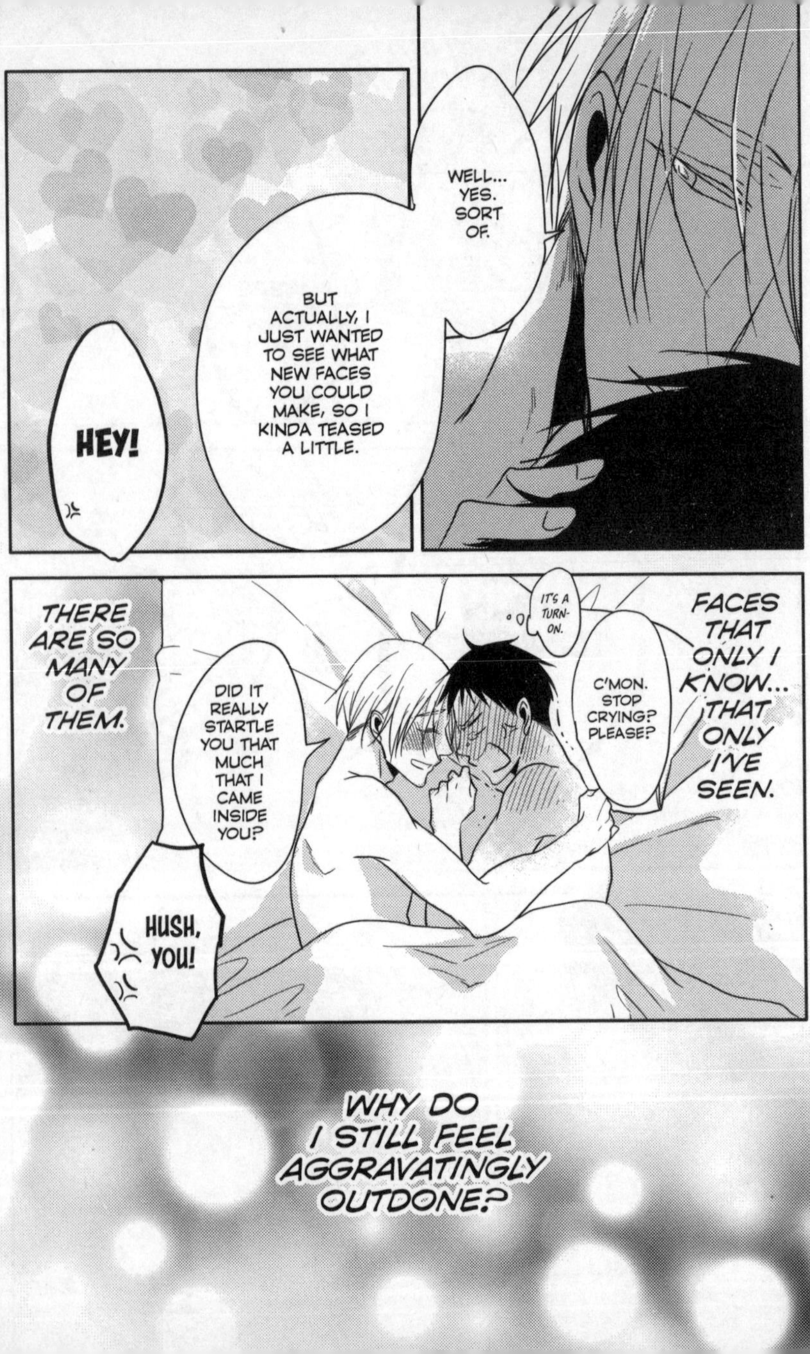
WELL... YES. SORT OF.
BUT ACTUALLY, I JUST WANTED TO SEE WHAT NEW FACES YOU COULD MAKE, SO I KINDA TEASED A LITTLE.
HEY!
FACES THAT ONLY I KNOW... THAT ONLY I'VE SEEN.
IT'S A TURN-ON.
C'MON. STOP CRYING? PLEASE?
DID IT REALLY STARTLE YOU THAT MUCH THAT I CAME INSIDE YOU?
THERE ARE SO MANY OF THEM.
HUSH, YOU!
WHY DO I STILL FEEL AGGRAVATINGLY OUTDONE?

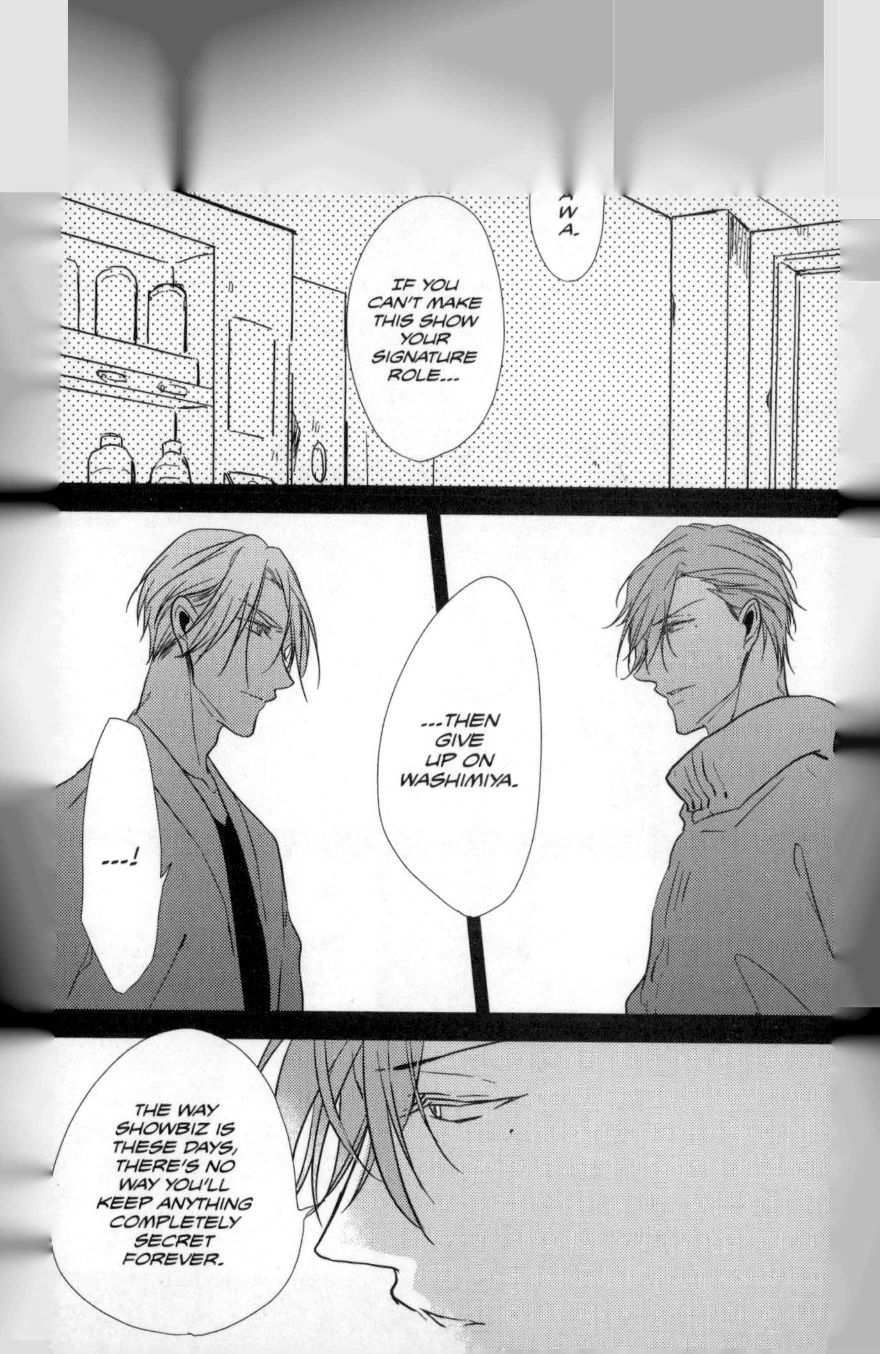
AWA.
IF YOU CAN'T MAKE THIS SHOW YOUR SIGNATURE ROLE...
...THEN GIVE UP ON WASHIMIYA.
...!
THE WAY SHOWBIZ IS THESE DAYS, THERE'S NO WAY YOU'LL KEEP ANYTHING COMPLETELY SECRET FOREVER.

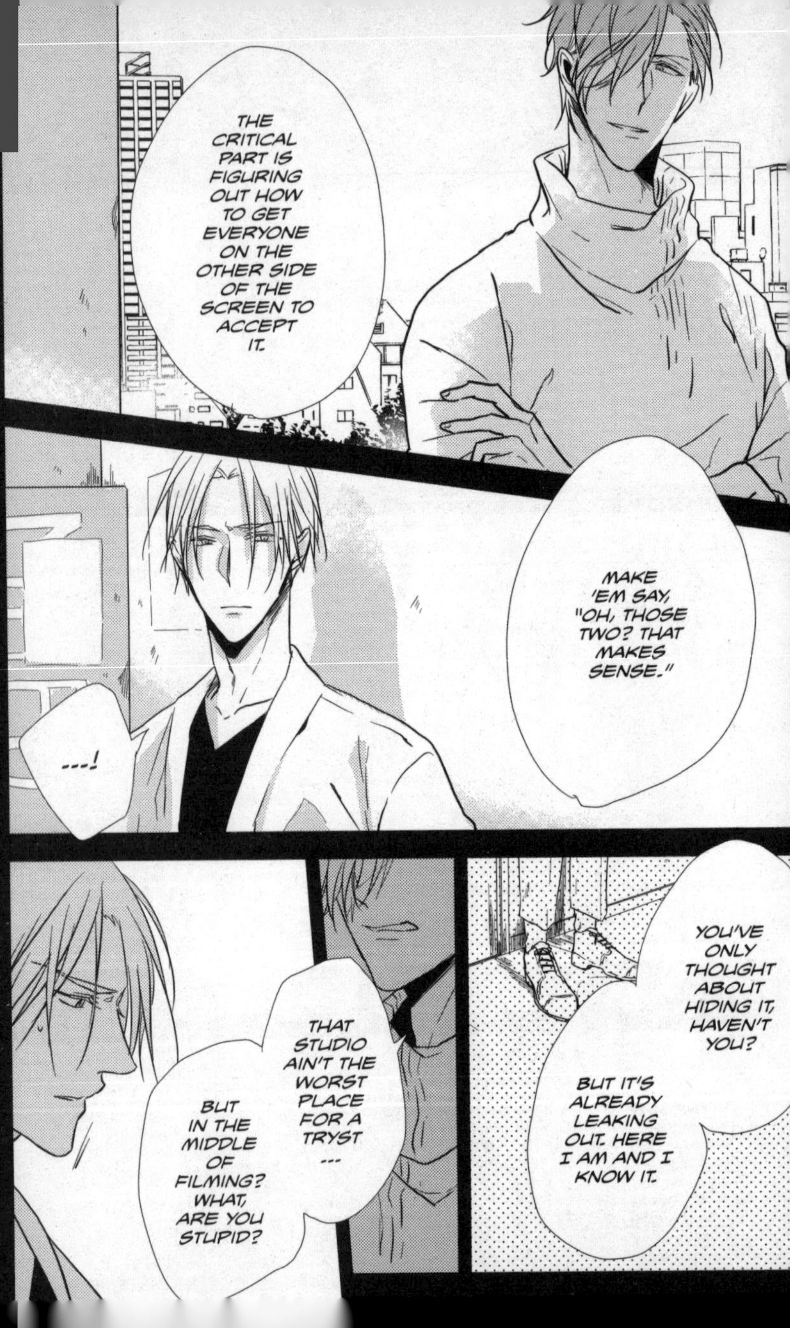
THE CRITICAL PART IS FIGURING OUT HOW TO GET EVERYONE ON THE OTHER SIDE OF THE SCREEN TO ACCEPT IT.
MAKE 'EM SAY, "OH, THOSE TWO? THAT MAKES SENSE."
---!
YOU'VE ONLY THOUGHT ABOUT HIDING IT, HAVEN'T YOU?
BUT IT'S ALREADY LEAKING OUT. HERE I AM AND I KNOW IT.
THAT STUDIO AIN'T THE WORST PLACE FOR A TRYST ---
BUT IN THE MIDDLE OF FILMING? WHAT, ARE YOU STUPID?

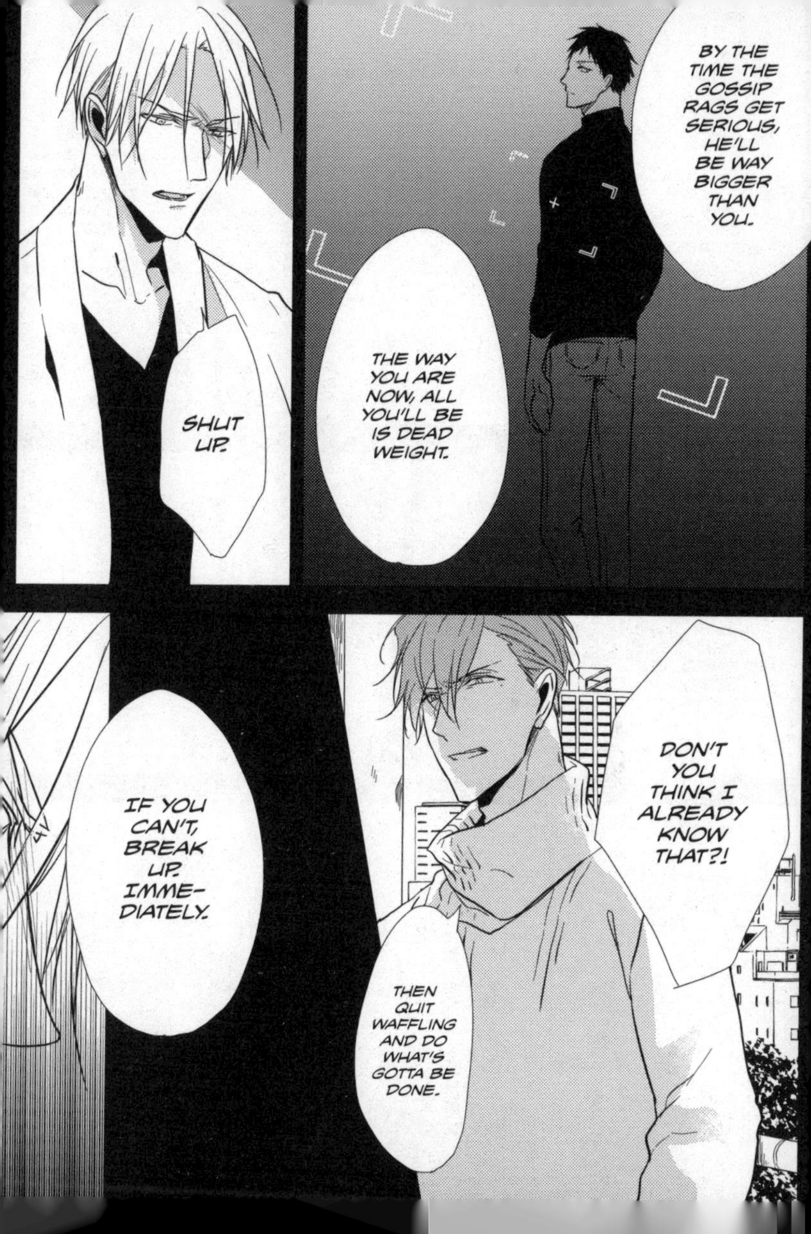
BY THE TIME THE GOSSIP RAGS GET SERIOUS, HE'LL BE WAY BIGGER THAN YOU.
THE WAY YOU ARE NOW, ALL YOU'LL BE IS DEAD WEIGHT.
SHUT UP.
DON'T YOU THINK I ALREADY KNOW THAT?!
THEN QUIT WAFFLING AND DO WHAT'S GOTTA BE DONE.
IF YOU CAN'T, BREAK UP. IMME-DIATELY.

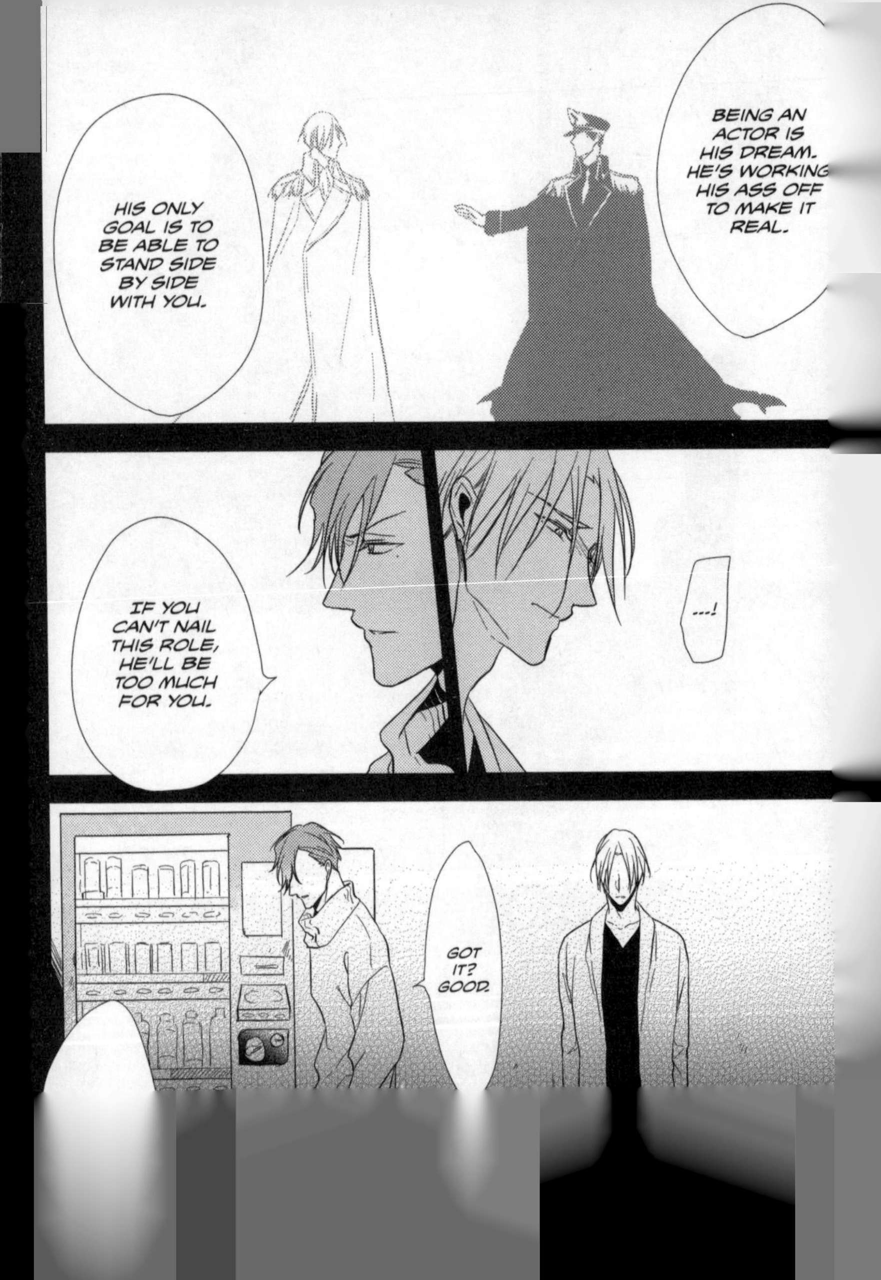
BEING AN ACTOR IS HIS DREAM. HE'S WORKING HIS ASS OFF TO MAKE IT REAL.
HIS ONLY GOAL IS TO BE ABLE TO STAND SIDE BY SIDE WITH YOU.
...!
IF YOU CAN'T NAIL THIS ROLE, HE'LL BE TOO MUCH FOR YOU.
GOT IT? GOOD.

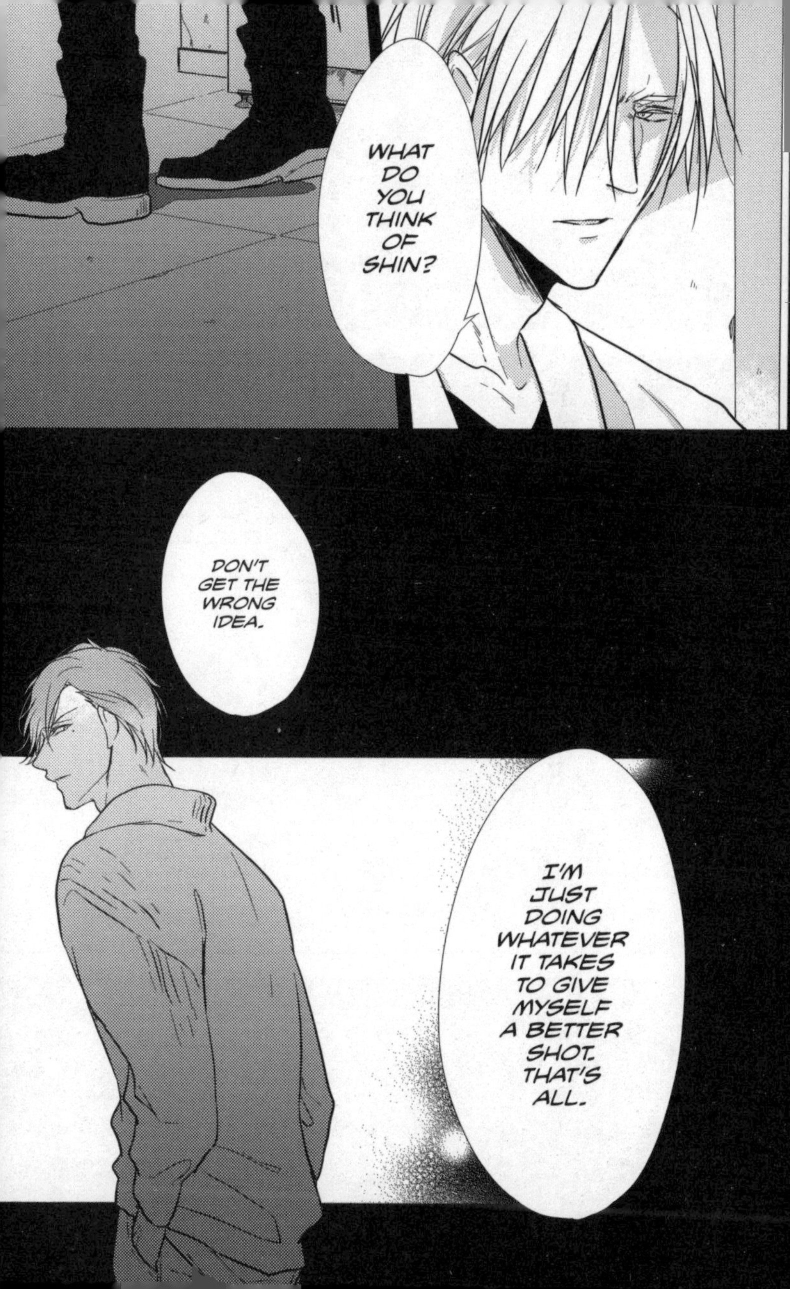
WHAT DO YOU THINK OF SHIN?
DON'T GET THE WRONG IDEA.
I'M JUST DOING WHATEVER IT TAKES TO GIVE MYSELF A BETTER SHOT. THAT'S ALL.

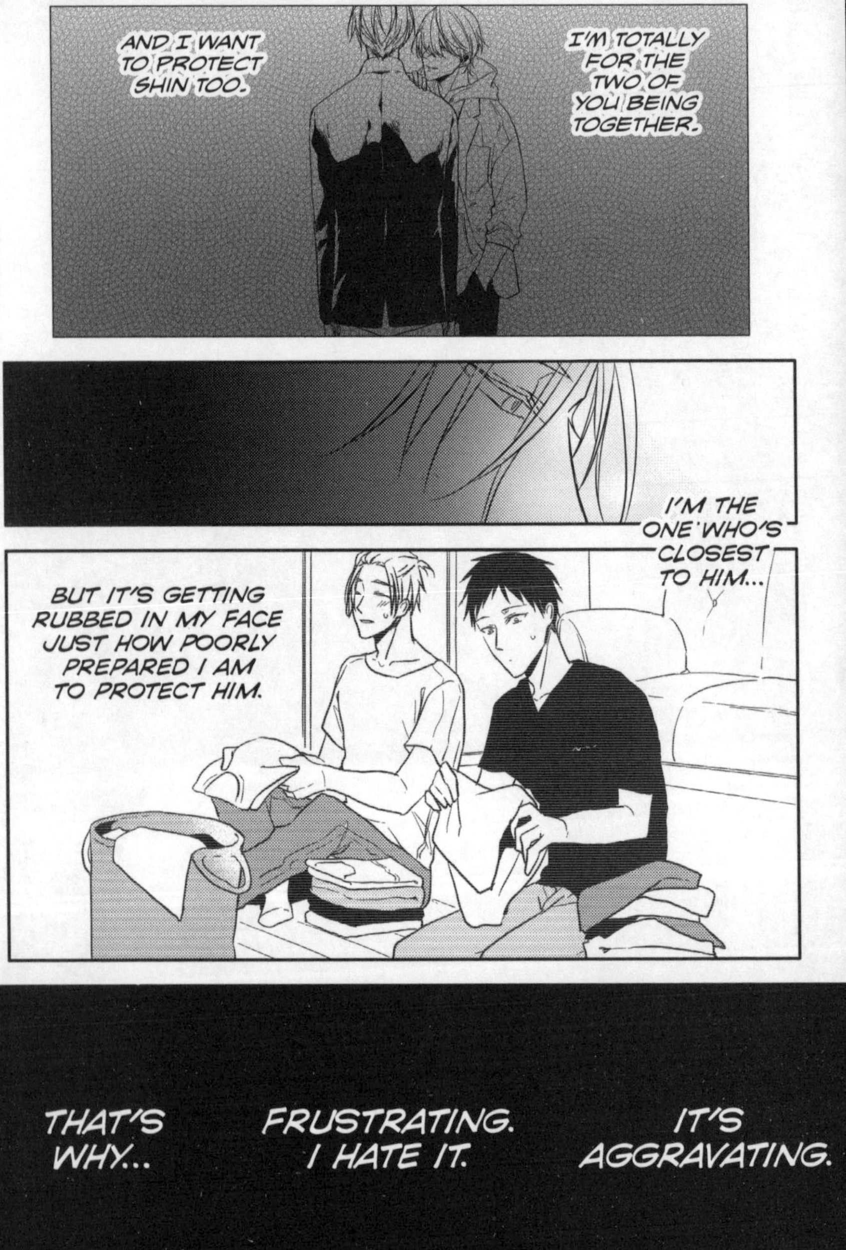
I'M TOTALLY FOR THE TWO OF YOU BEING TOGETHER.
AND I WANT TO PROTECT SHIN TOO.
I'M THE ONE WHO'S CLOSEST TO HIM...
BUT IT'S GETTING RUBBED IN MY FACE JUST HOW POORLY PREPARED I AM TO PROTECT HIM.
IT'S AGGRAVATING.
FRUSTRATING. I HATE IT.
THAT'S WHY...

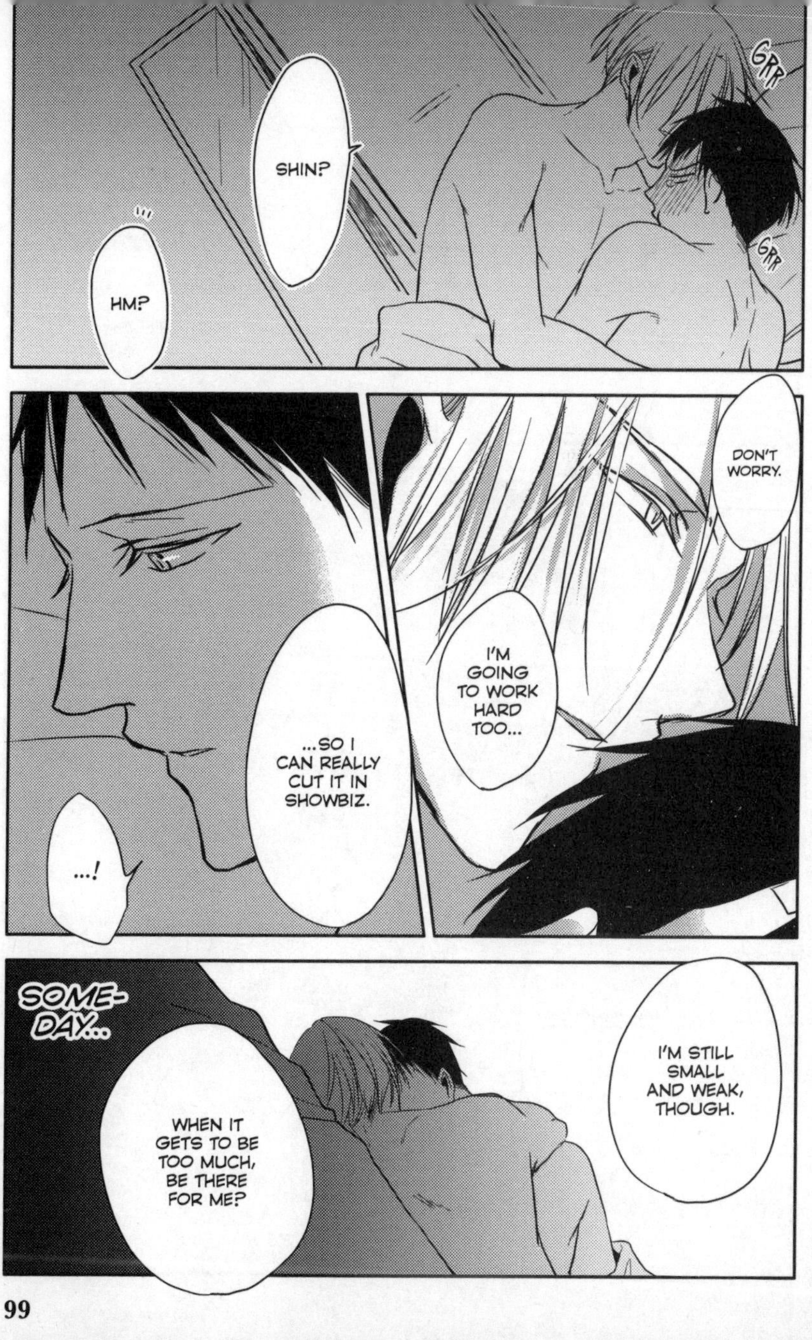
GRR
GRR
SHIN?
HM?
DON'T WORRY.
I'M GOING TO WORK HARD TOO...
...SO I CAN REALLY CUT IT IN SHOWBIZ.
...!
I'M STILL SMALL AND WEAK, THOUGH.
SOME-DAY...
WHEN IT GETS TO BE TOO MUCH, BE THERE FOR ME?

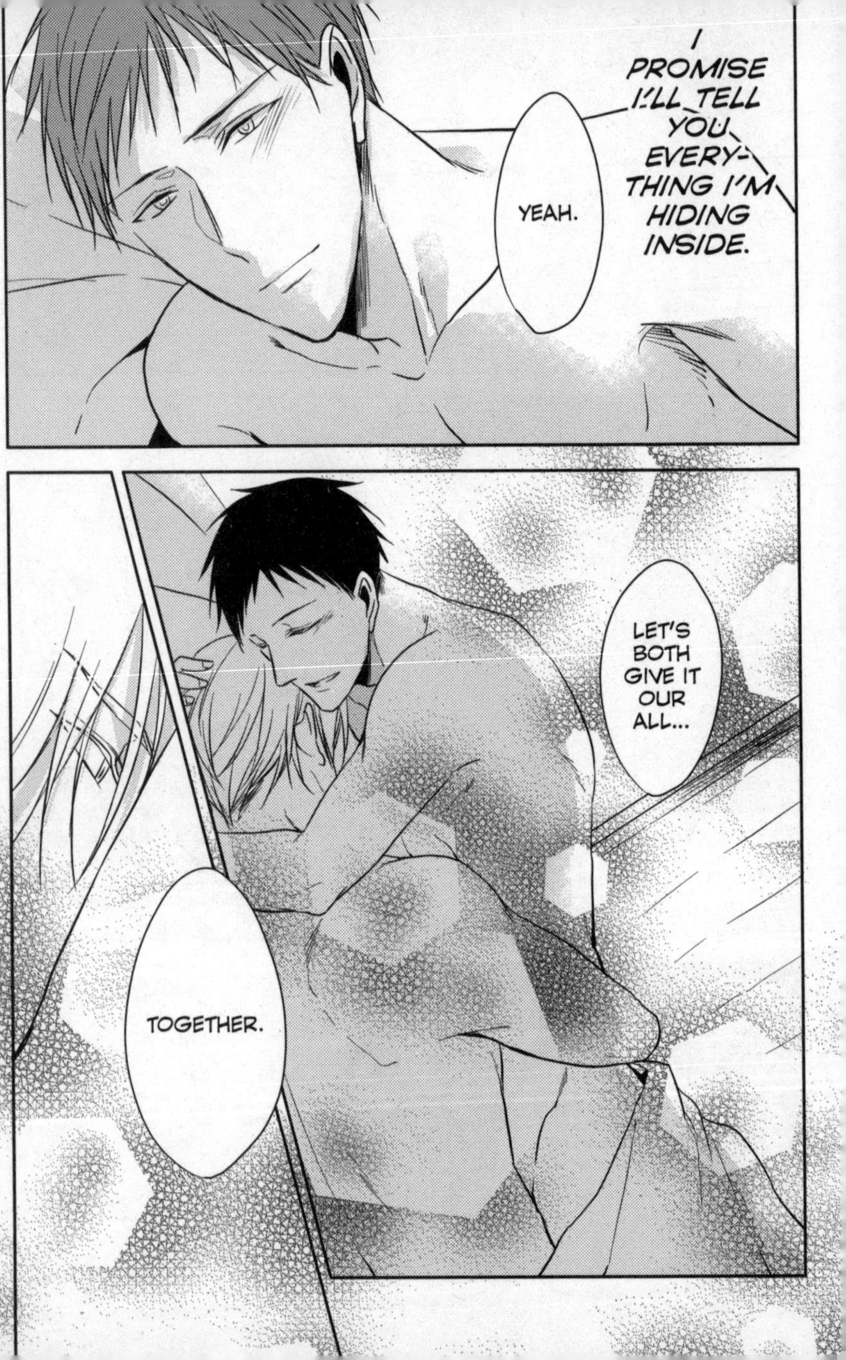
I PROMISE I'LL TELL YOU EVERYTHING I'M HIDING INSIDE.
YEAH.
LET'S BOTH GIVE IT OUR ALL...
TOGETHER.

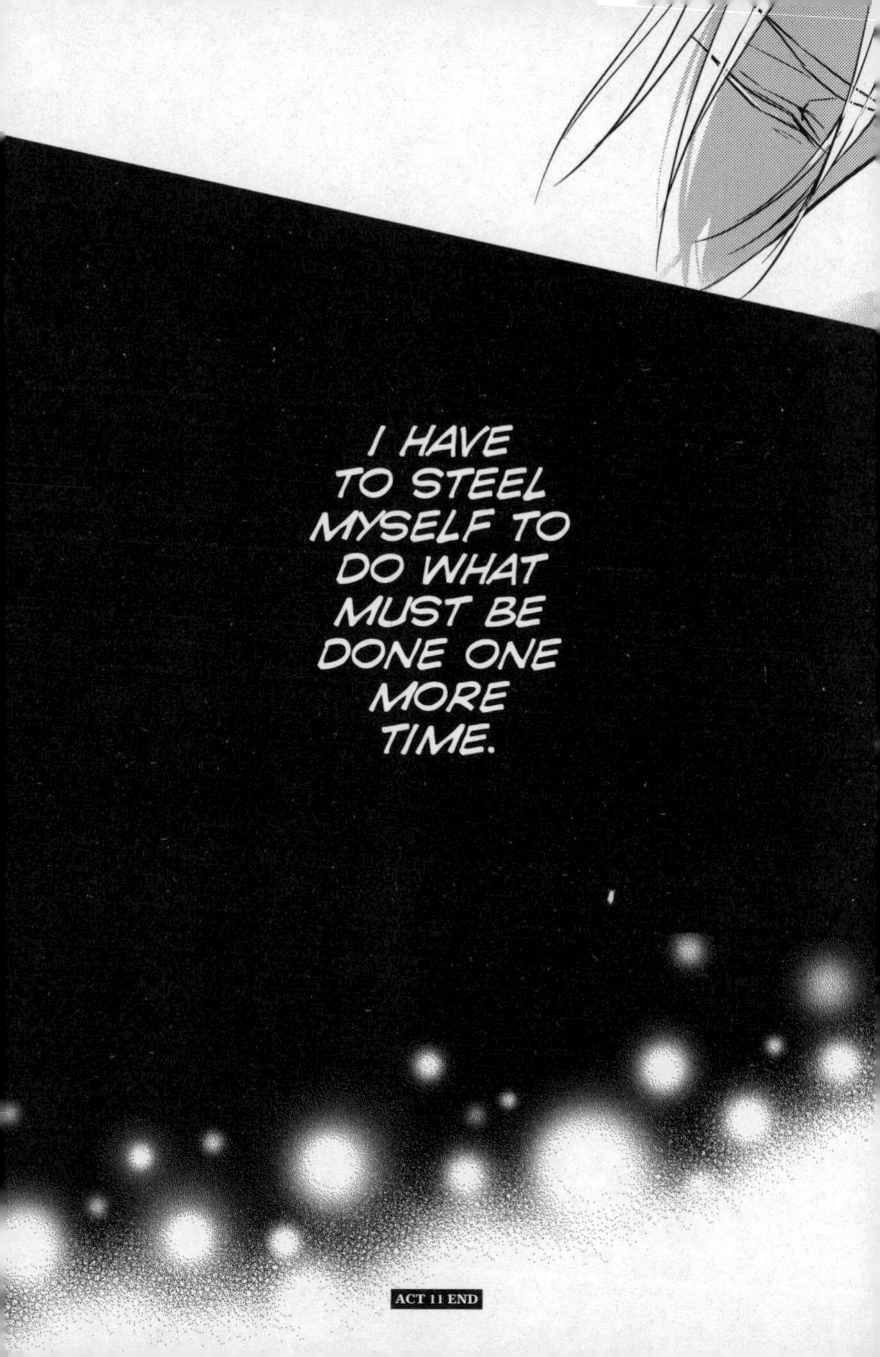
I HAVE TO STEEL MYSELF TO DO WHAT MUST BE DONE ONE MORE TIME.
ACT 11 END

Black
or White

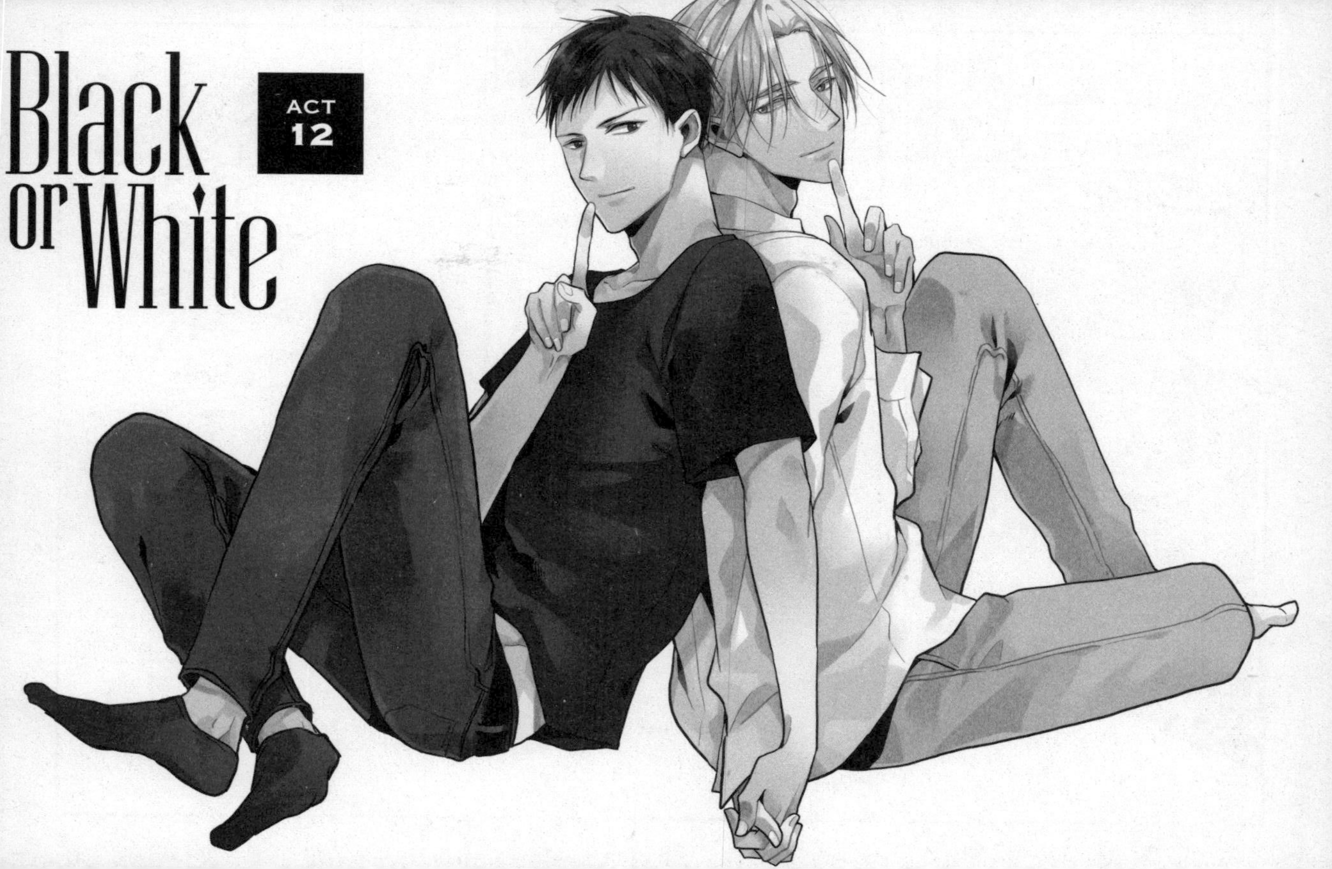
Black or White
ACT 12

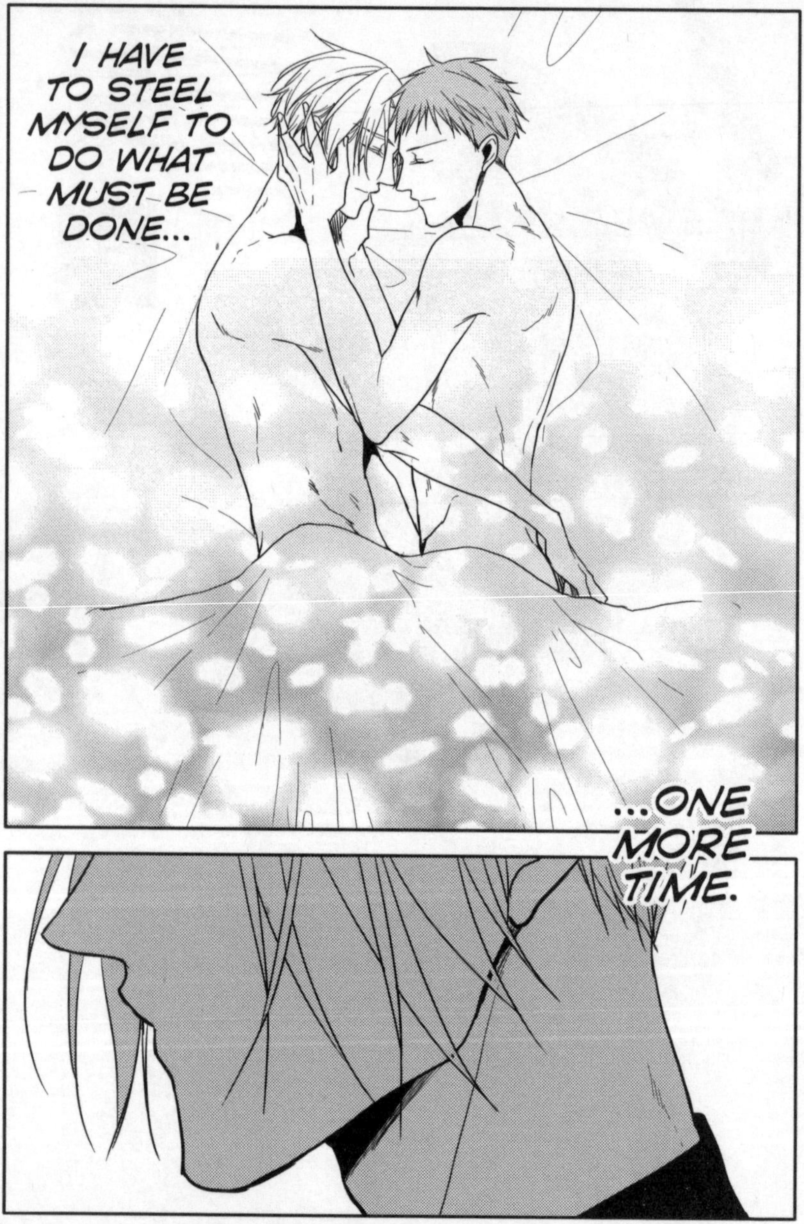
I HAVE TO STEEL MYSELF TO DO WHAT MUST BE DONE...
...ONE MORE TIME.

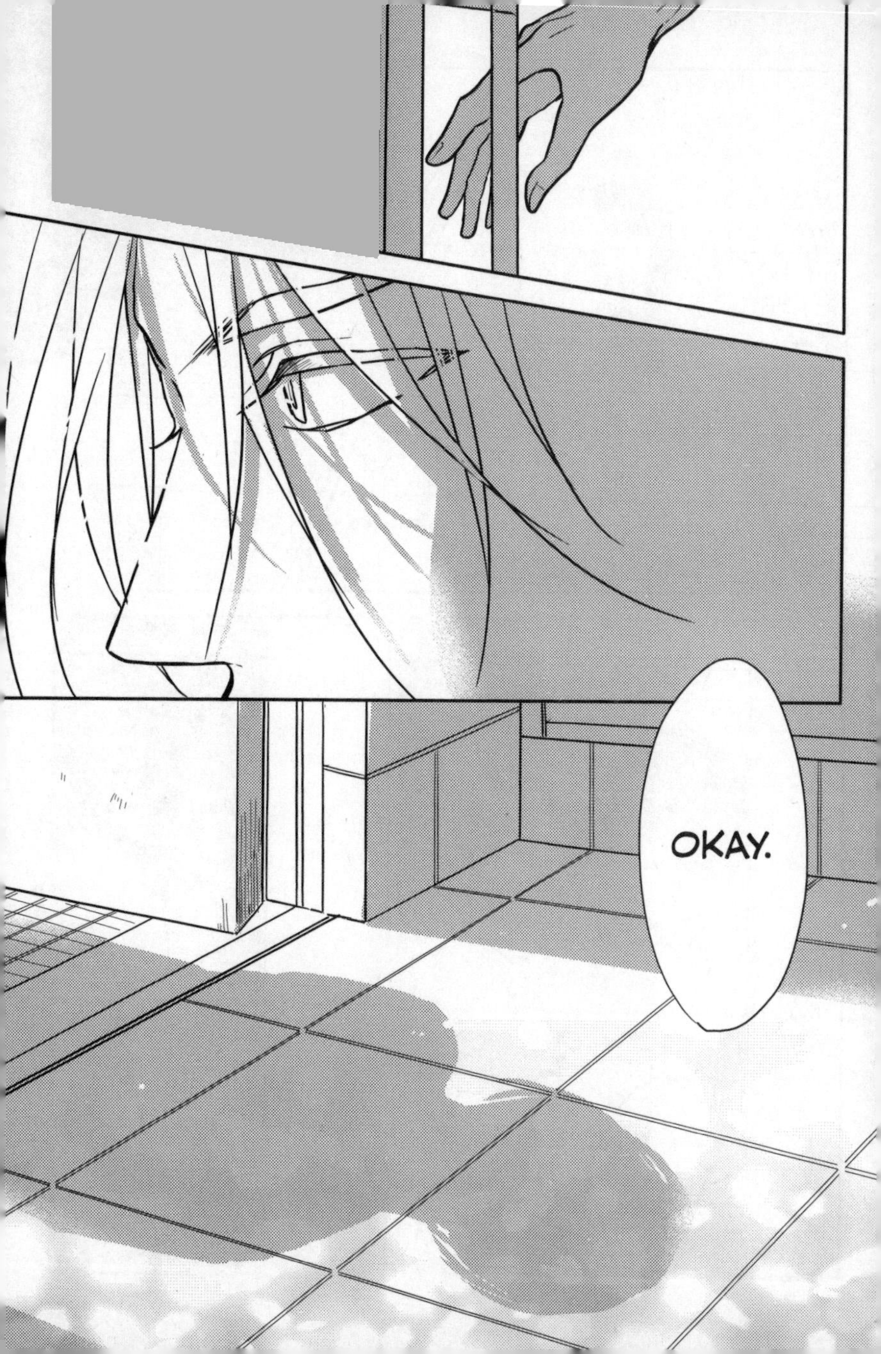
OKAY.

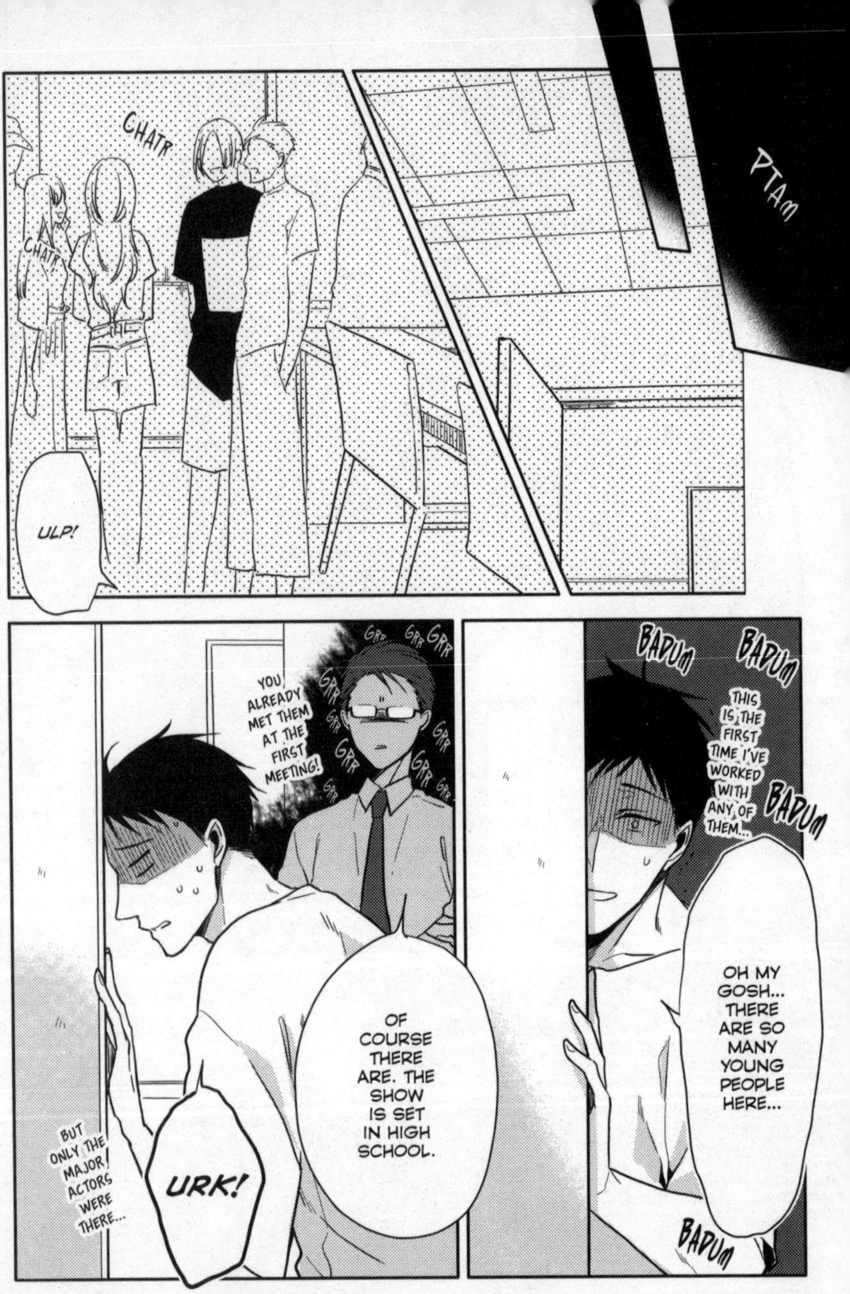
PTAM
CHATR
CHATR
ULP!
BADUM
BADUM
THIS IS THE FIRST TIME I'VE WORKED WITH ANY OF THEM...
BADUM
OH MY GOSH... THERE ARE SO MANY YOUNG PEOPLE HERE...
BADUM
GRR GRR GRR
YOU ALREADY MET THEM AT THE FIRST MEETING!
OF COURSE THERE ARE. THE SHOW IS SET IN HIGH SCHOOL.
URK!
BUT ONLY THE MAJOR ACTORS WERE THERE...

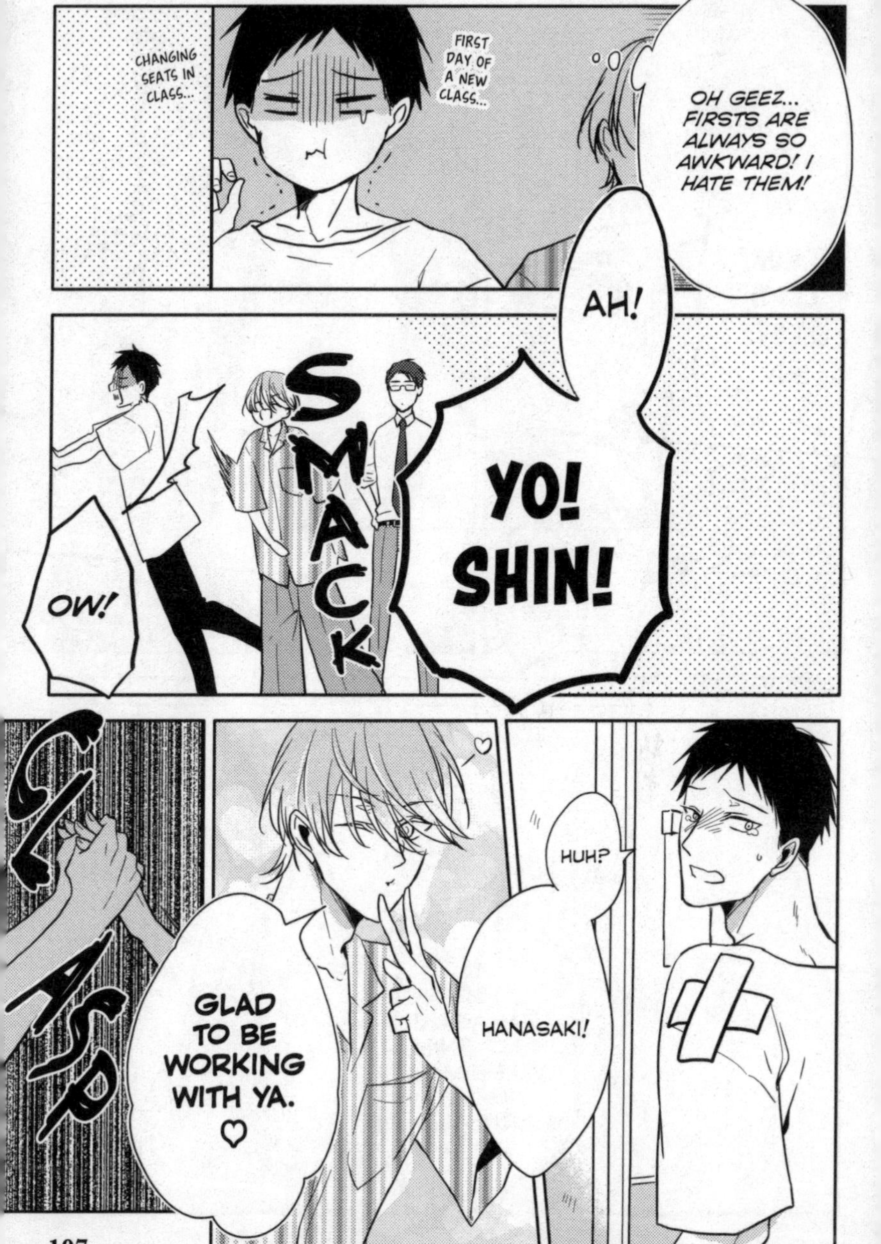
FIRST DAY OF A NEW CLASS...
OH GEEZ... FIRSTS ARE ALWAYS SO AWKWARD! I HATE THEM!
CHANGING SEATS IN CLASS...
AH!
YO! SHIN!
SMACK
OW!
HUH?
HANASAKI!
GLAD TO BE WORKING WITH YA. ♡
CLASP

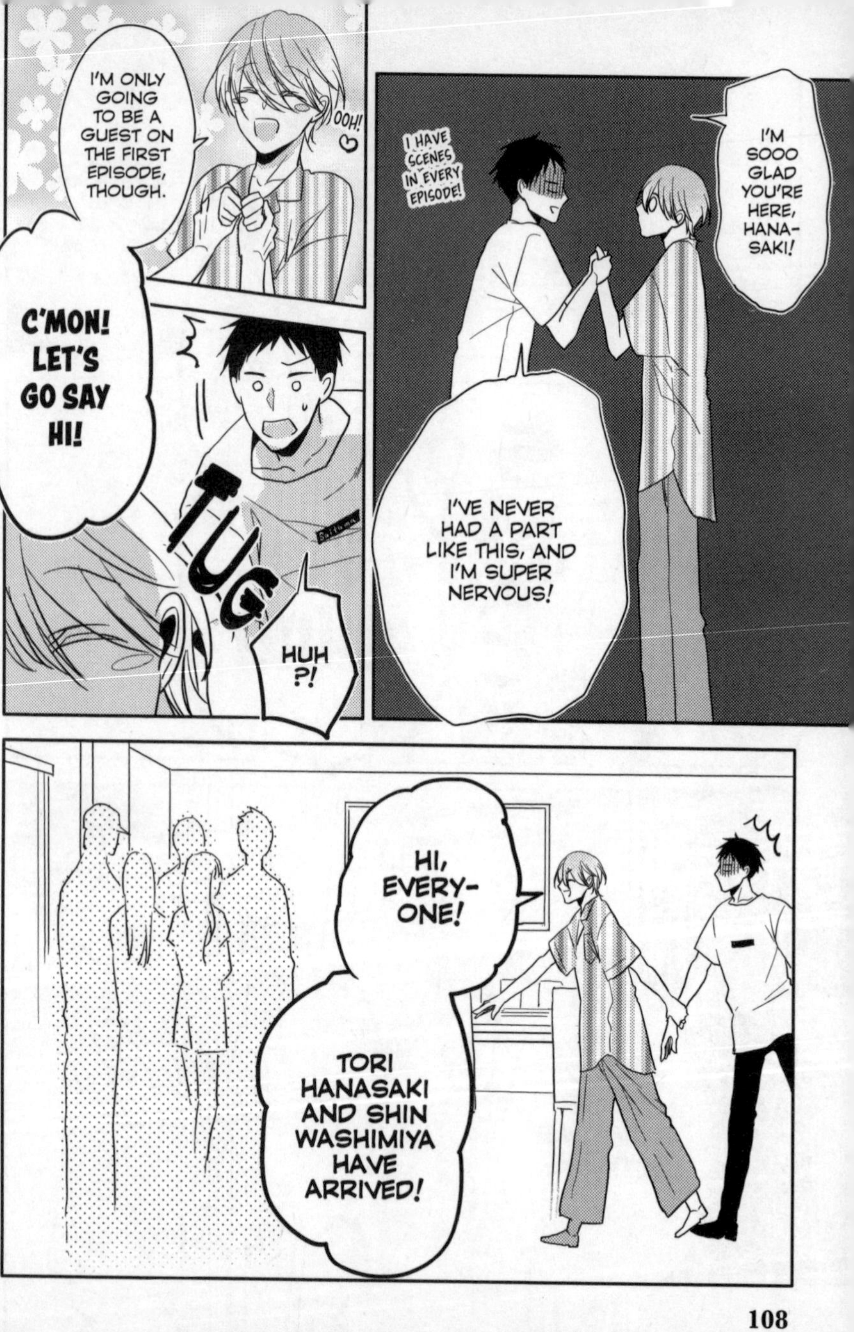
I'M SOOO GLAD YOU'RE HERE, HANA-SAKI!
I HAVE SCENES IN EVERY EPISODE!
I'VE NEVER HAD A PART LIKE THIS, AND I'M SUPER NERVOUS!
I'M ONLY GOING TO BE A GUEST ON THE FIRST EPISODE, THOUGH.
OOH!
C'MON! LET'S GO SAY HI!
TUG
HUH?!
HI, EVERY-ONE!
TORI HANASAKI AND SHIN WASHIMIYA HAVE ARRIVED!

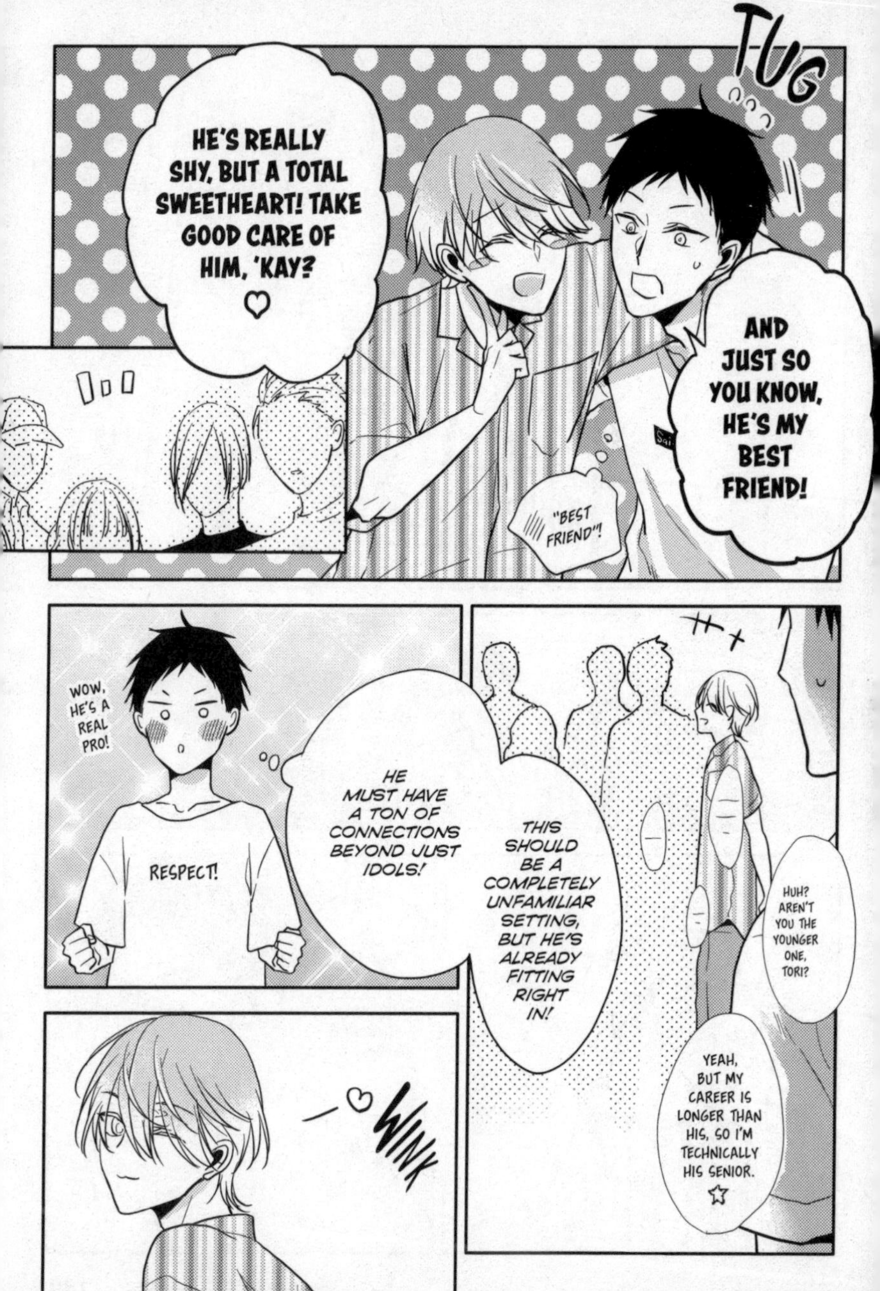
TUG
HE'S REALLY SHY, BUT A TOTAL SWEETHEART! TAKE GOOD CARE OF HIM, 'KAY? ♡
AND JUST SO YOU KNOW, HE'S MY BEST FRIEND!
"BEST FRIEND"!
HUH? AREN'T YOU THE YOUNGER ONE, TORI?
YEAH, BUT MY CAREER IS LONGER THAN HIS, SO I'M TECHNICALLY HIS SENIOR. ☆
THIS SHOULD BE A COMPLETELY UNFAMILIAR SETTING, BUT HE'S ALREADY FITTING RIGHT IN!
HE MUST HAVE A TON OF CONNECTIONS BEYOND JUST IDOLS!
WOW, HE'S A REAL PRO!
RESPECT!
WINK

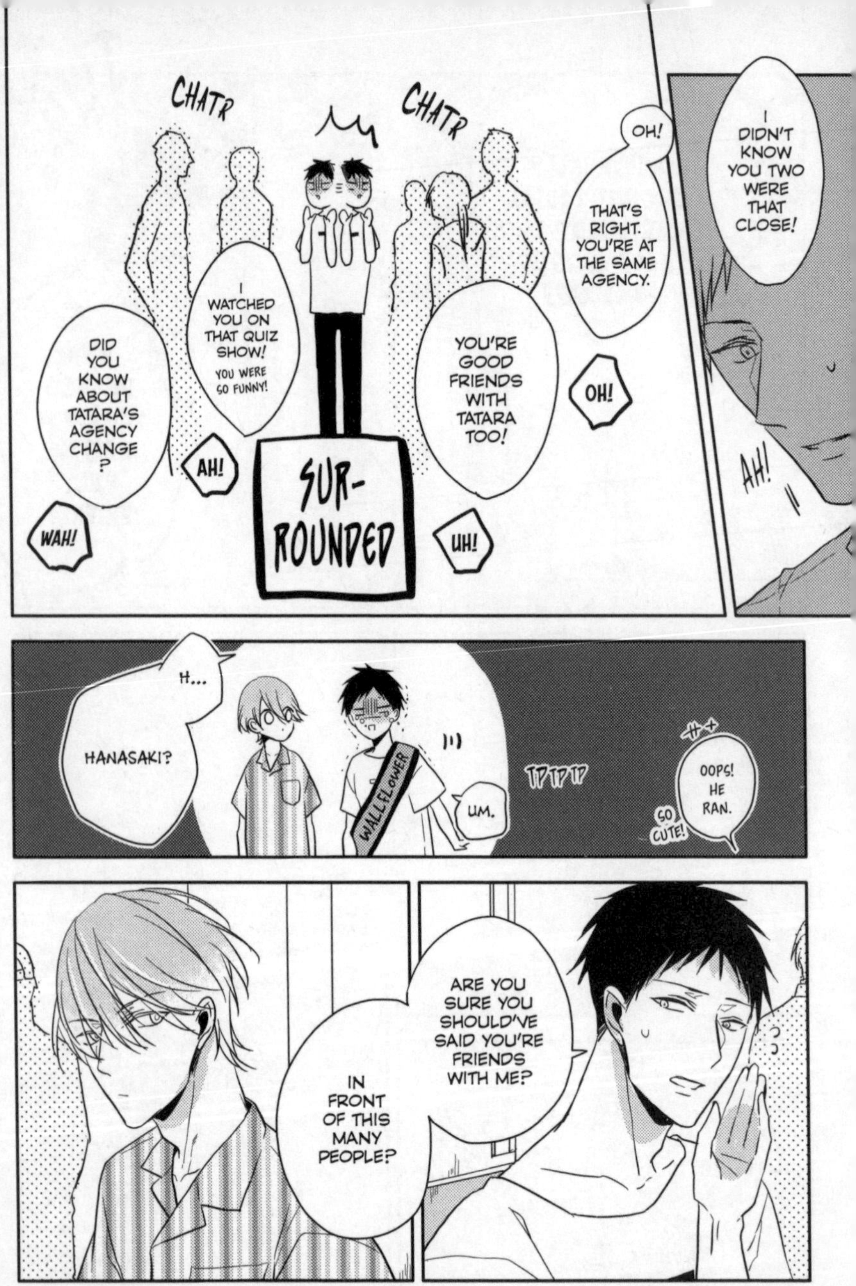
I DIDN'T KNOW YOU TWO WERE THAT CLOSE!
AH!
OH!
THAT'S RIGHT. YOU'RE AT THE SAME AGENCY.
CHATR
OH!
YOU'RE GOOD FRIENDS WITH TATARA TOO!
CHATR
UH!
I WATCHED YOU ON THAT QUIZ SHOW! YOU WERE SO FUNNY!
SUR-ROUNDED
DID YOU KNOW ABOUT TATARA'S AGENCY CHANGE?
AH!
WAH!
OOPS! HE RAN.
SO CUTE!
TPTPTP
UM.
WALLFLOWER
H...
HANASAKI?
ARE YOU SURE YOU SHOULD'VE SAID YOU'RE FRIENDS WITH ME?
IN FRONT OF THIS MANY PEOPLE?

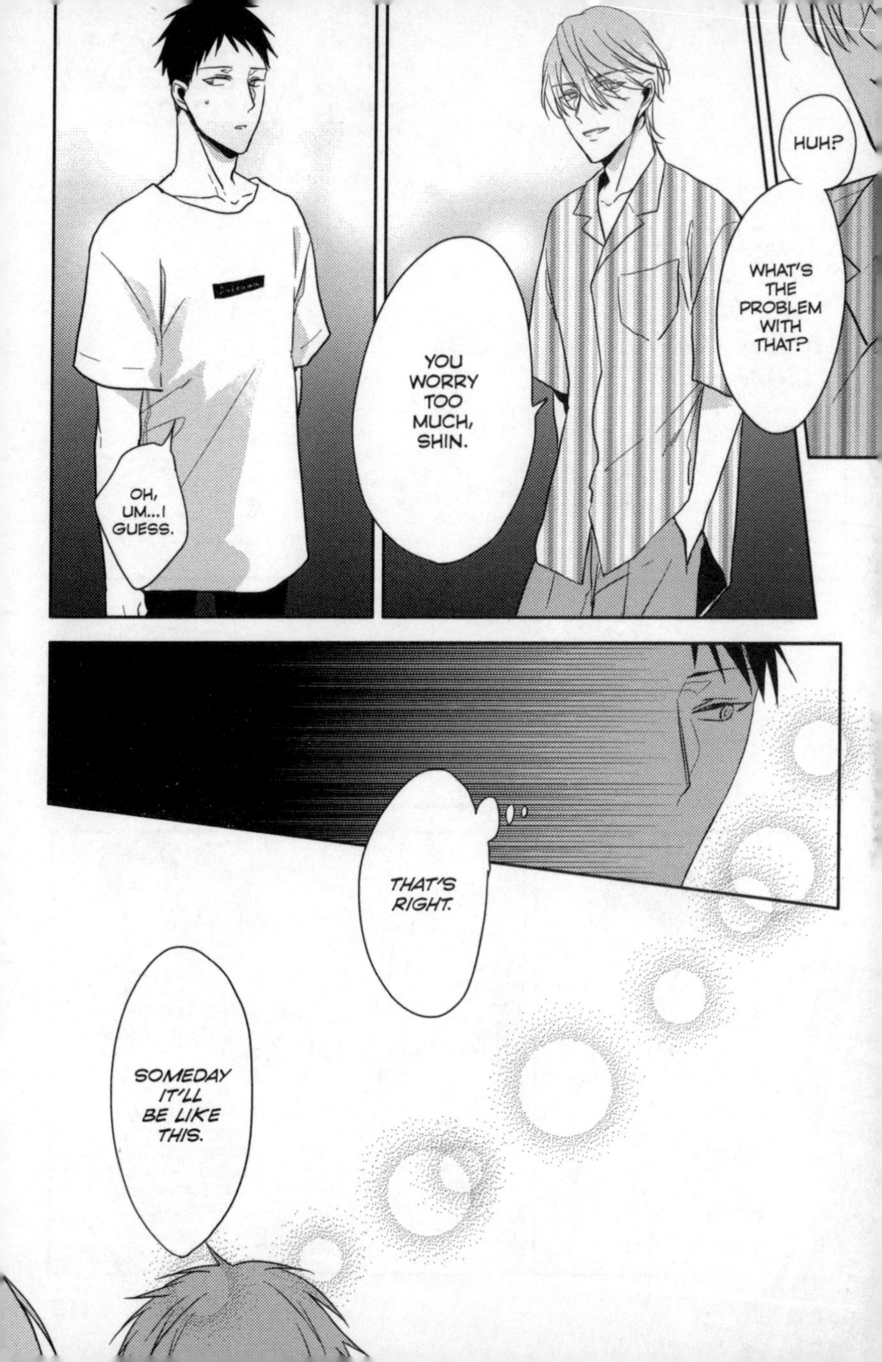
HUH?
WHAT'S THE PROBLEM WITH THAT?
YOU WORRY TOO MUCH, SHIN.
OH, UM...I GUESS.
THAT'S RIGHT.
SOMEDAY IT'LL BE LIKE THIS.

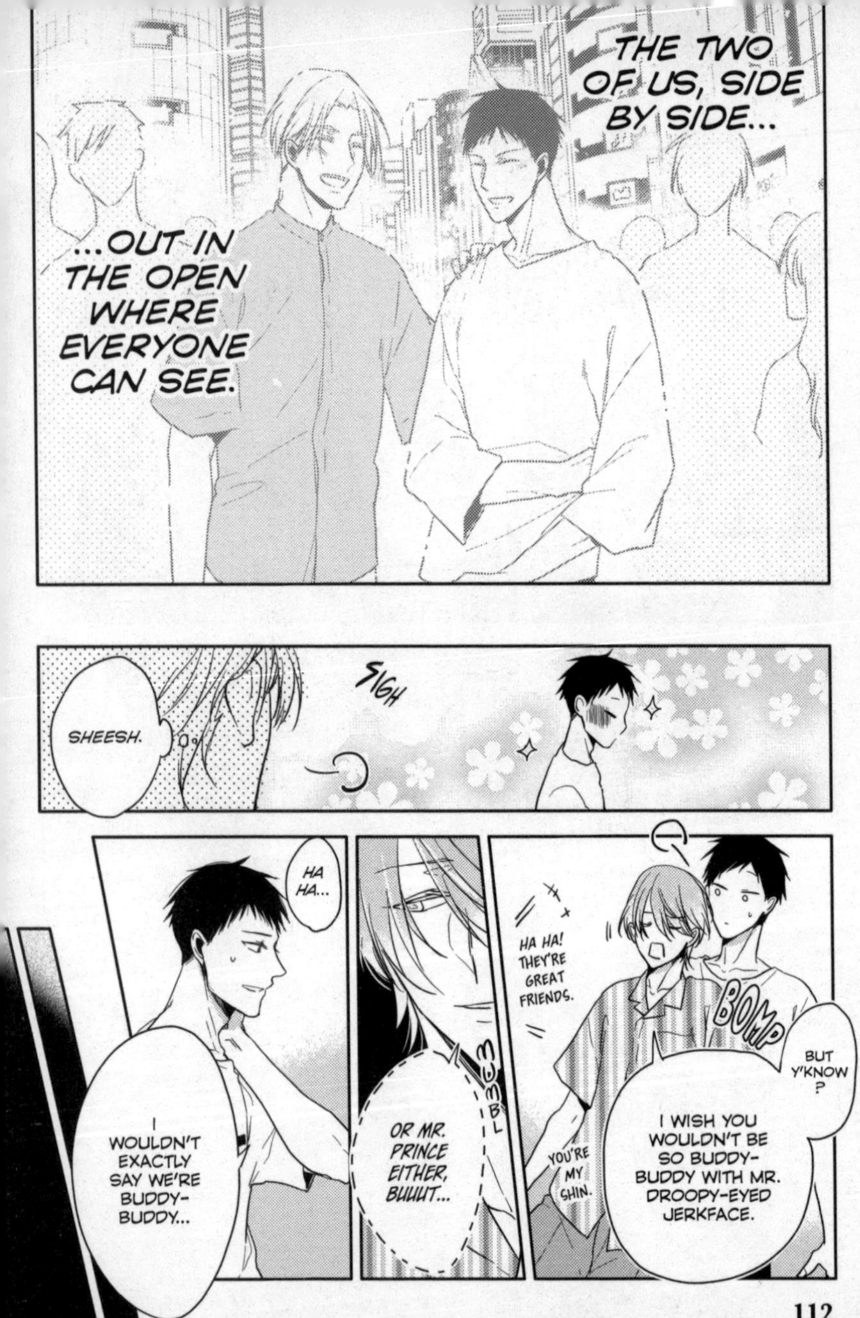
THE TWO OF US, SIDE BY SIDE...
...OUT IN THE OPEN WHERE EVERYONE CAN SEE.
SIGH
SHEESH.
BUT Y'KNOW?
BOMP
I WISH YOU WOULDN'T BE SO BUDDY-BUDDY WITH MR. DROOPY-EYED JERKFACE.
YOU'RE MY SHIN.
HA HA! THEY'RE GREAT FRIENDS.
MUMBL
OR MR. PRINCE EITHER, BUUUT...
HA HA...
I WOULDN'T EXACTLY SAY WE'RE BUDDY-BUDDY...

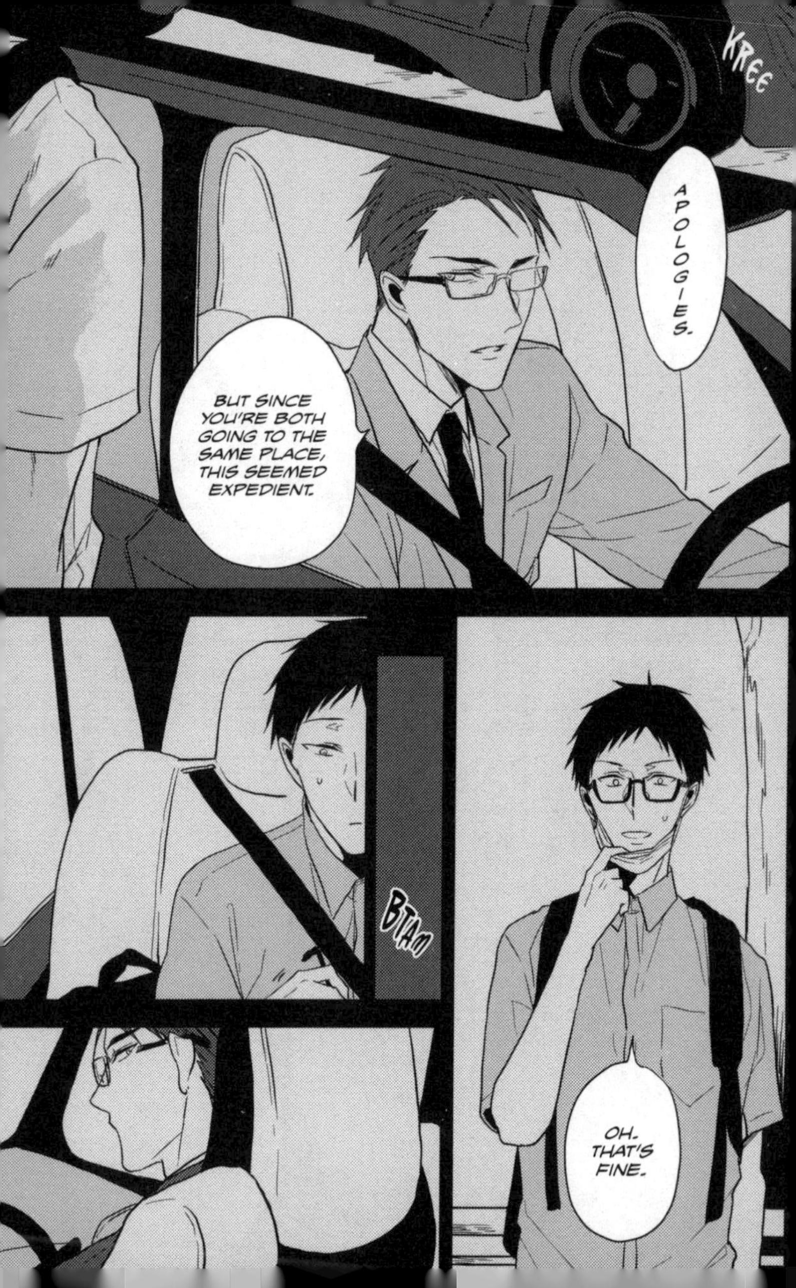
KREE
APOLOGIES.
BUT SINCE YOU'RE BOTH GOING TO THE SAME PLACE, THIS SEEMED EXPEDIENT.
OH. THAT'S FINE.
BTAM

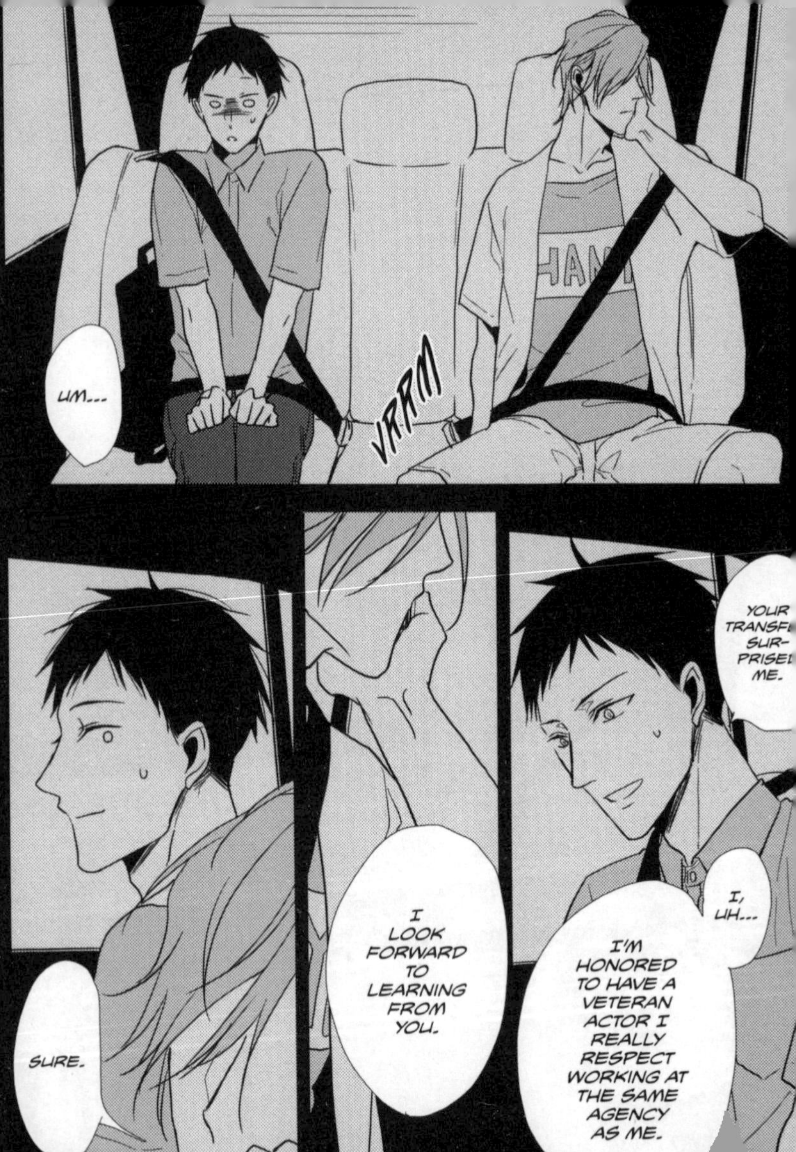
VRRM
UM...
YOUR TRANSFE SUR- PRISED ME.
I, UH...
I'M HONORED TO HAVE A VETERAN ACTOR I REALLY RESPECT WORKING AT THE SAME AGENCY AS ME.
I LOOK FORWARD TO LEARNING FROM YOU.
SURE.

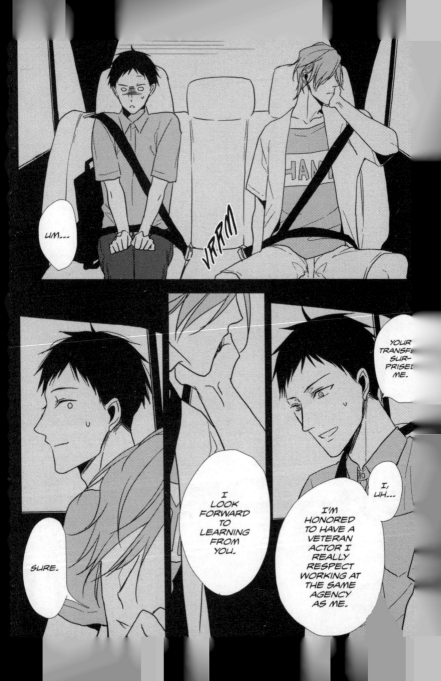

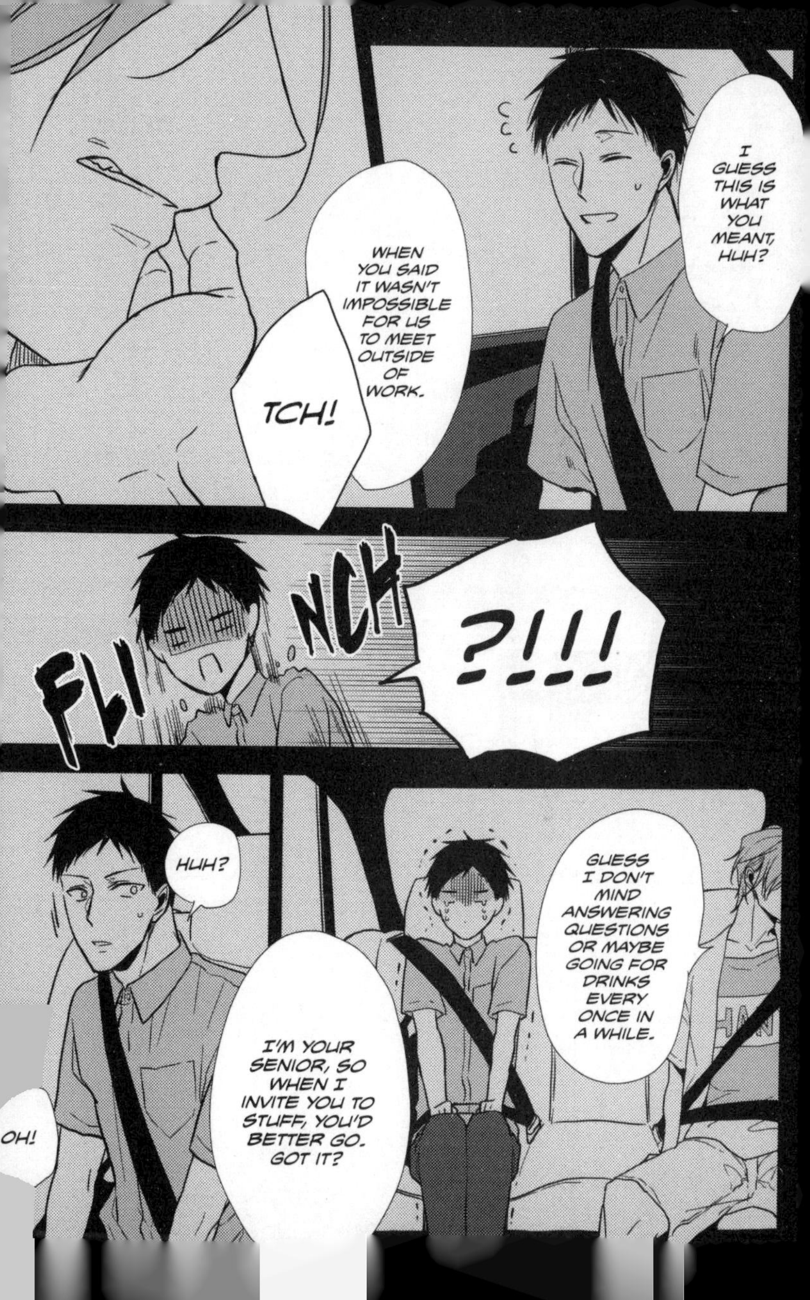
I GUESS THIS IS WHAT YOU MEANT, HUH?
WHEN YOU SAID IT WASN'T IMPOSSIBLE FOR US TO MEET OUTSIDE OF WORK.
TCH!
?!!!
FLINCH
GUESS I DON'T MIND ANSWERING QUESTIONS OR MAYBE GOING FOR DRINKS EVERY ONCE IN A WHILE.
I'M YOUR SENIOR, SO WHEN I INVITE YOU TO STUFF, YOU'D BETTER GO. GOT IT?
HUH?
OH!

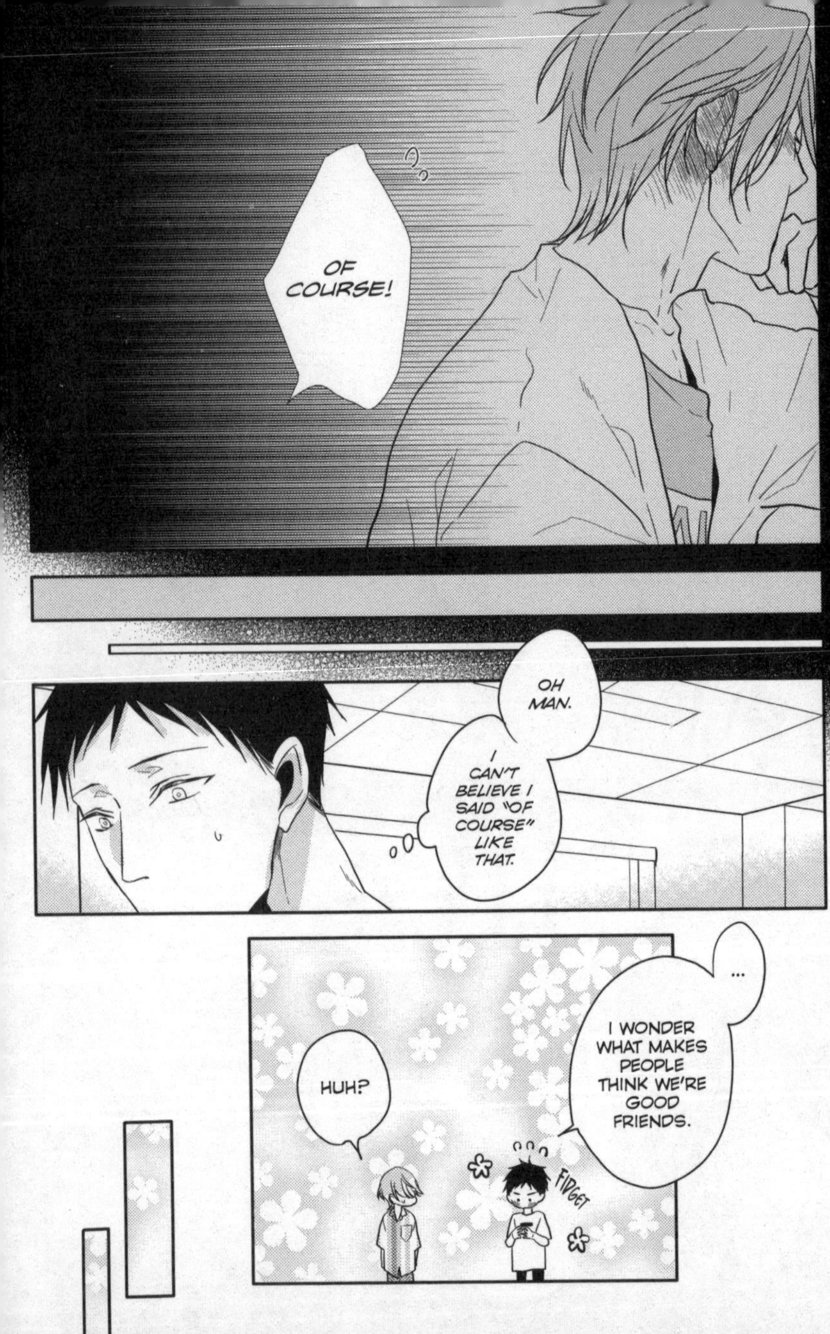
OF COURSE!
OH MAN.
I CAN'T BELIEVE I SAID "OF COURSE" LIKE THAT.
...
I WONDER WHAT MAKES PEOPLE THINK WE'RE GOOD FRIENDS.
FIDGET
HUH?

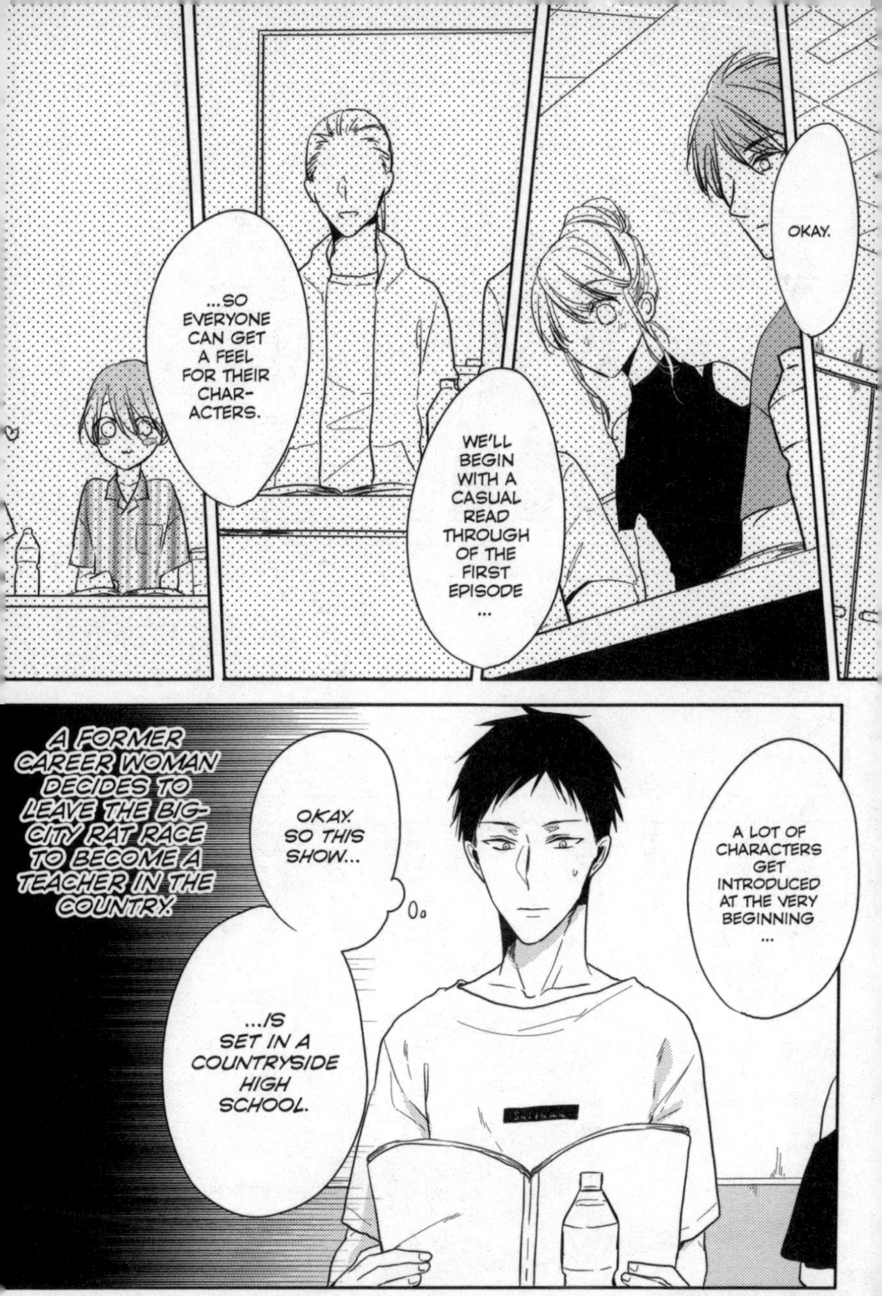
OKAY.
WE'LL BEGIN WITH A CASUAL READ THROUGH OF THE FIRST EPISODE ...
...SO EVERYONE CAN GET A FEEL FOR THEIR CHAR-ACTERS.
A LOT OF CHARACTERS GET INTRODUCED AT THE VERY BEGINNING ...
OKAY. SO THIS SHOW...
...IS SET IN A COUNTRYSIDE HIGH SCHOOL.
A FORMER CAREER WOMAN DECIDES TO LEAVE THE BIG-CITY RAT RACE TO BECOME A TEACHER IN THE COUNTRY.

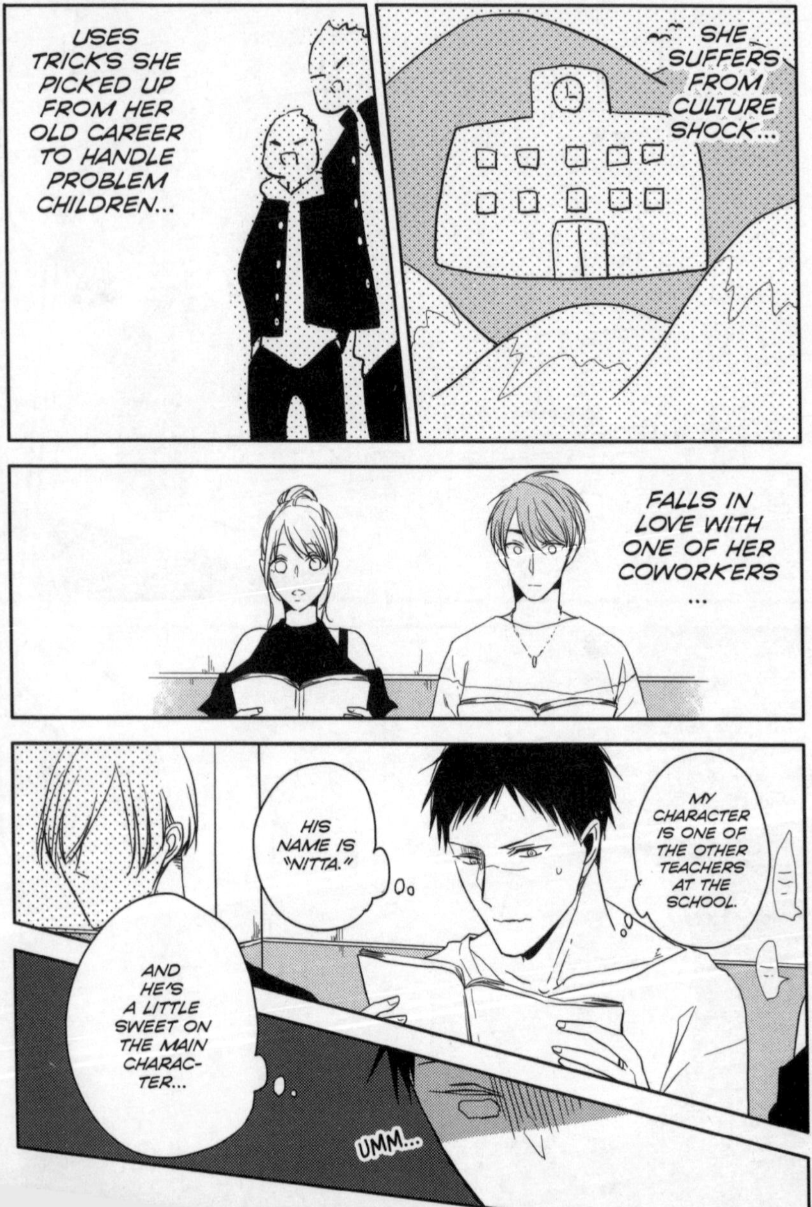
SHE SUFFERS FROM CULTURE SHOCK...
USES TRICKS SHE PICKED UP FROM HER OLD CAREER TO HANDLE PROBLEM CHILDREN...
FALLS IN LOVE WITH ONE OF HER COWORKERS ...
MY CHARACTER IS ONE OF THE OTHER TEACHERS AT THE SCHOOL.
HIS NAME IS "NITTA."
AND HE'S A LITTLE SWEET ON THE MAIN CHARAC-TER...
UMM...

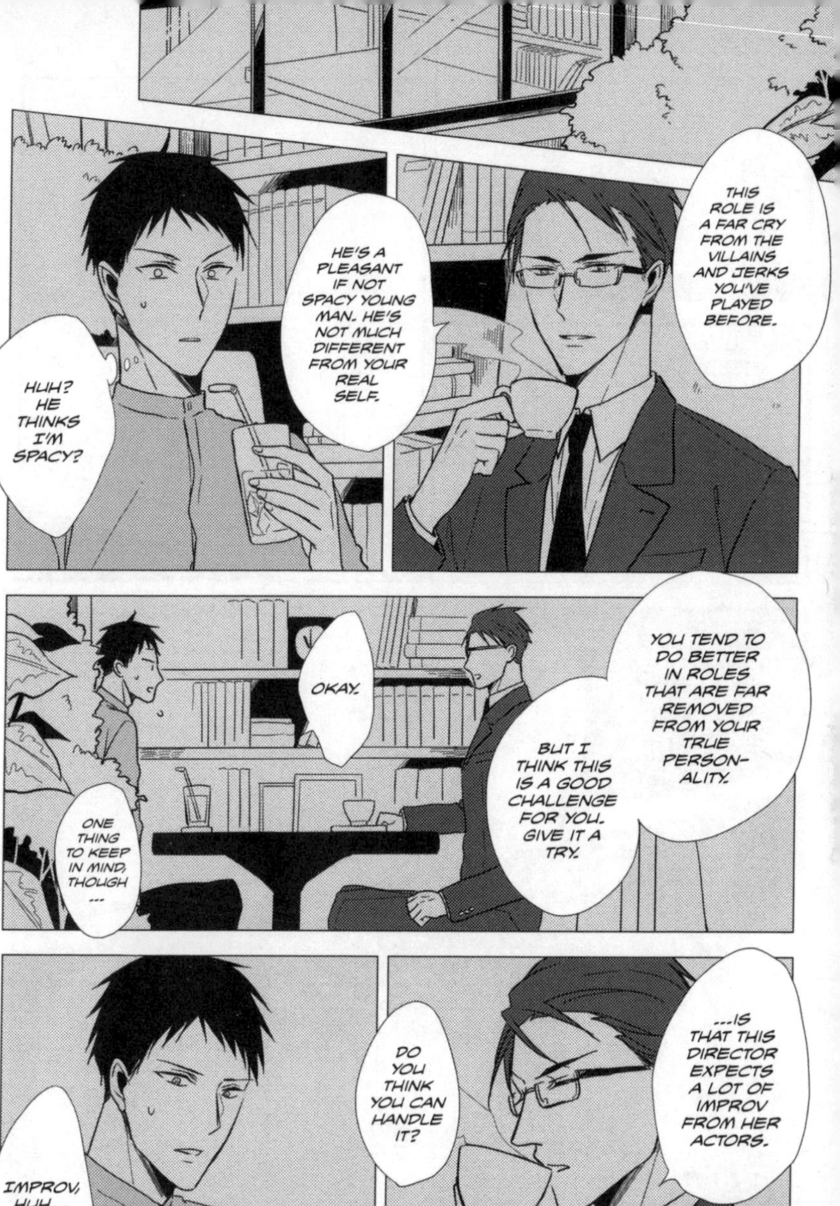
THIS ROLE IS A FAR CRY FROM THE VILLAINS AND JERKS YOU'VE PLAYED BEFORE.
HE'S A PLEASANT IF NOT SPACY YOUNG MAN. HE'S NOT MUCH DIFFERENT FROM YOUR REAL SELF.
HUH? HE THINKS I'M SPACY?
YOU TEND TO DO BETTER IN ROLES THAT ARE FAR REMOVED FROM YOUR TRUE PERSON-ALITY.
BUT I THINK THIS IS A GOOD CHALLENGE FOR YOU. GIVE IT A TRY.
OKAY.
ONE THING TO KEEP IN MIND, THOUGH...
...IS THAT THIS DIRECTOR EXPECTS A LOT OF IMPROV FROM HER ACTORS.
DO YOU THINK YOU CAN HANDLE IT?
IMPROV, HUH...

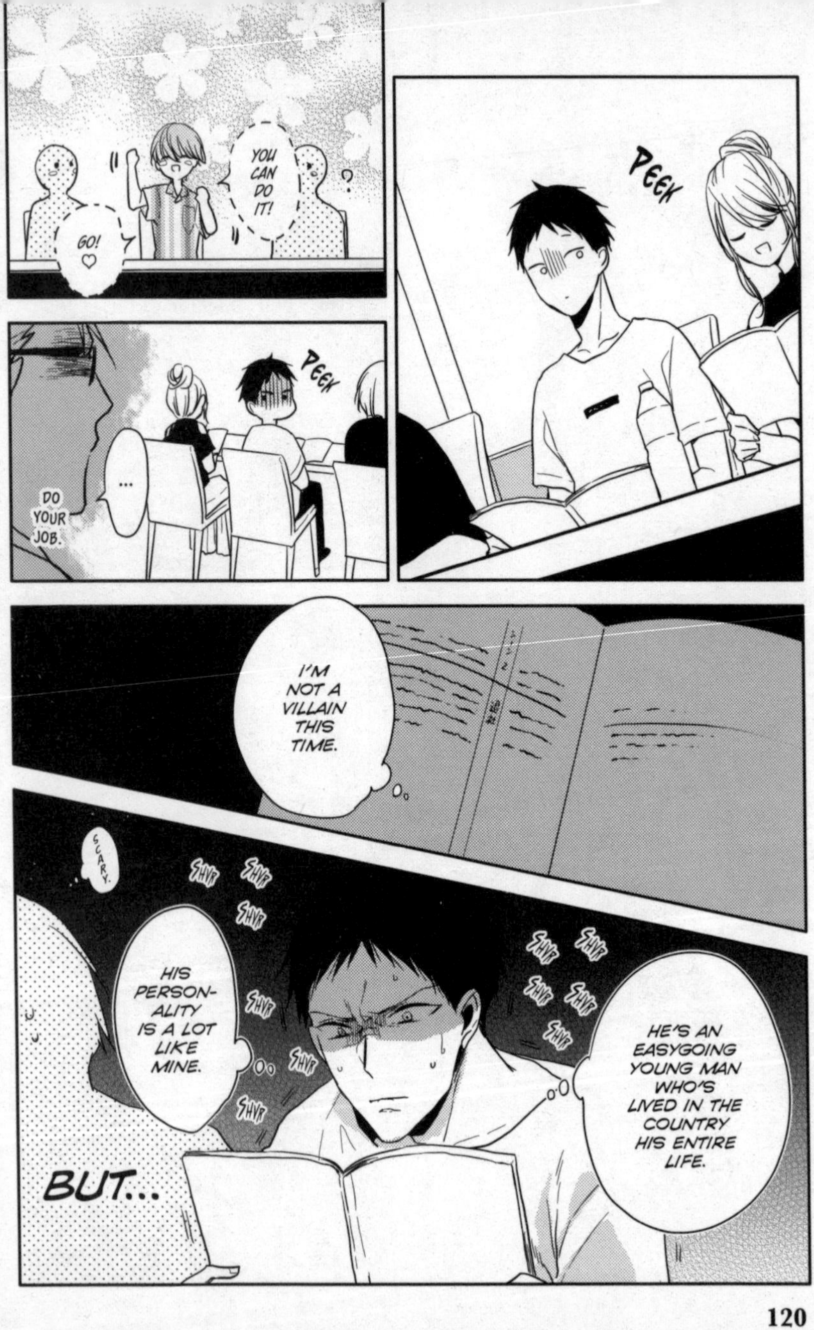
PEEK
YOU CAN DO IT!
GO! ♡
?
PEEK
...
DO YOUR JOB.
I'M NOT A VILLAIN THIS TIME.
HE'S AN EASYGOING YOUNG MAN WHO'S LIVED IN THE COUNTRY HIS ENTIRE LIFE.
SHVR SHVR SHVR SHVR SHVR
HIS PERSONALITY IS A LOT LIKE MINE.
SHVR SHVR SHVR SHVR SHVR
SCARY.
BUT...

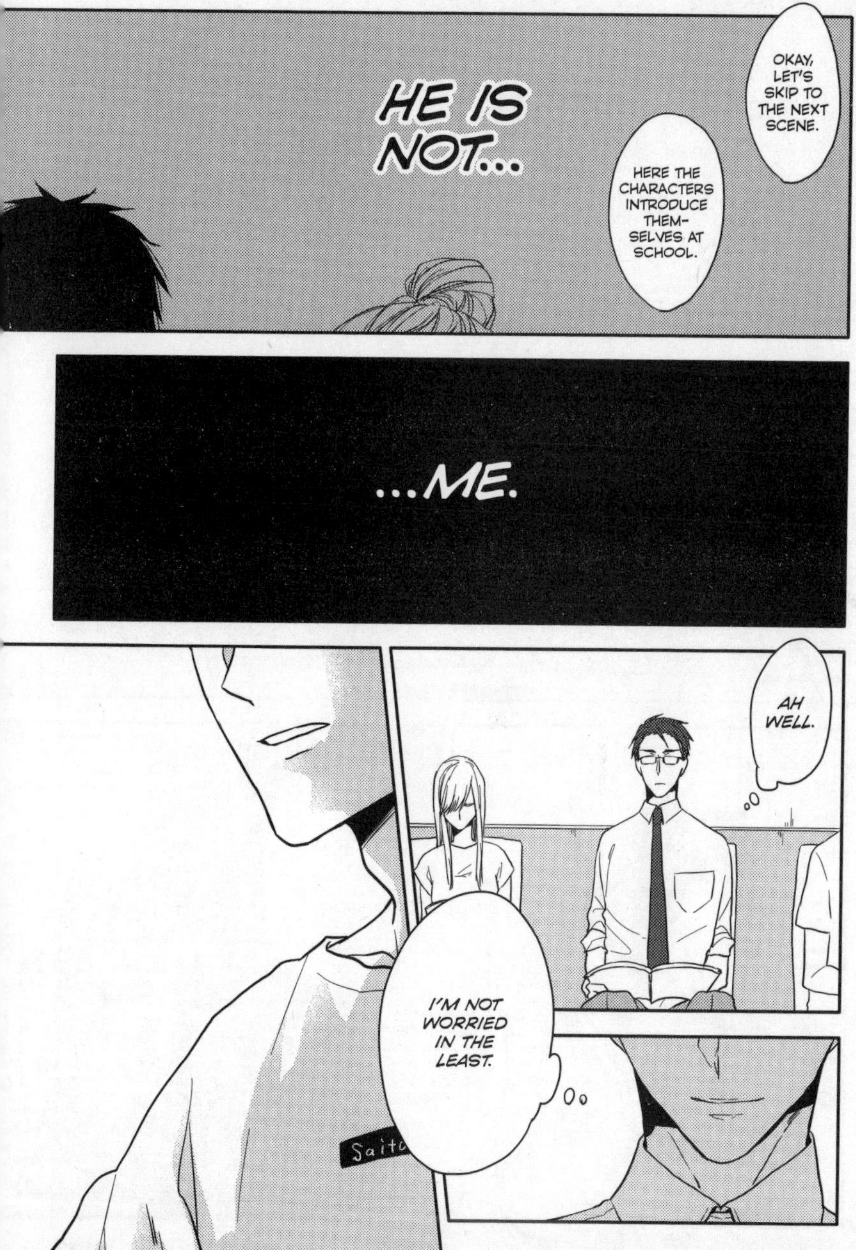
OKAY, LET'S SKIP TO THE NEXT SCENE.
HERE THE CHARACTERS INTRODUCE THEM-SELVES AT SCHOOL.
HE IS NOT...
...ME.
AH WELL.
I'M NOT WORRIED IN THE LEAST.

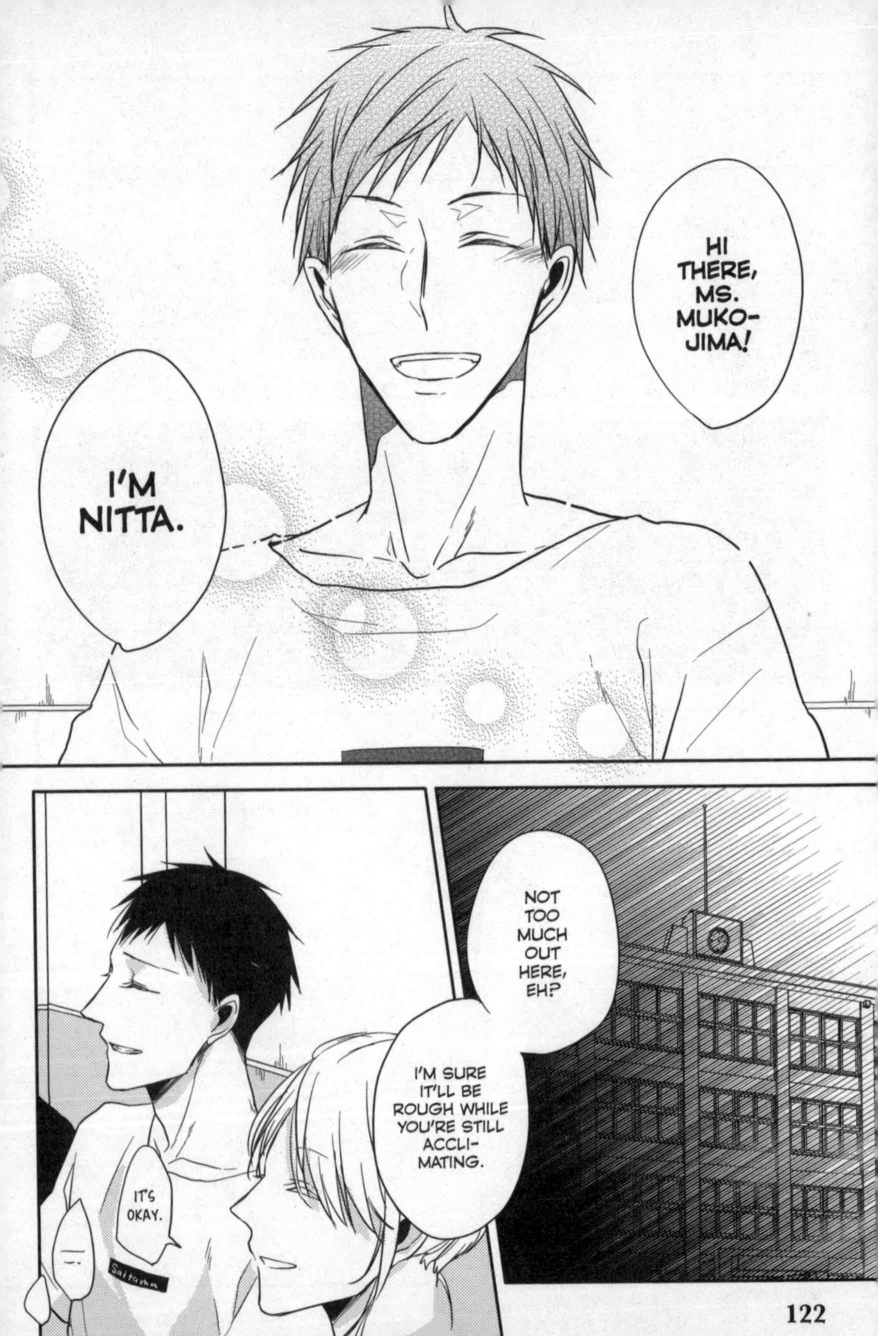
HI THERE, MS. MUKOJIMA!
I'M NITTA.
NOT TOO MUCH OUT HERE, EH?
I'M SURE IT'LL BE ROUGH WHILE YOU'RE STILL ACCLIMATING.
IT'S OKAY.
Saitama

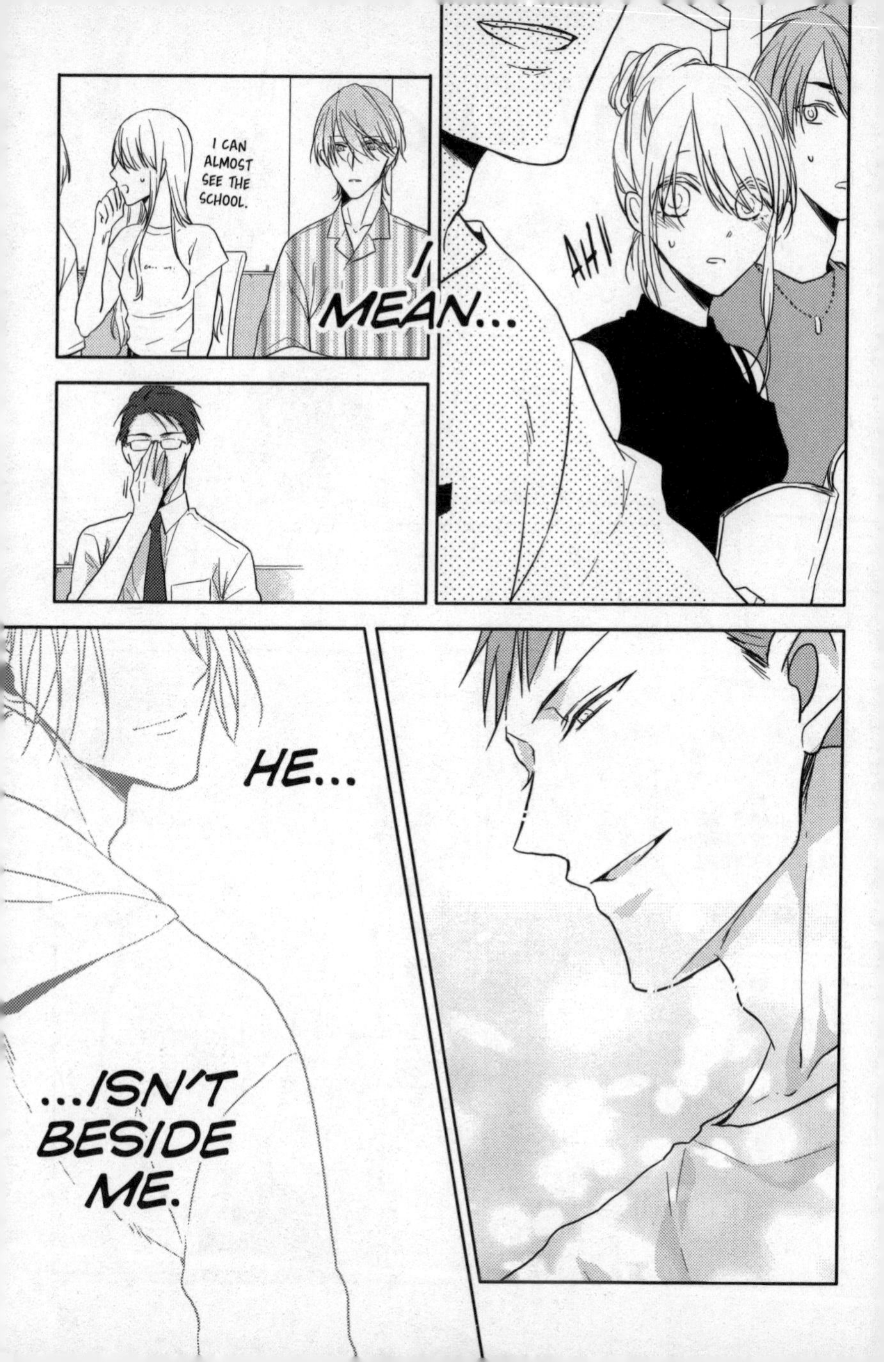
AH!
I MEAN...
I CAN ALMOST SEE THE SCHOOL.
HE...
...ISN'T BESIDE ME.

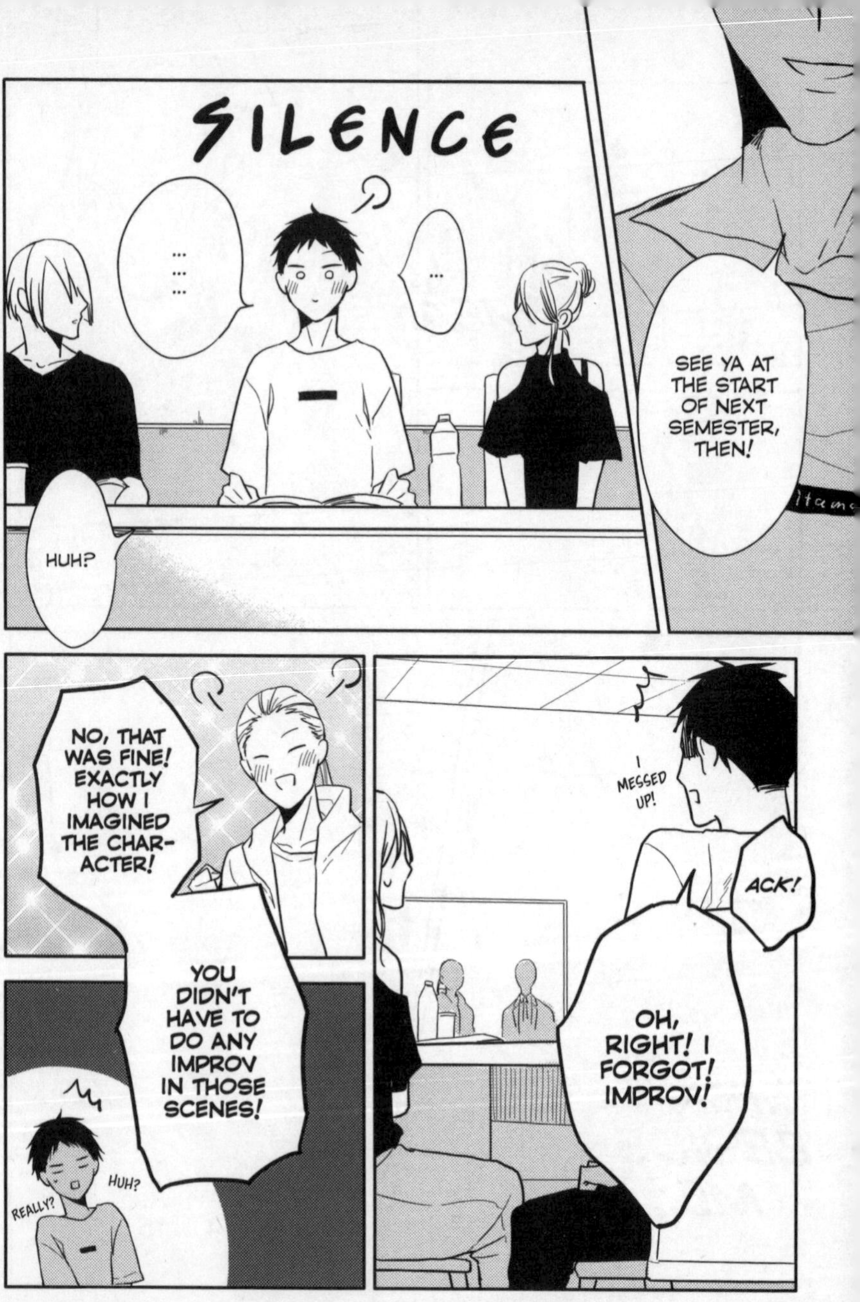
SEE YA AT THE START OF NEXT SEMESTER, THEN!
SILENCE
...
... ...
HUH?
I MESSED UP!
ACK!
OH, RIGHT! I FORGOT! IMPROV!
NO, THAT WAS FINE! EXACTLY HOW I IMAGINED THE CHAR-ACTER!
YOU DIDN'T HAVE TO DO ANY IMPROV IN THOSE SCENES!
HUH?
REALLY?

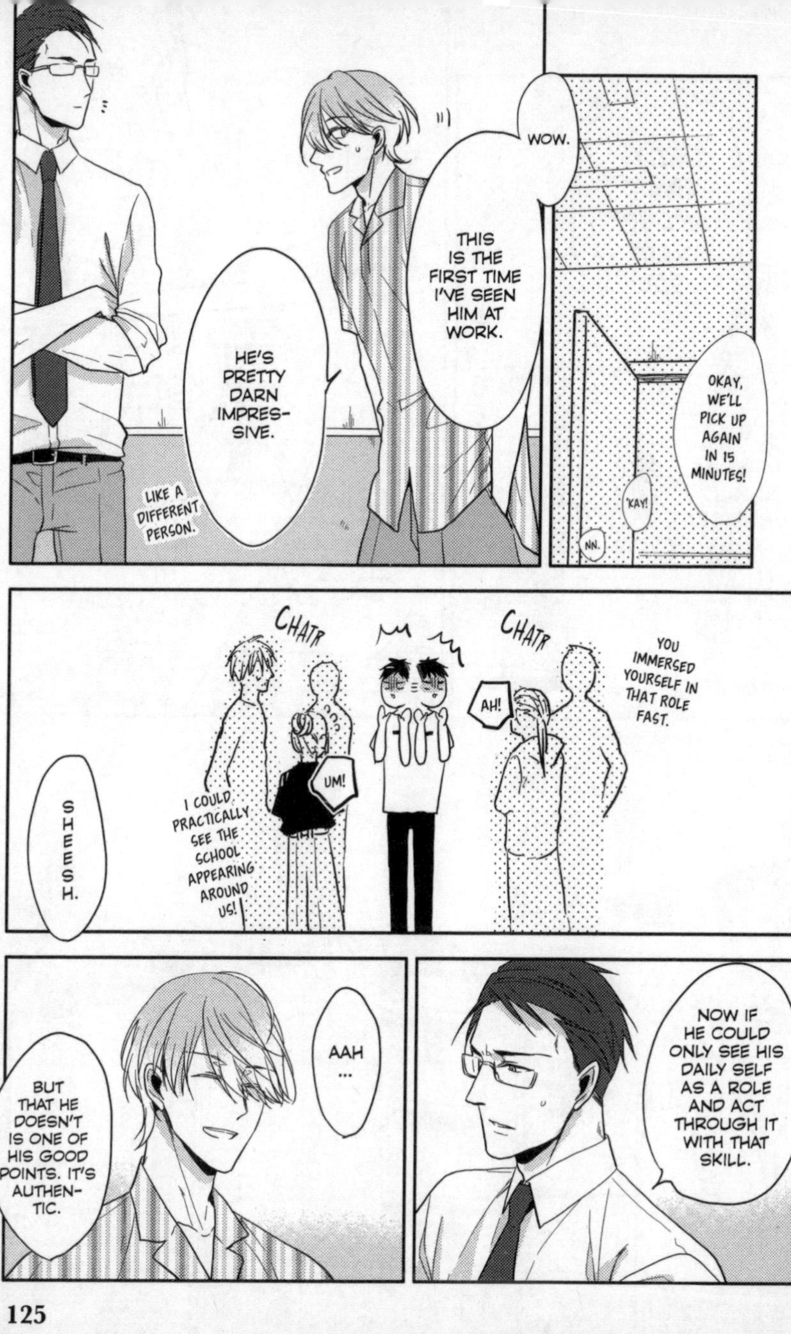
OKAY, WE'LL PICK UP AGAIN IN 15 MINUTES!
'KAY!
NN.
WOW.
THIS IS THE FIRST TIME I'VE SEEN HIM AT WORK.
HE'S PRETTY DARN IMPRESSIVE.
LIKE A DIFFERENT PERSON.
YOU IMMERSED YOURSELF IN THAT ROLE FAST.
CHATR
AH!
CHATR
UM!
I COULD PRACTICALLY SEE THE SCHOOL APPEARING AROUND US!
SHEESH.
NOW IF HE COULD ONLY SEE HIS DAILY SELF AS A ROLE AND ACT THROUGH IT WITH THAT SKILL.
AAH ...
BUT THAT HE DOESN'T IS ONE OF HIS GOOD POINTS. IT'S AUTHENTIC.

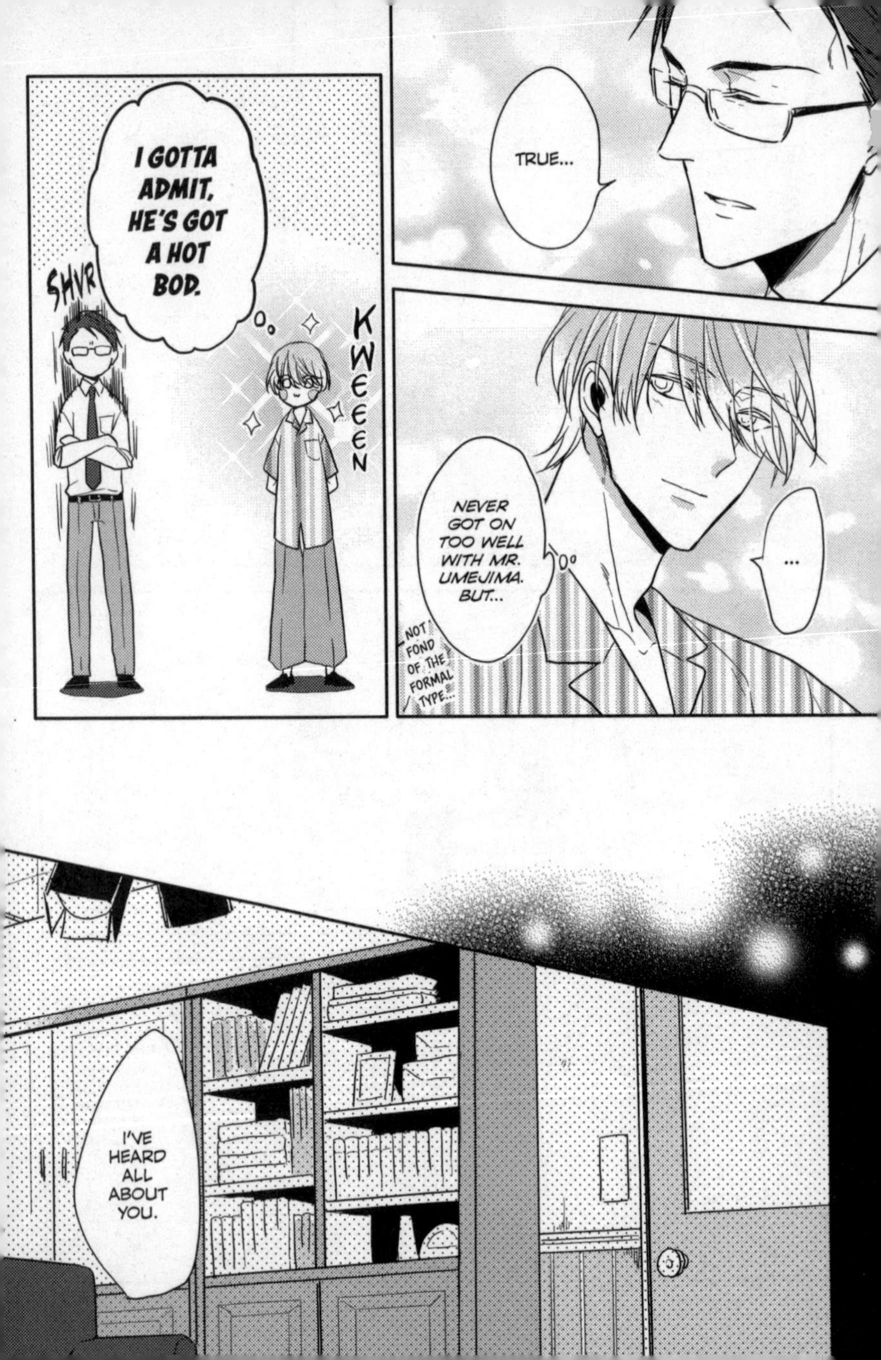
TRUE...
...
NEVER GOT ON TOO WELL WITH MR. UMEJIMA. BUT...
NOT FOND OF THE FORMAL TYPE...
KWEEEEN
I GOTTA ADMIT, HE'S GOT A HOT BOD.
SHVR
I'VE HEARD ALL ABOUT YOU.

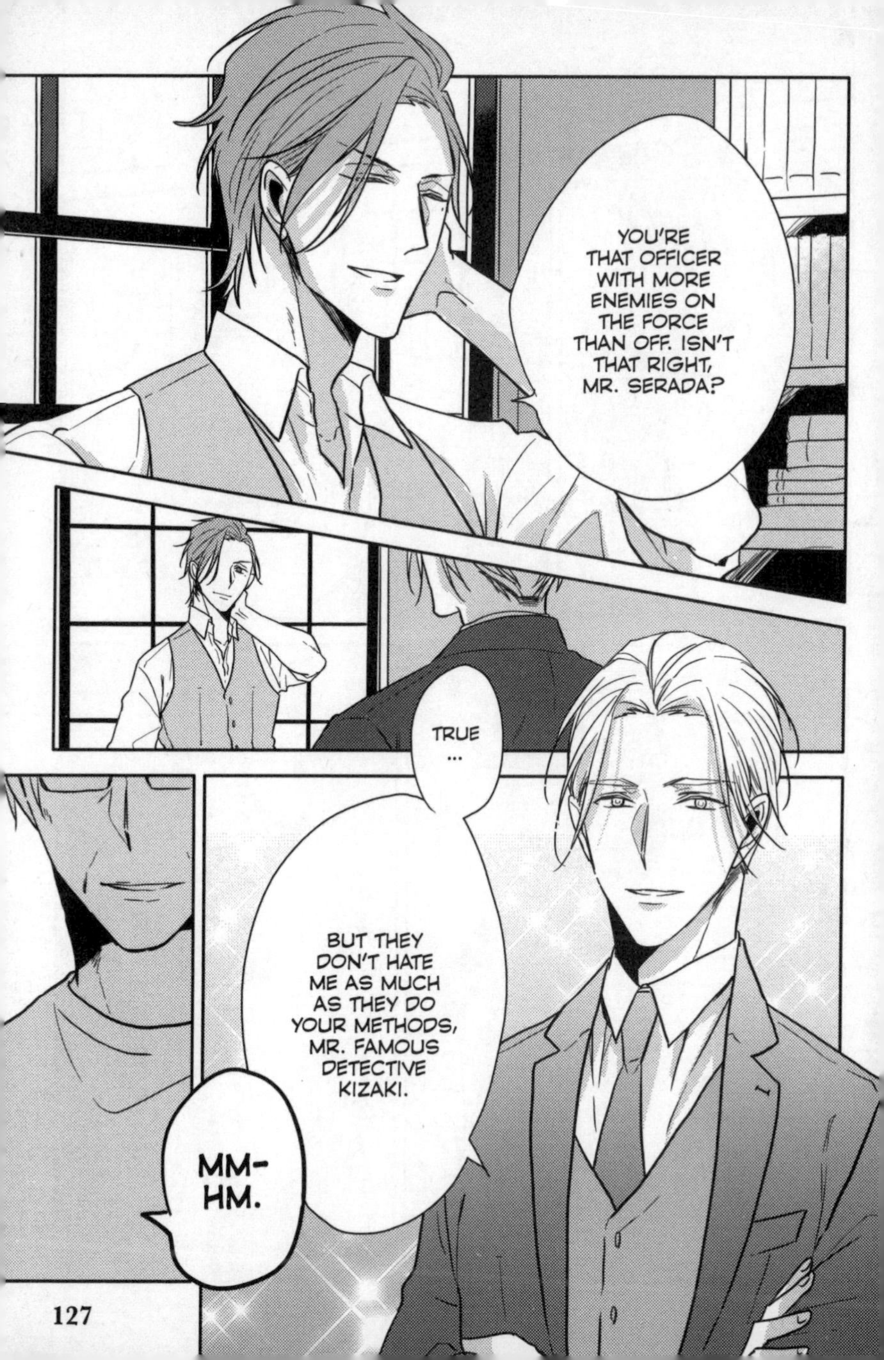
YOU'RE THAT OFFICER WITH MORE ENEMIES ON THE FORCE THAN OFF. ISN'T THAT RIGHT, MR. SERADA?
TRUE ...
BUT THEY DON'T HATE ME AS MUCH AS THEY DO YOUR METHODS, MR. FAMOUS DETECTIVE KIZAKI.
MM-HM.

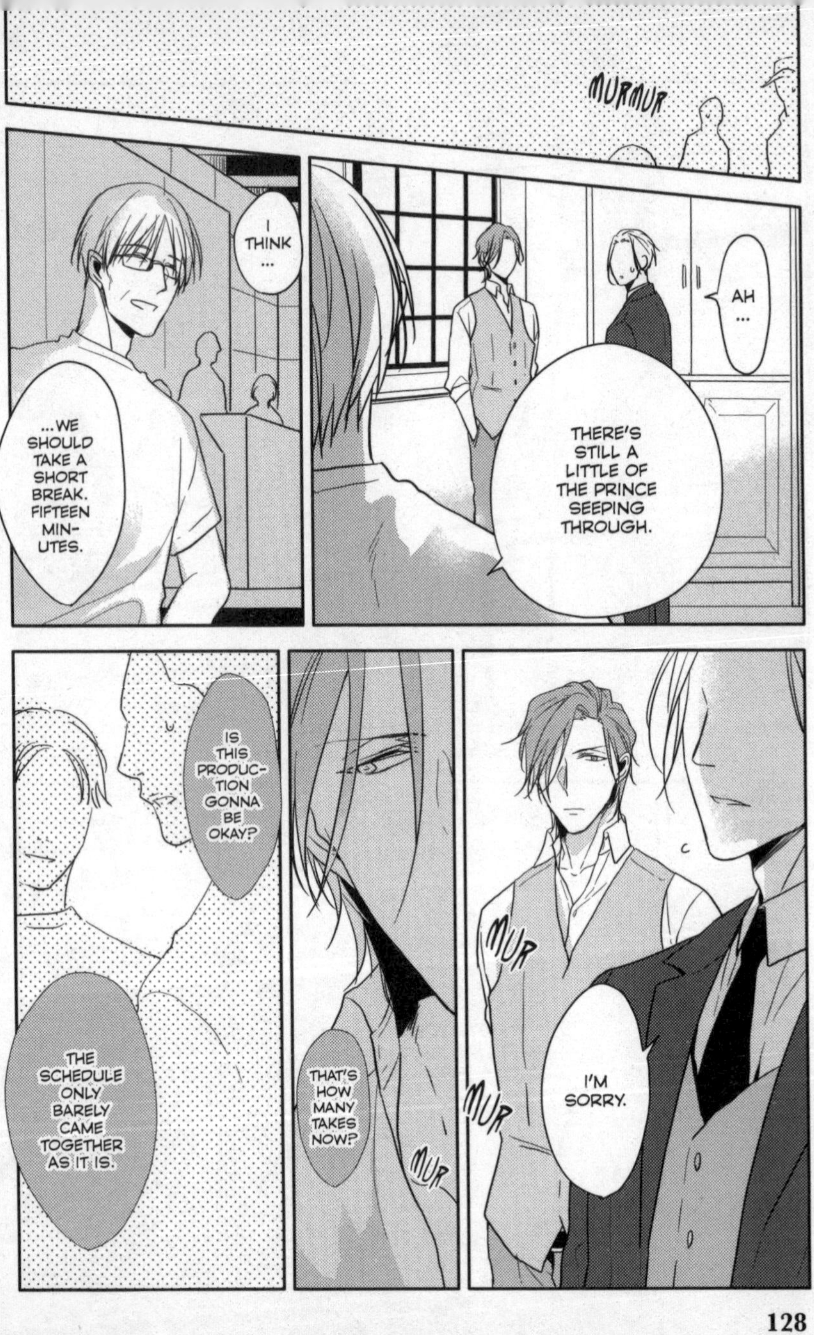
MURMUR
AH...
THERE'S STILL A LITTLE OF THE PRINCE SEEPING THROUGH.
I THINK...
...WE SHOULD TAKE A SHORT BREAK. FIFTEEN MINUTES.
MUR
I'M SORRY.
MUR
MUR
THAT'S HOW MANY TAKES NOW?
IS THIS PRODUCTION GONNA BE OKAY?
THE SCHEDULE ONLY BARELY CAME TOGETHER AS IT IS.

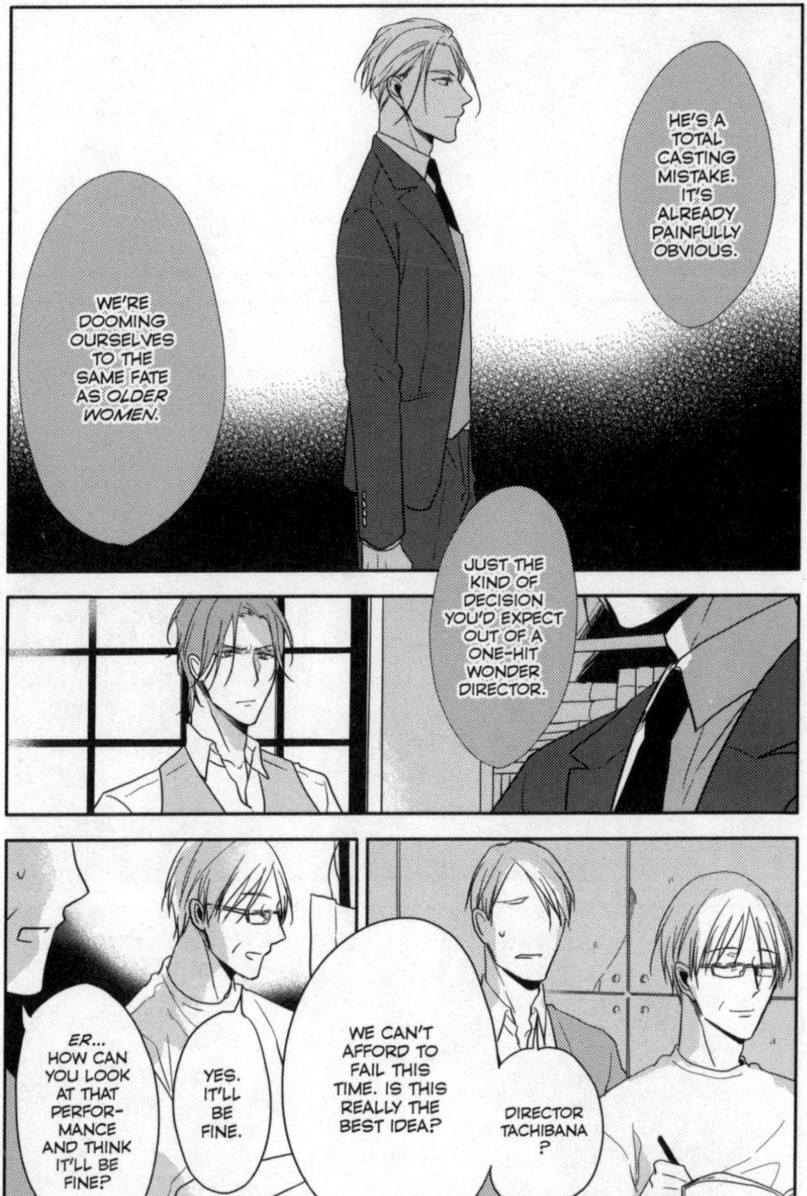
HE'S A TOTAL CASTING MISTAKE. IT'S ALREADY PAINFULLY OBVIOUS.
WE'RE DOOMING OURSELVES TO THE SAME FATE AS *OLDER WOMEN*.
JUST THE KIND OF DECISION YOU'D EXPECT OUT OF A ONE-HIT WONDER DIRECTOR.
DIRECTOR TACHIBANA?
WE CAN'T AFFORD TO FAIL THIS TIME. IS THIS REALLY THE BEST IDEA?
YES. IT'LL BE FINE.
ER... HOW CAN YOU LOOK AT THAT PERFORMANCE AND THINK IT'LL BE FINE?

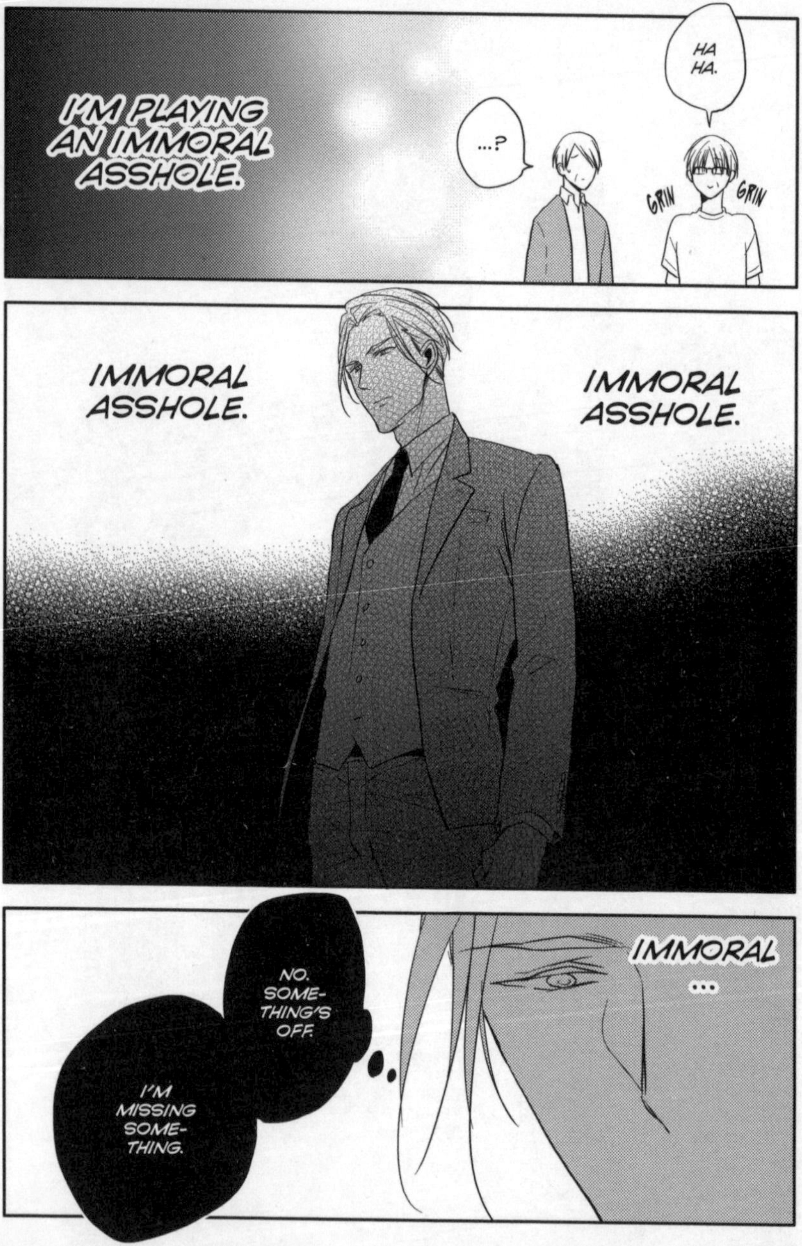
HA HA.
...?
GRIN GRIN
I'M PLAYING AN IMMORAL ASSHOLE.
IMMORAL ASSHOLE.
IMMORAL ASSHOLE.
IMMORAL...
NO. SOME-THING'S OFF.
I'M MISSING SOME-THING.

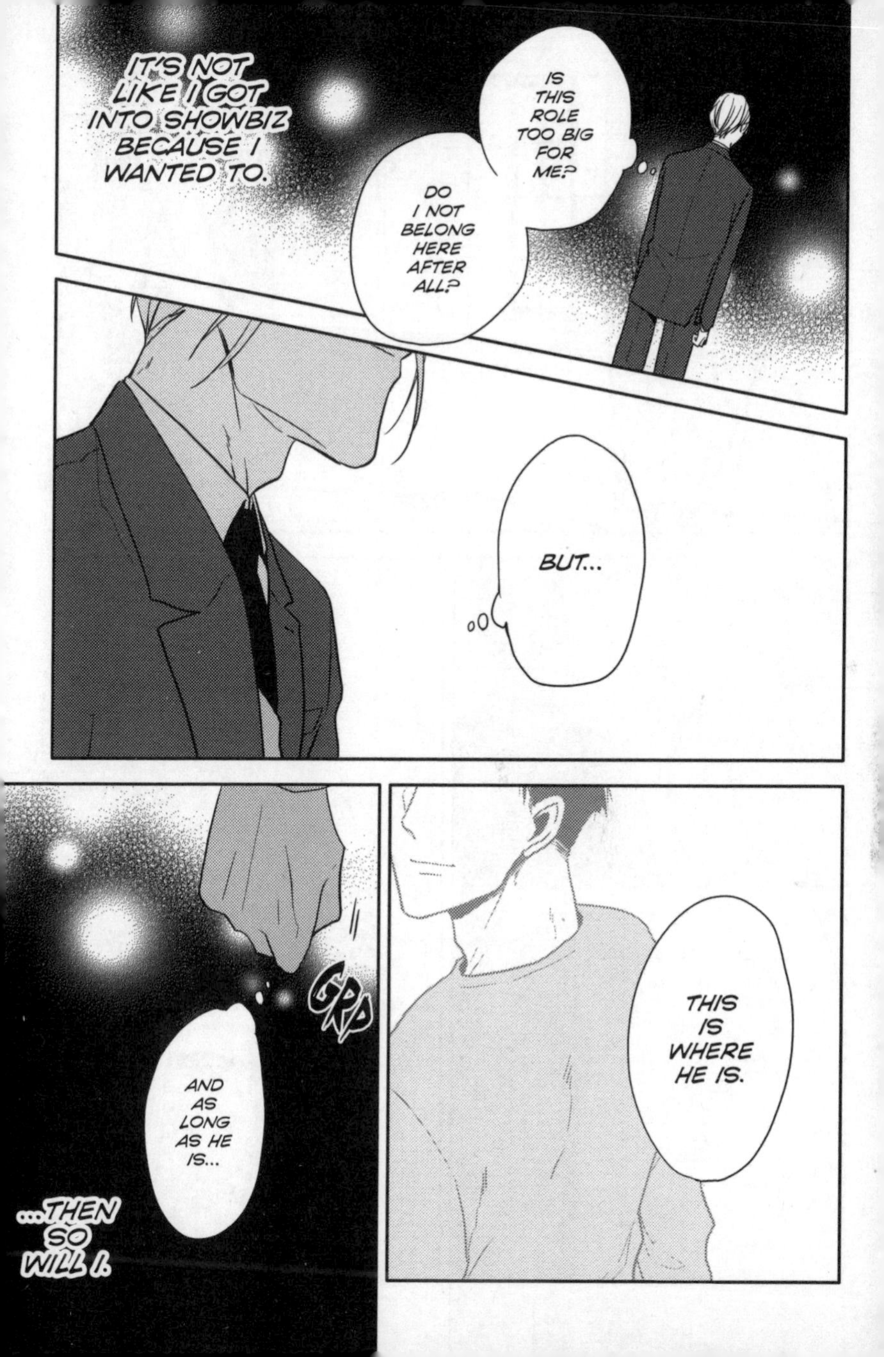
IS THIS ROLE TOO BIG FOR ME?
DO I NOT BELONG HERE AFTER ALL?
IT'S NOT LIKE I GOT INTO SHOWBIZ BECAUSE I WANTED TO.
BUT...
THIS IS WHERE HE IS.
GRP
AND AS LONG AS HE IS...
...THEN SO WILL I.

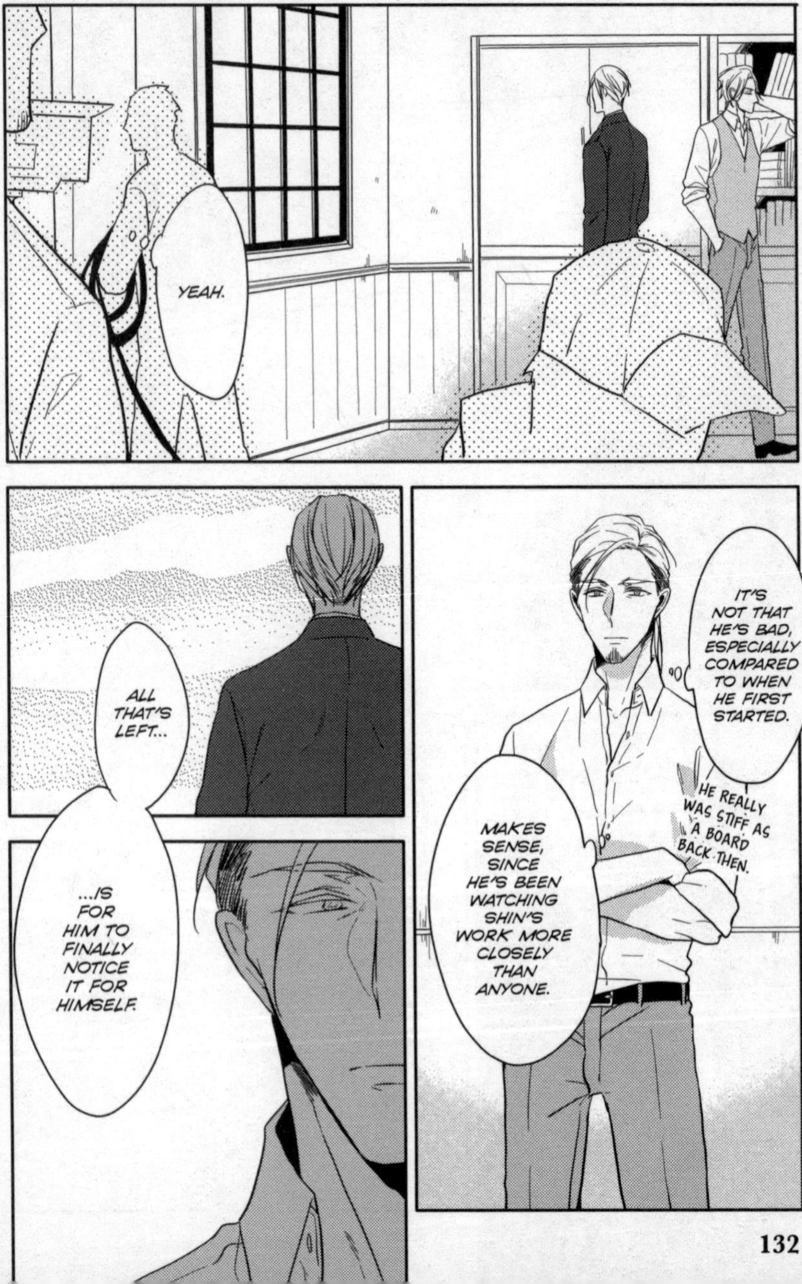
YEAH.
IT'S NOT THAT HE'S BAD, ESPECIALLY COMPARED TO WHEN HE FIRST STARTED.
HE REALLY WAS STIFF AS A BOARD BACK THEN.
MAKES SENSE, SINCE HE'S BEEN WATCHING SHIN'S WORK MORE CLOSELY THAN ANYONE.
ALL THAT'S LEFT...
...IS FOR HIM TO FINALLY NOTICE IT FOR HIMSELF.

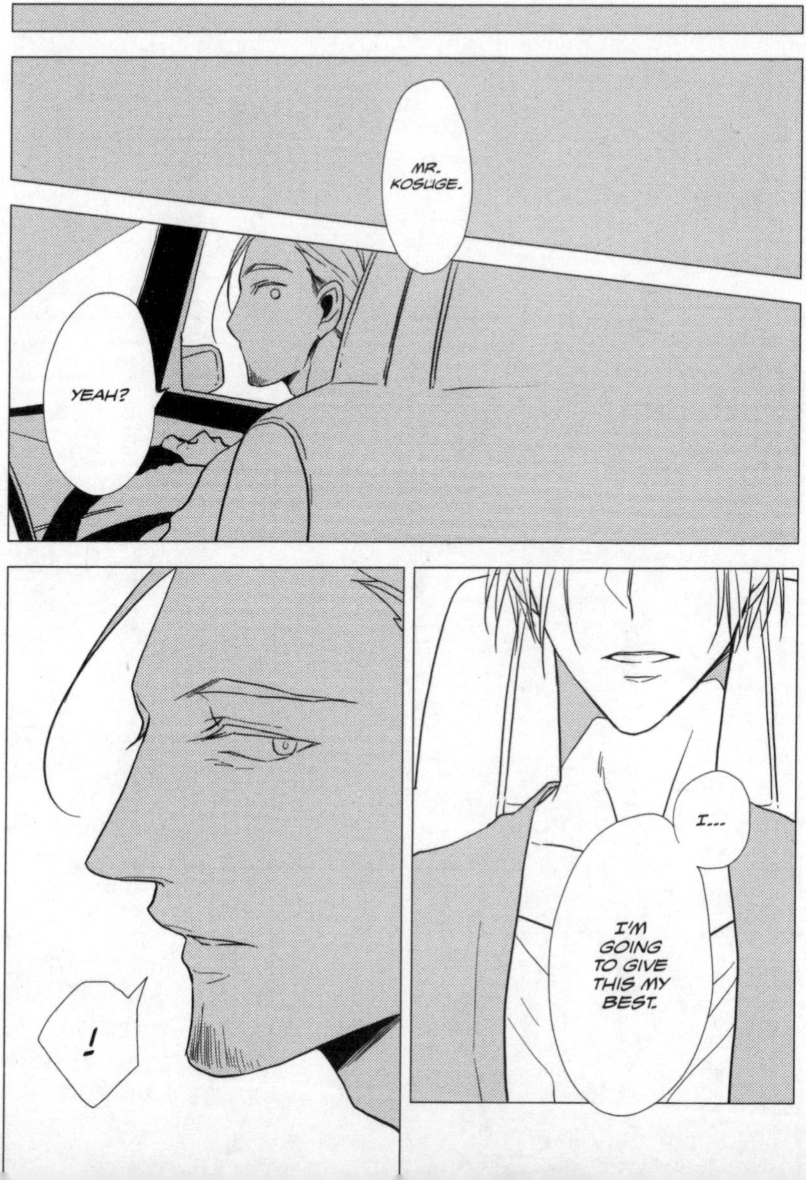
MR. KOSUGE.
YEAH?
I...
I'M GOING TO GIVE THIS MY BEST.
!

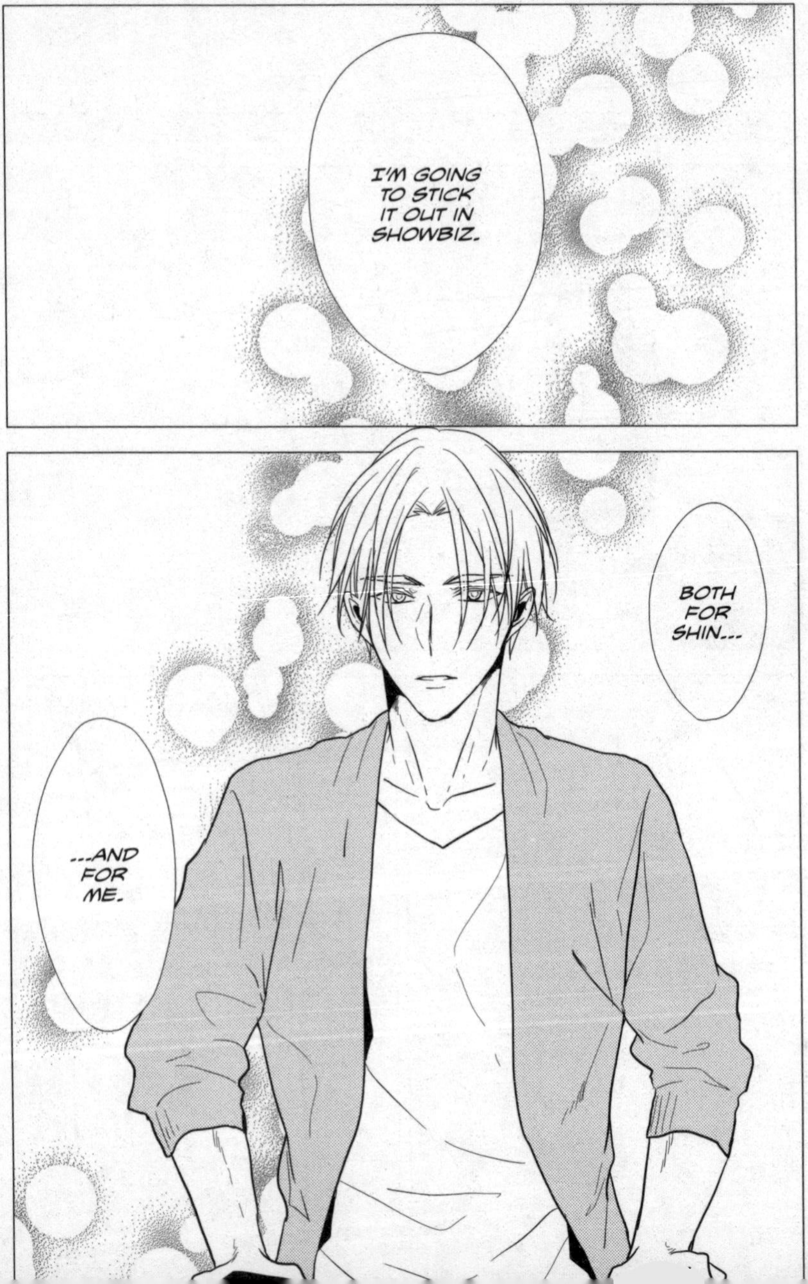
I'M GOING TO STICK IT OUT IN SHOWBIZ.
BOTH FOR SHIN...
...AND FOR ME.

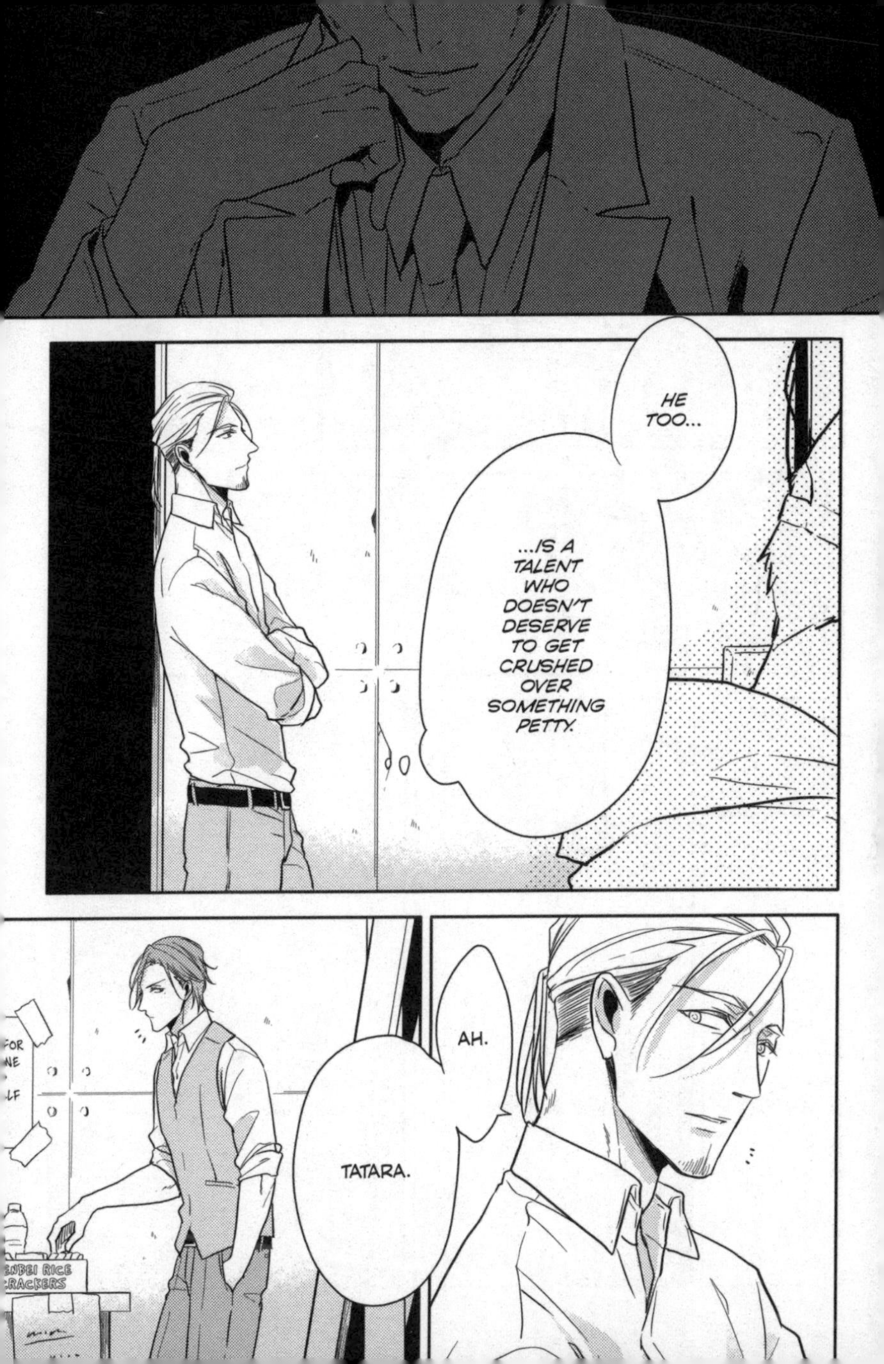
HE TOO...
...IS A TALENT WHO DOESN'T DESERVE TO GET CRUSHED OVER SOMETHING PETTY.
AH.
TATARA.

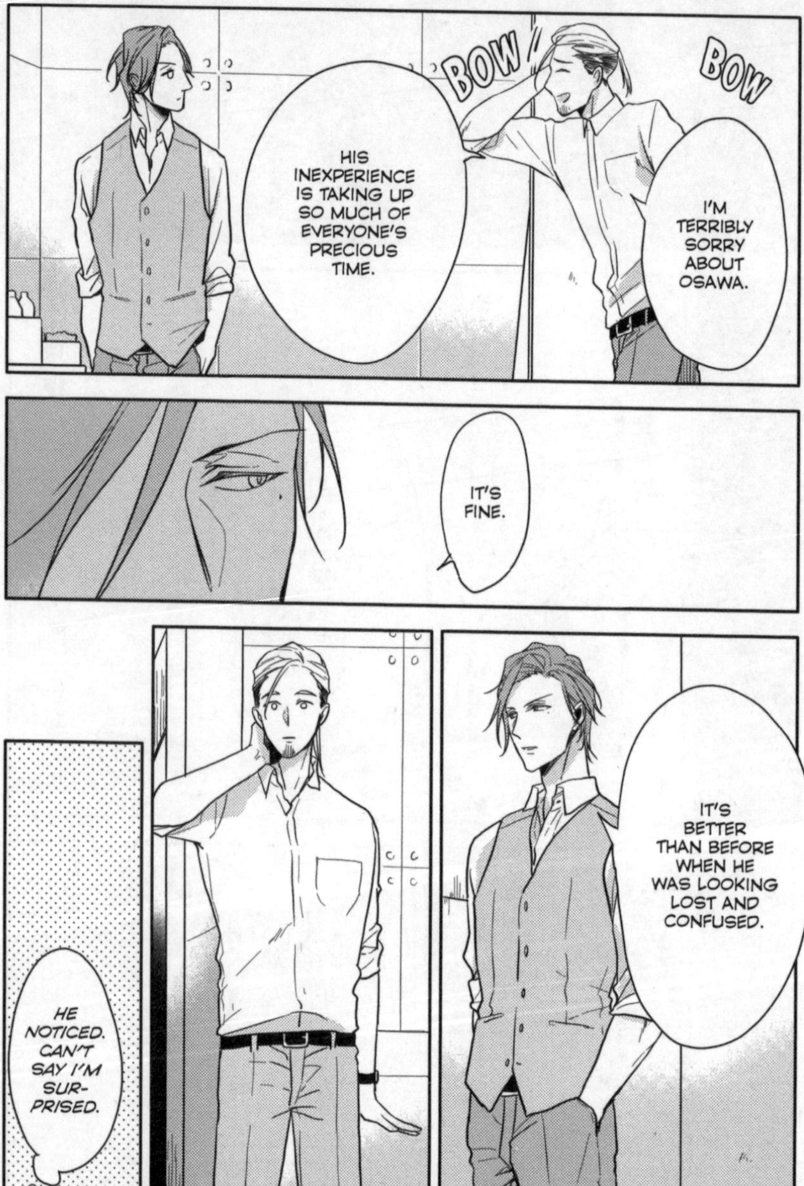
BOW
BOW
I'M TERRIBLY SORRY ABOUT OSAWA.
HIS INEXPERIENCE IS TAKING UP SO MUCH OF EVERYONE'S PRECIOUS TIME.
IT'S FINE.
IT'S BETTER THAN BEFORE WHEN HE WAS LOOKING LOST AND CONFUSED.
HE NOTICED. CAN'T SAY I'M SUR-PRISED.

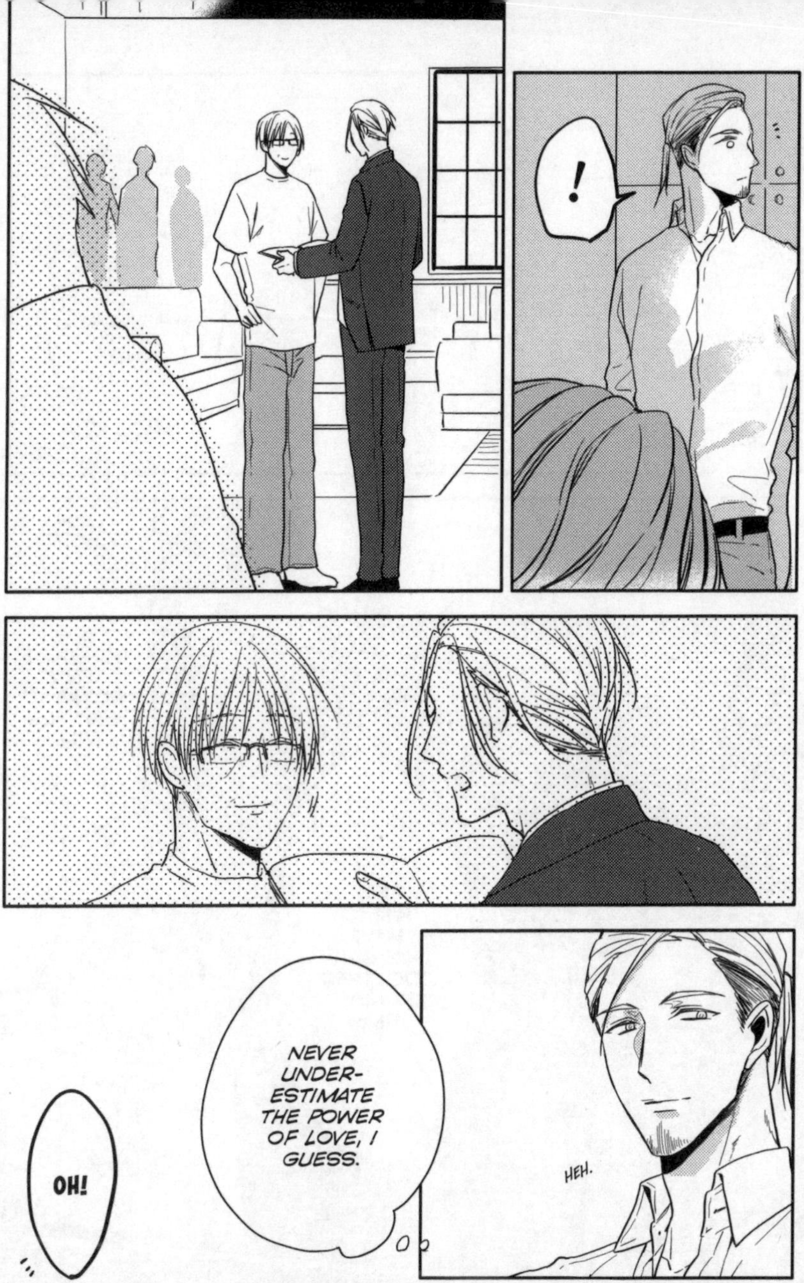
!
HEH.
NEVER UNDER-ESTIMATE THE POWER OF LOVE, I GUESS.
OH!

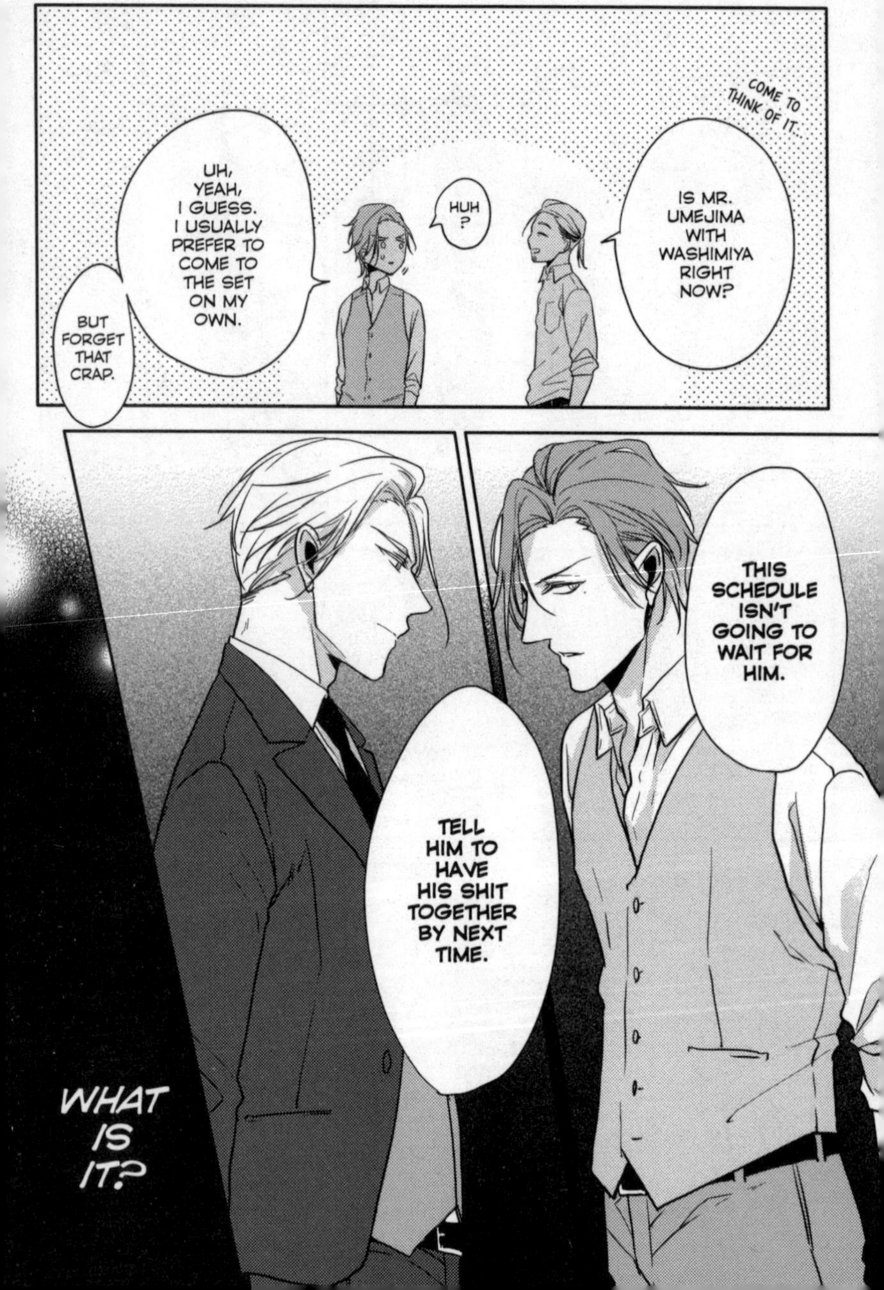
COME TO THINK OF IT...
IS MR. UMEJIMA WITH WASHIMIYA RIGHT NOW?
HUH?
UH, YEAH, I GUESS. I USUALLY PREFER TO COME TO THE SET ON MY OWN.
BUT FORGET THAT CRAP.
THIS SCHEDULE ISN'T GOING TO WAIT FOR HIM.
TELL HIM TO HAVE HIS SHIT TOGETHER BY NEXT TIME.
WHAT IS IT?

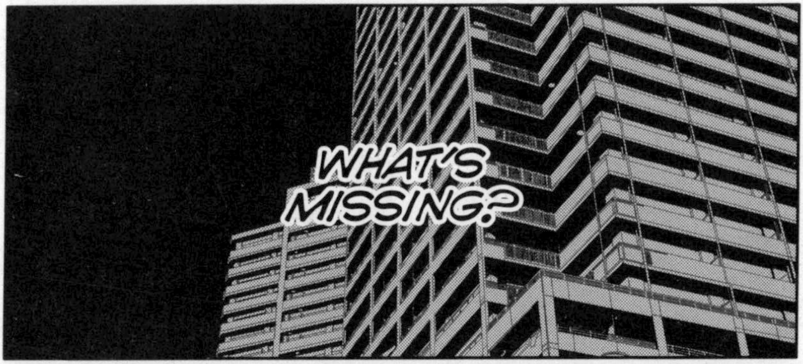
WHAT'S MISSING?

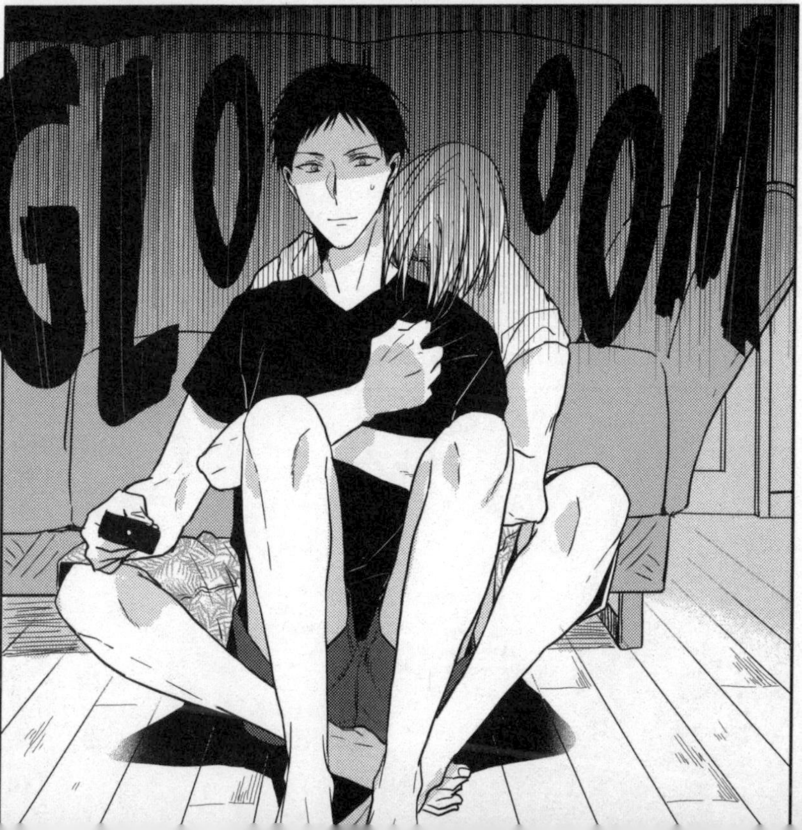
GLOOOM

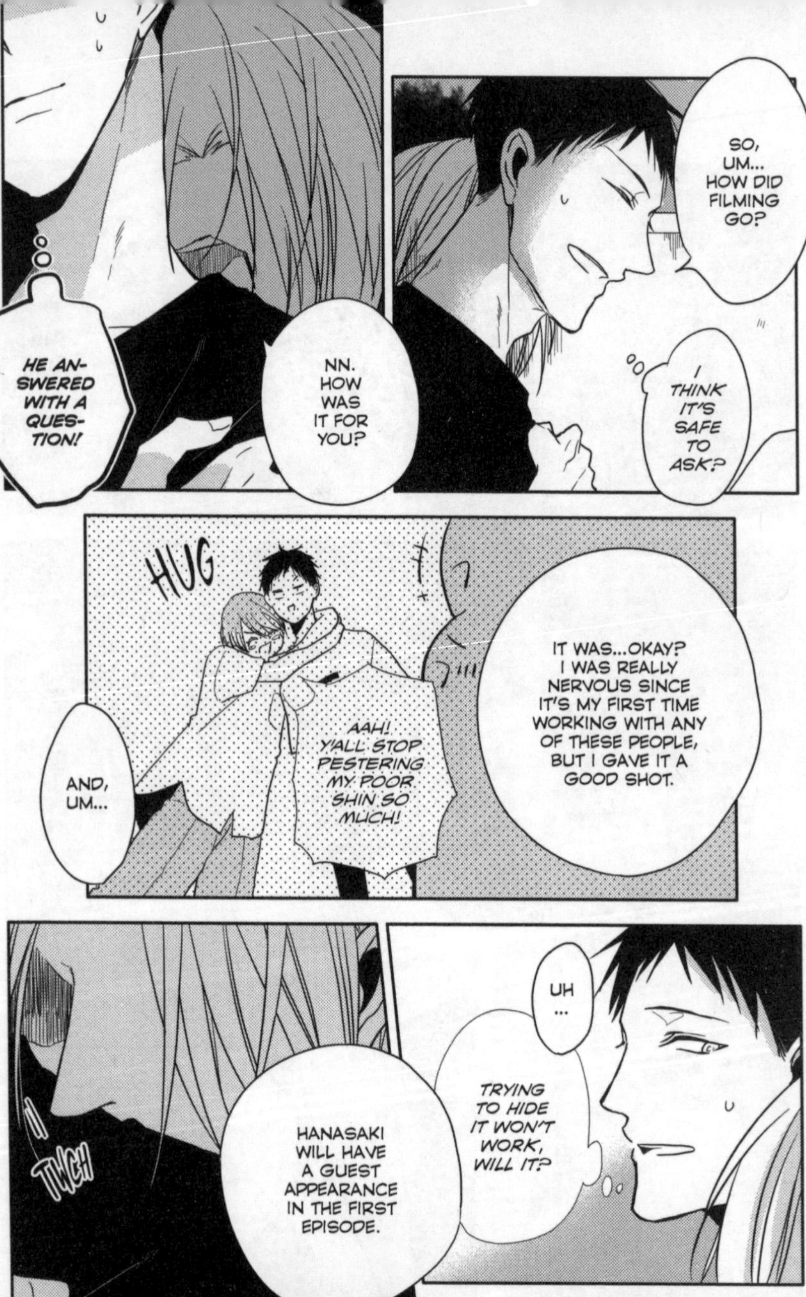
SO, UM... HOW DID FILMING GO?
I THINK IT'S SAFE TO ASK?
NN. HOW WAS IT FOR YOU?
HE AN-SWERED WITH A QUES-TION!
IT WAS...OKAY? I WAS REALLY NERVOUS SINCE IT'S MY FIRST TIME WORKING WITH ANY OF THESE PEOPLE, BUT I GAVE IT A GOOD SHOT.
HUG
AAH! Y'ALL STOP PESTERING MY POOR SHIN SO MUCH!
AND, UM...
UH ...
TRYING TO HIDE IT WON'T WORK, WILL IT?
HANASAKI WILL HAVE A GUEST APPEARANCE IN THE FIRST EPISODE.
TWCH

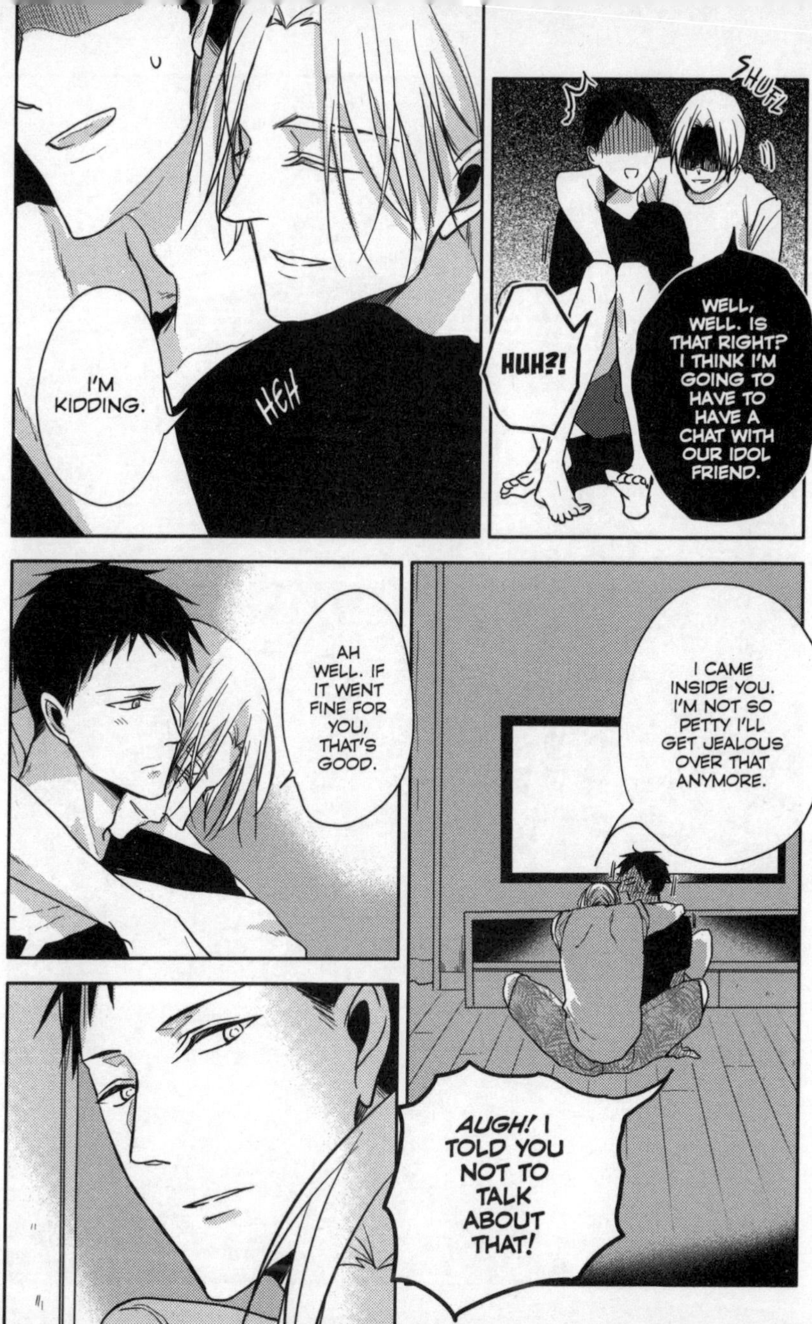
SHUFL
WELL, WELL. IS THAT RIGHT? I THINK I'M GOING TO HAVE TO HAVE A CHAT WITH OUR IDOL FRIEND.
HUH?!
I'M KIDDING.
HEH
I CAME INSIDE YOU. I'M NOT SO PETTY I'LL GET JEALOUS OVER THAT ANYMORE.
AH WELL. IF IT WENT FINE FOR YOU, THAT'S GOOD.
AUGH! I TOLD YOU NOT TO TALK ABOUT THAT!

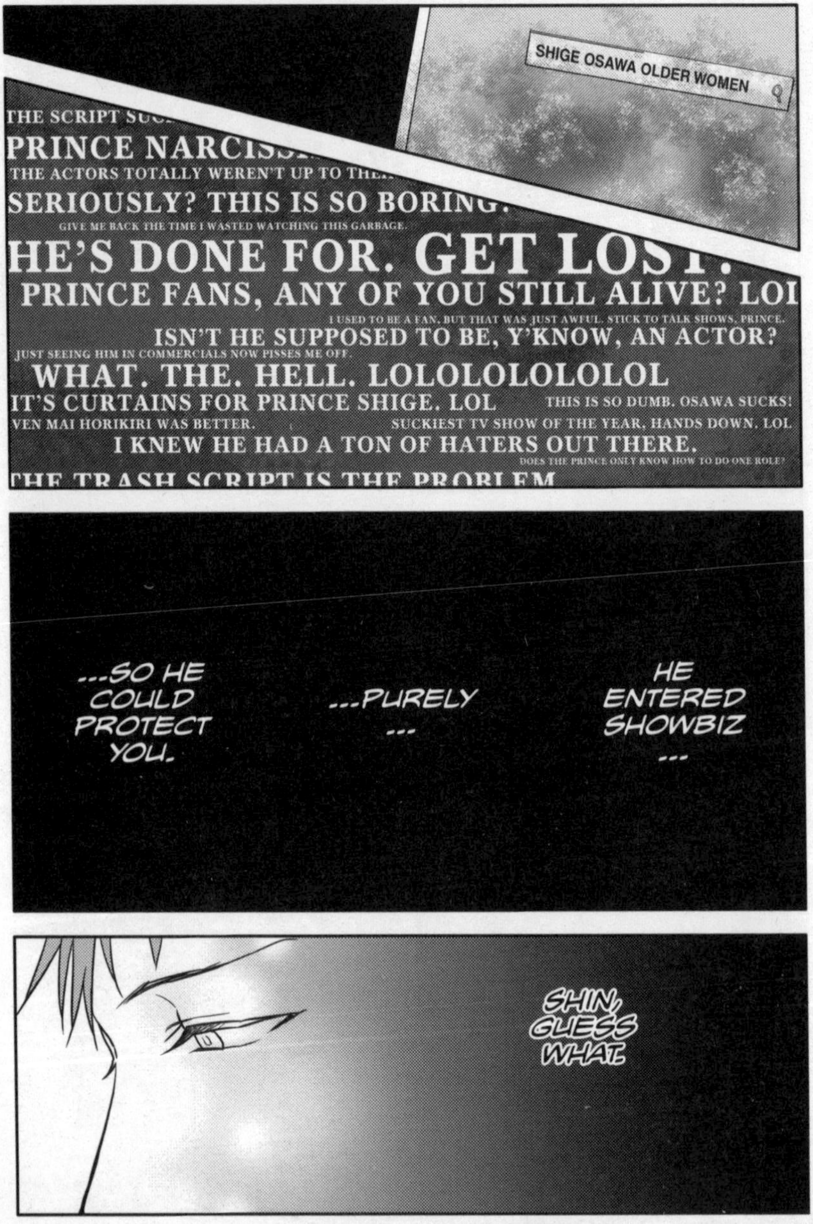
SHIGE OSAWA OLDER WOMEN
THE SCRIPT
PRINCE
THE ACTORS TOTALLY WEREN'T UP TO
SERIOUSLY? THIS IS SO
GIVE ME BACK THE TIME I WASTED WATCHING THIS GARBAGE.
HE'S DONE FOR. GET
PRINCE FANS, ANY OF YOU STILL ALIVE? LOL
I USED TO BE A FAN, BUT THAT WAS JUST AWFUL. STICK TO TALK SHOWS, PRINCE.
ISN'T HE SUPPOSED TO BE, Y'KNOW, AN ACTOR?
JUST SEEING HIM IN COMMERCIALS NOW PISSES ME OFF.
WHAT. THE. HELL. LOLOLOLOLOLOL
IT'S CURTAINS FOR PRINCE SHIGE. LOL
THIS IS SO DUMB. OSAWA SUCKS!
MAI HORIKIRI WAS BETTER.
SUCKIEST TV SHOW OF THE YEAR, HANDS DOWN. LOL
I KNEW HE HAD A TON OF HATERS OUT THERE.
DOES THE PRINCE ONLY KNOW HOW TO DO ONE ROLE?
HE ENTERED SHOWBIZ...
...PURELY...
...SO HE COULD PROTECT YOU.
SHIN, GUESS WHAT.

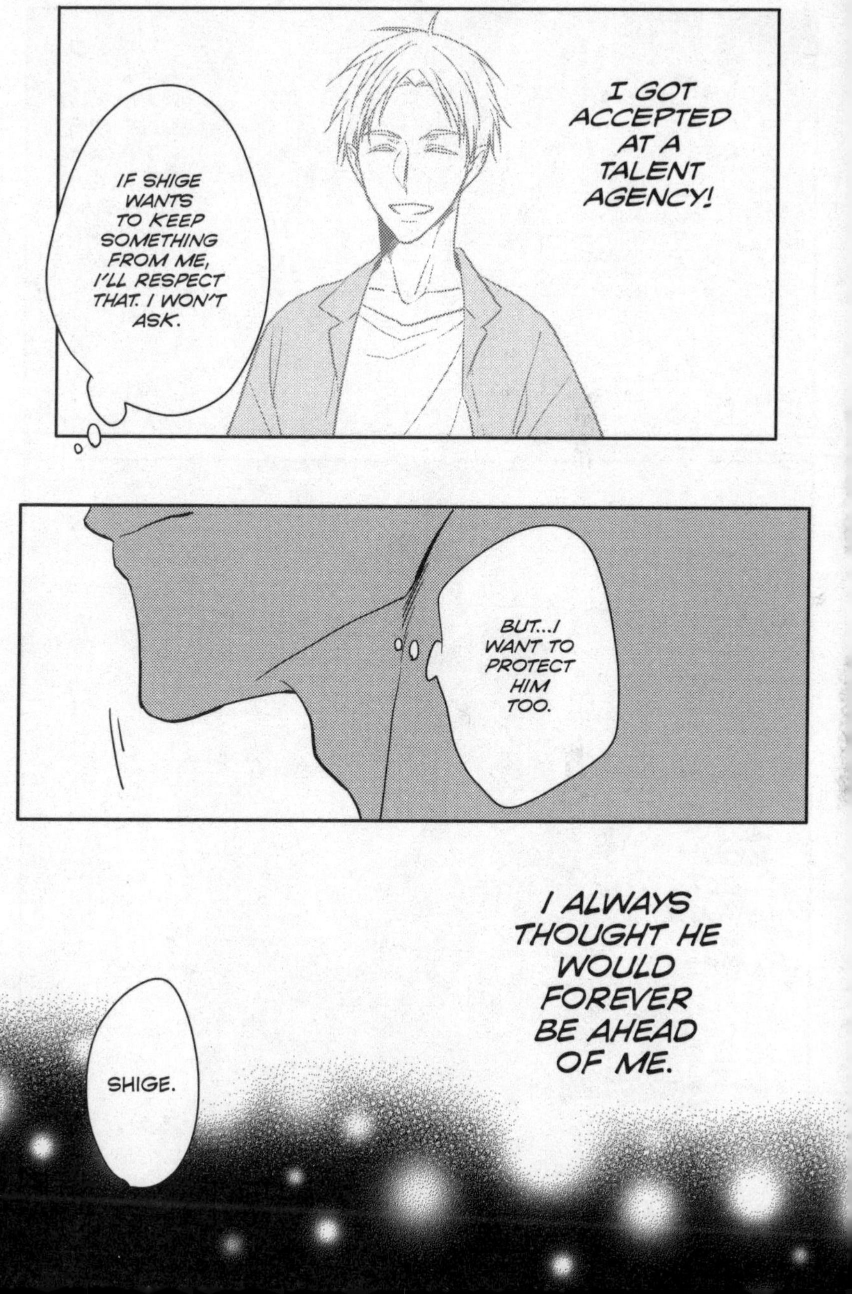
I GOT ACCEPTED AT A TALENT AGENCY!
IF SHIGE WANTS TO KEEP SOMETHING FROM ME, I'LL RESPECT THAT. I WON'T ASK.
BUT...I WANT TO PROTECT HIM TOO.
I ALWAYS THOUGHT HE WOULD FOREVER BE AHEAD OF ME.
SHIGE.

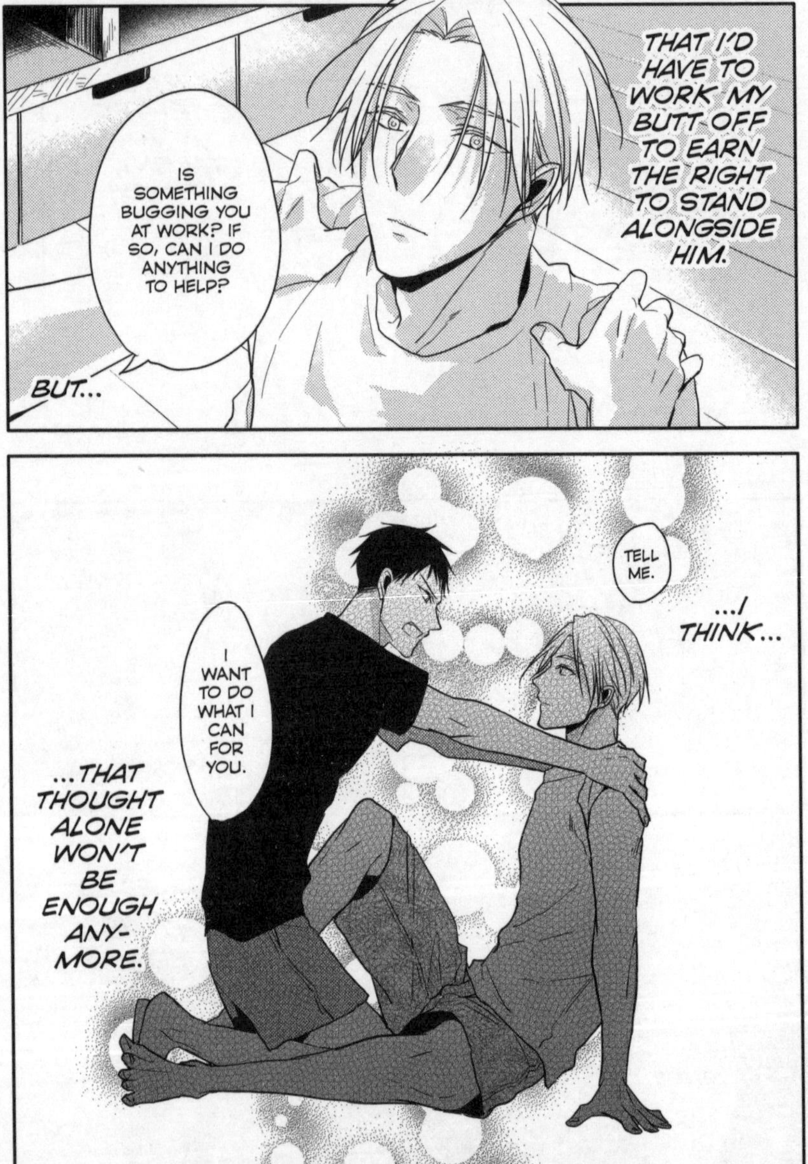
THAT I'D HAVE TO WORK MY BUTT OFF TO EARN THE RIGHT TO STAND ALONGSIDE HIM.
IS SOMETHING BUGGING YOU AT WORK? IF SO, CAN I DO ANYTHING TO HELP?
BUT...
TELL ME.
...I THINK...
I WANT TO DO WHAT I CAN FOR YOU.
...THAT THOUGHT ALONE WON'T BE ENOUGH ANY-MORE.

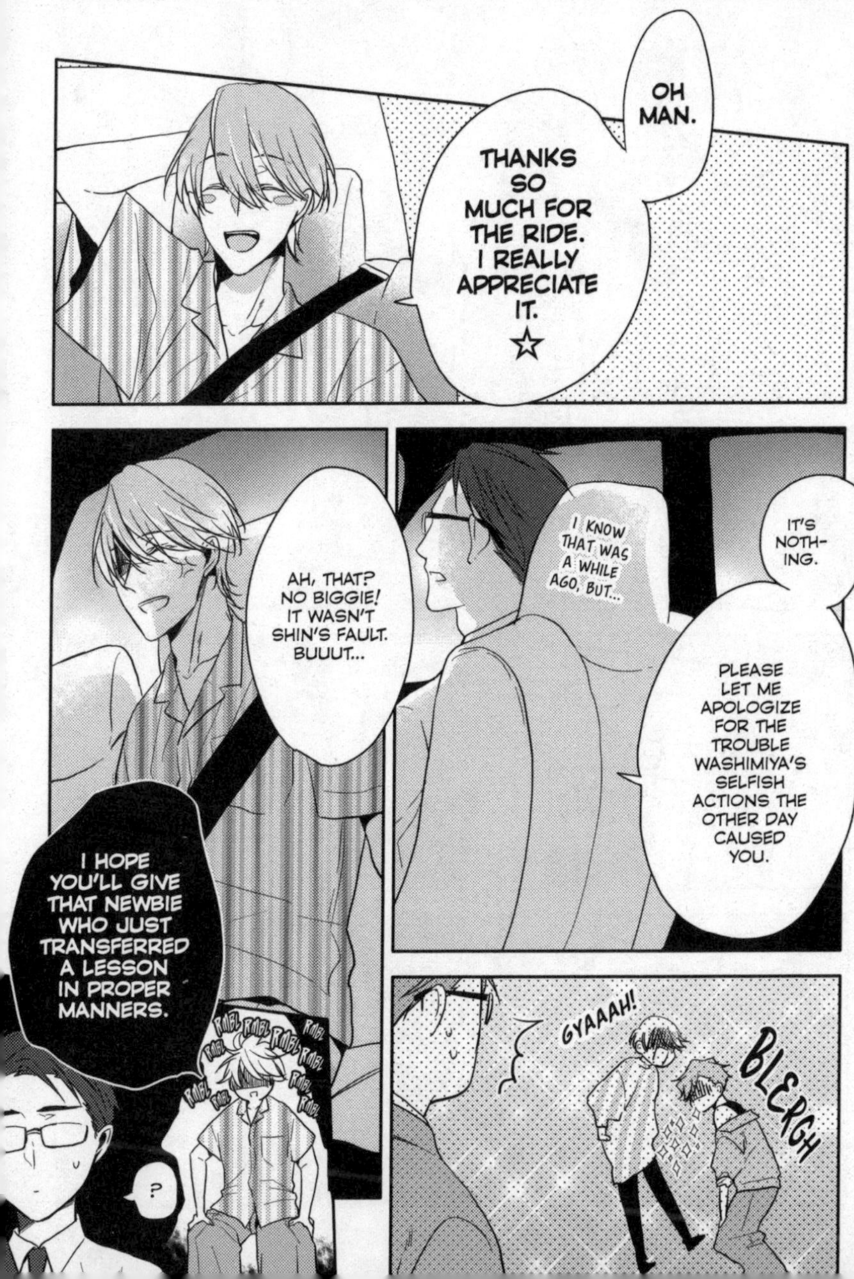
OH MAN.
THANKS SO MUCH FOR THE RIDE. I REALLY APPRECIATE IT. ☆
IT'S NOTHING.
PLEASE LET ME APOLOGIZE FOR THE TROUBLE WASHIMIYA'S SELFISH ACTIONS THE OTHER DAY CAUSED YOU.
I KNOW THAT WAS A WHILE AGO, BUT...
AH, THAT? NO BIGGIE! IT WASN'T SHIN'S FAULT. BUUUT...
I HOPE YOU'LL GIVE THAT NEWBIE WHO JUST TRANSFERRED A LESSON IN PROPER MANNERS.
GYAAAH!
BLERGH
RMBL RMBL RMBL RMBL
?

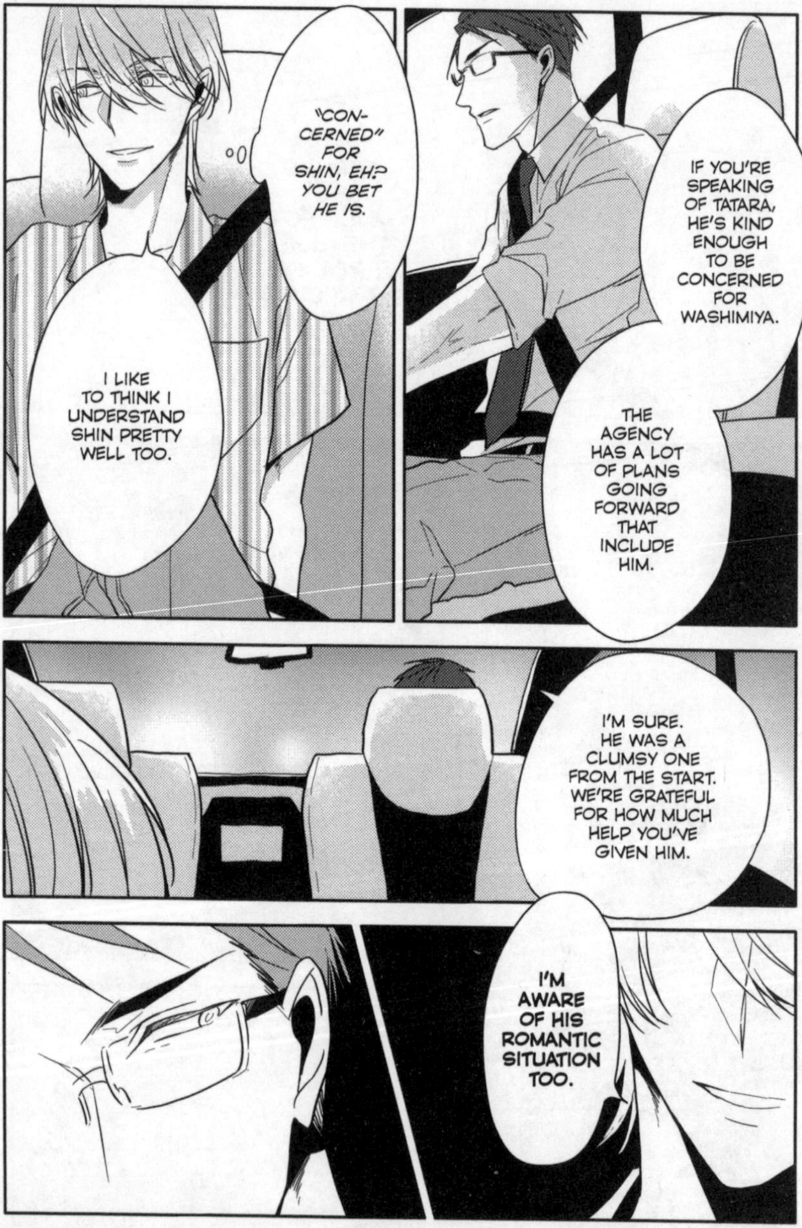
IF YOU'RE SPEAKING OF TATARA, HE'S KIND ENOUGH TO BE CONCERNED FOR WASHIMIYA.
THE AGENCY HAS A LOT OF PLANS GOING FORWARD THAT INCLUDE HIM.
"CON-CERNED" FOR SHIN, EH? YOU BET HE IS.
I LIKE TO THINK I UNDERSTAND SHIN PRETTY WELL TOO.
I'M SURE. HE WAS A CLUMSY ONE FROM THE START. WE'RE GRATEFUL FOR HOW MUCH HELP YOU'VE GIVEN HIM.
I'M AWARE OF HIS ROMANTIC SITUATION TOO.

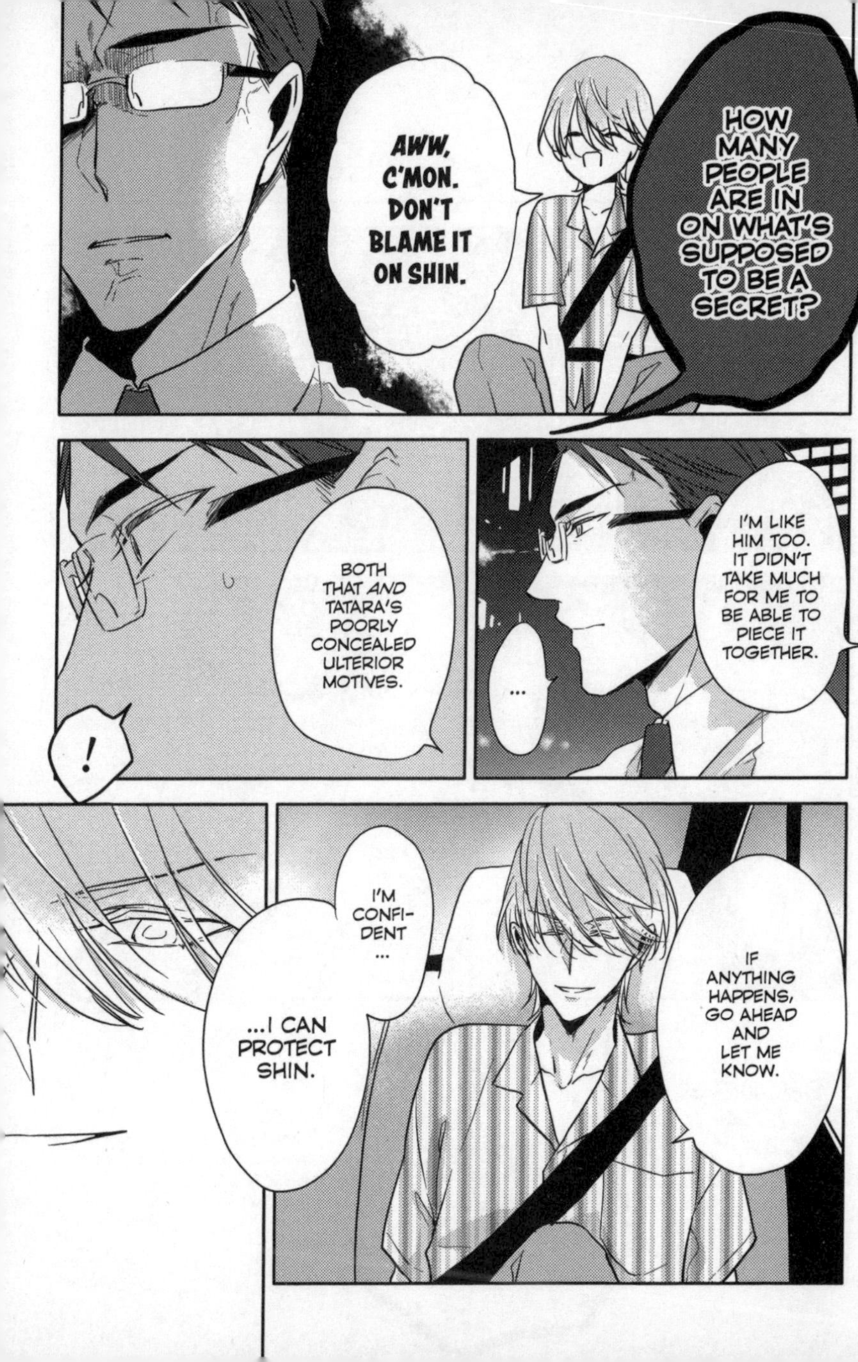
HOW MANY PEOPLE ARE IN ON WHAT'S SUPPOSED TO BE A SECRET?
AWW, C'MON. DON'T BLAME IT ON SHIN.
I'M LIKE HIM TOO. IT DIDN'T TAKE MUCH FOR ME TO BE ABLE TO PIECE IT TOGETHER.
...
BOTH THAT *AND* TATARA'S POORLY CONCEALED ULTERIOR MOTIVES.
!
IF ANYTHING HAPPENS, GO AHEAD AND LET ME KNOW.
I'M CONFI-DENT ...
...I CAN PROTECT SHIN.

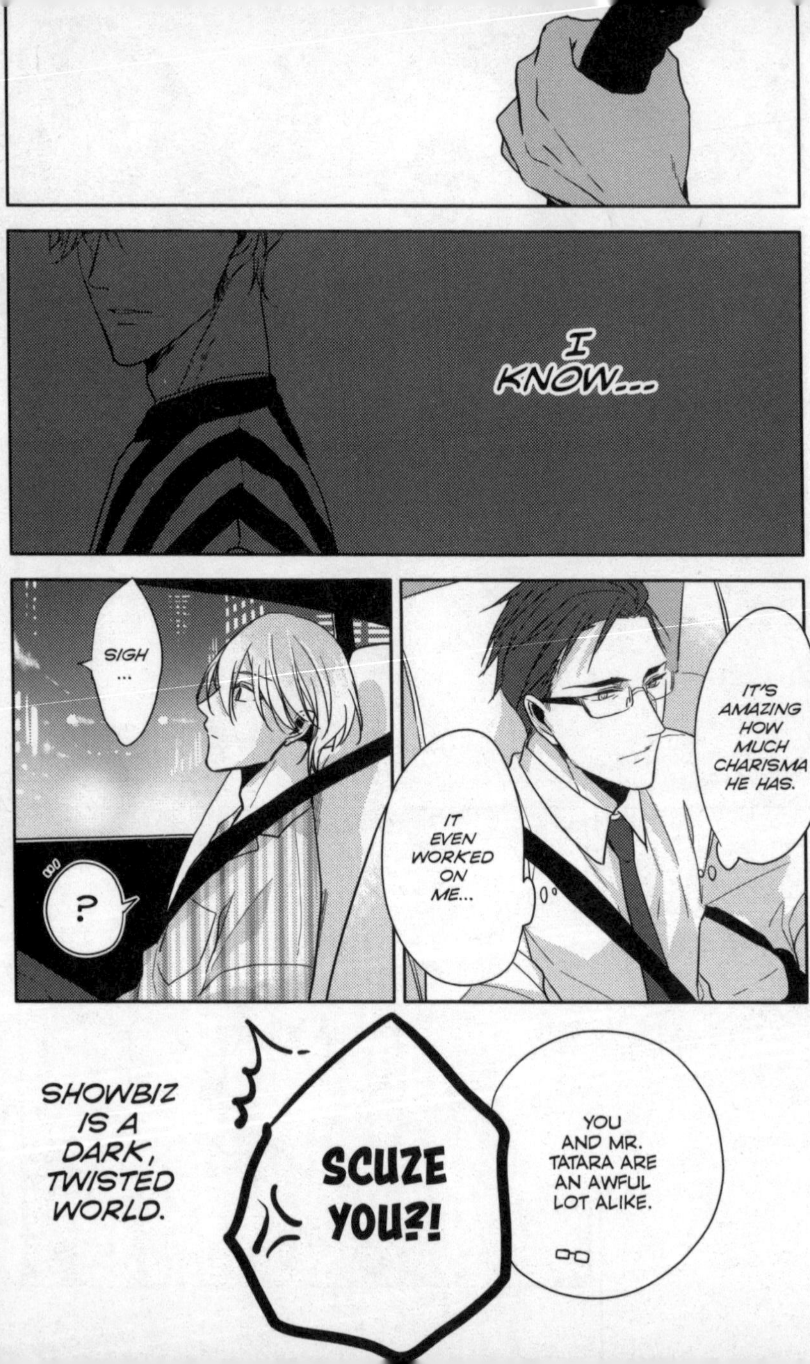
I KNOW...
IT'S AMAZING HOW MUCH CHARISMA HE HAS.
IT EVEN WORKED ON ME...
SIGH ...
?
YOU AND MR. TATARA ARE AN AWFUL LOT ALIKE.
SCUZE YOU?!
SHOWBIZ IS A DARK, TWISTED WORLD.

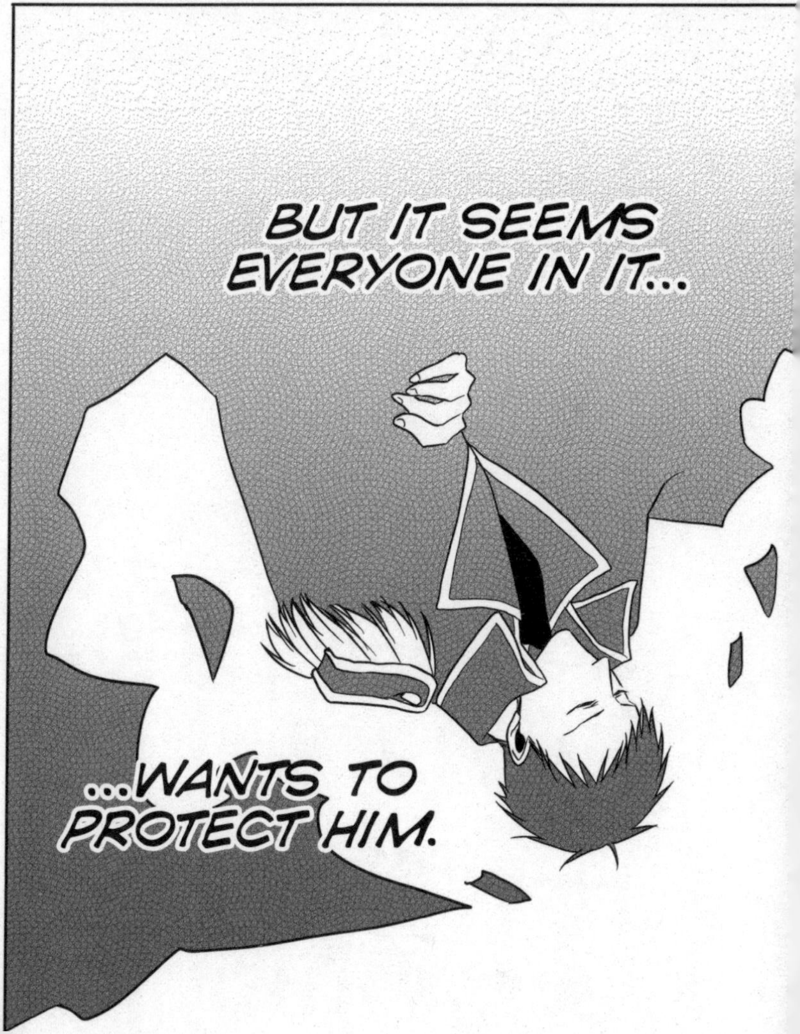
BUT IT SEEMS EVERYONE IN IT...
...WANTS TO PROTECT HIM.

Black
or White

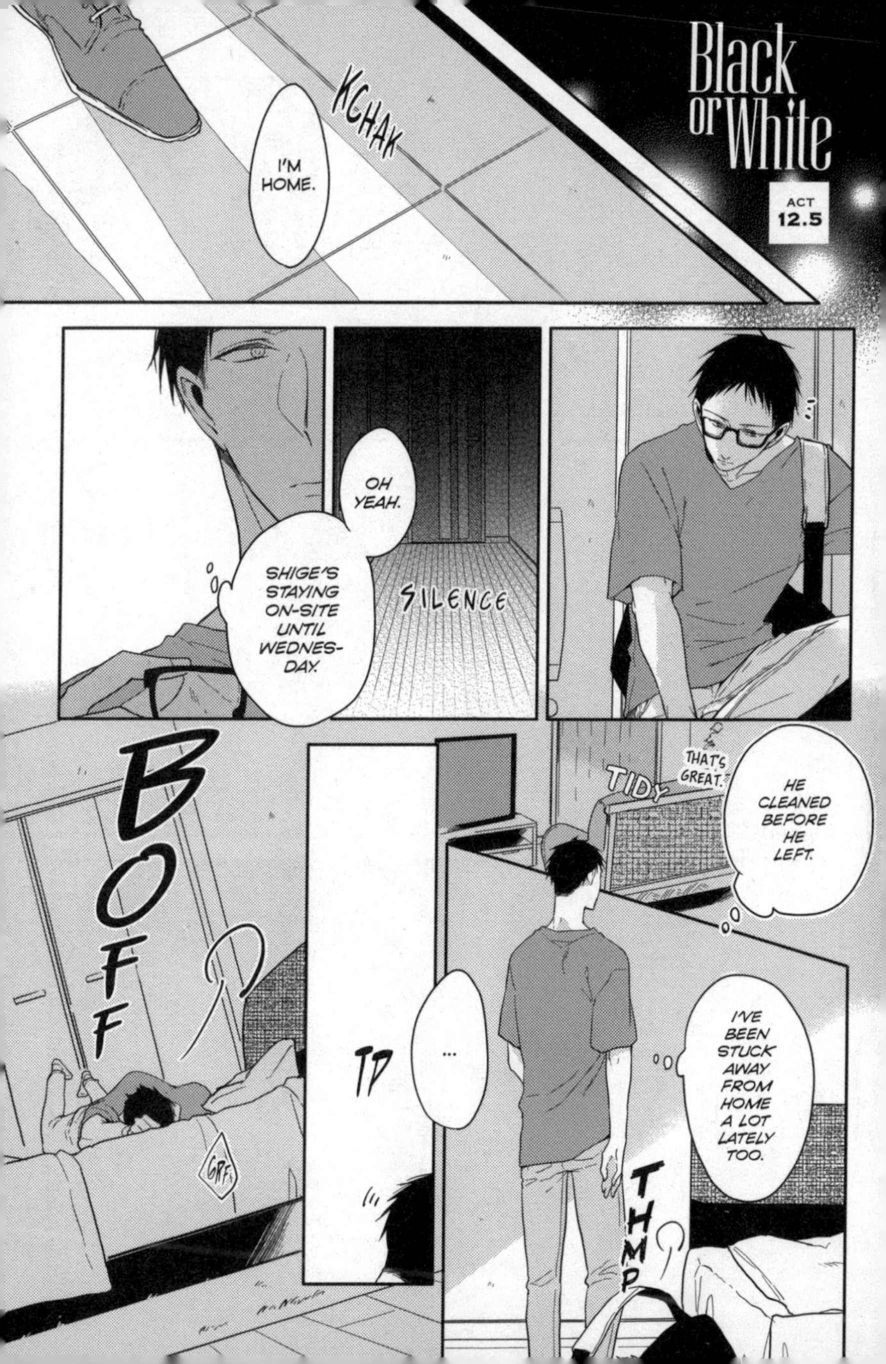
Black or White
ACT 12.5
KCHAK
I'M HOME.
OH YEAH.
SILENCE
SHIGE'S STAYING ON-SITE UNTIL WEDNES-DAY.
TIDY
THAT'S GREAT.
HE CLEANED BEFORE HE LEFT.
I'VE BEEN STUCK AWAY FROM HOME A LOT LATELY TOO.
THMP
...
TD
BOFF
GRF

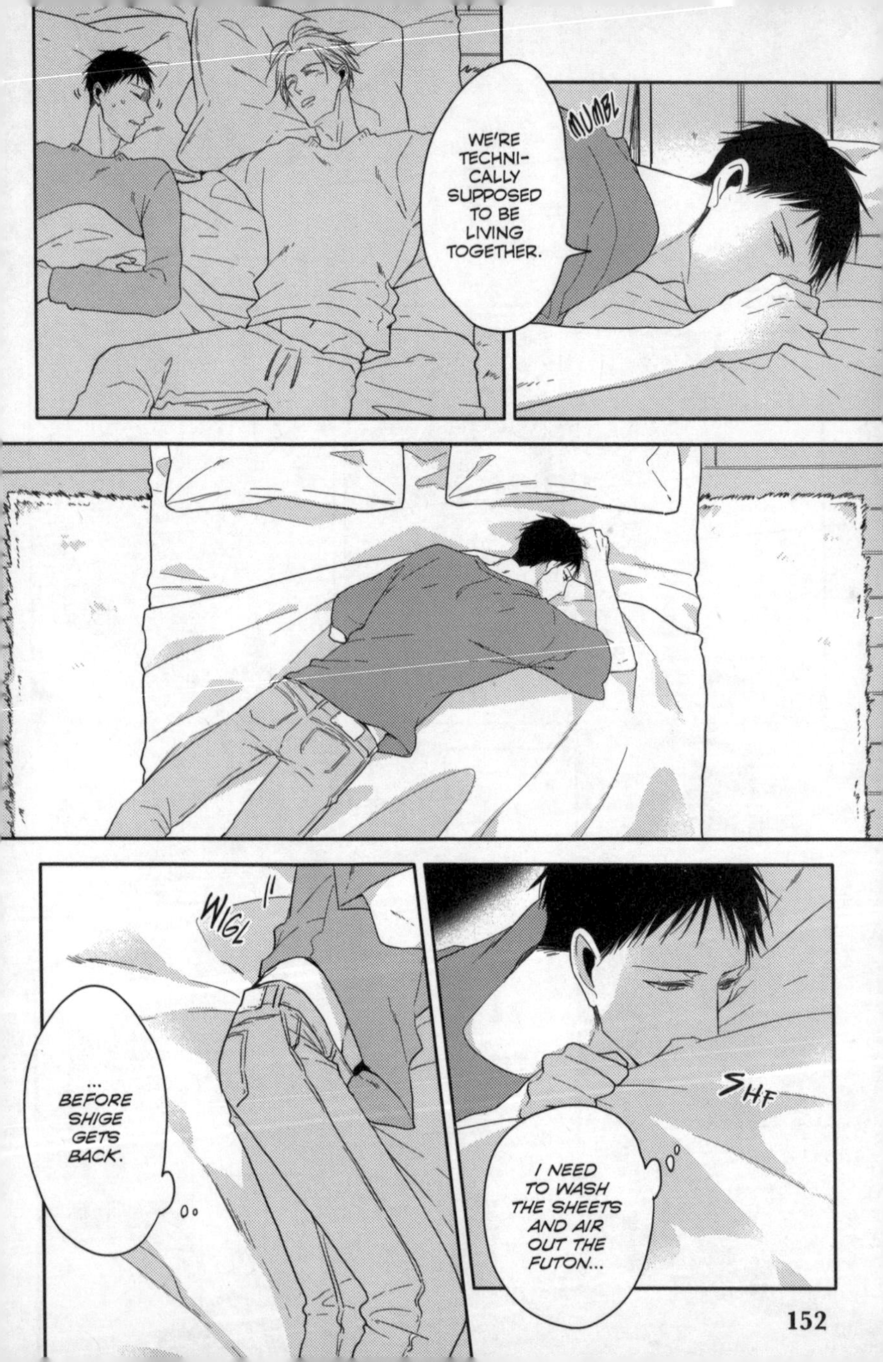
MUMBL
WE'RE TECHNI-CALLY SUPPOSED TO BE LIVING TOGETHER.
SHF
I NEED TO WASH THE SHEETS AND AIR OUT THE FUTON...
WIGL
... BEFORE SHIGE GETS BACK.

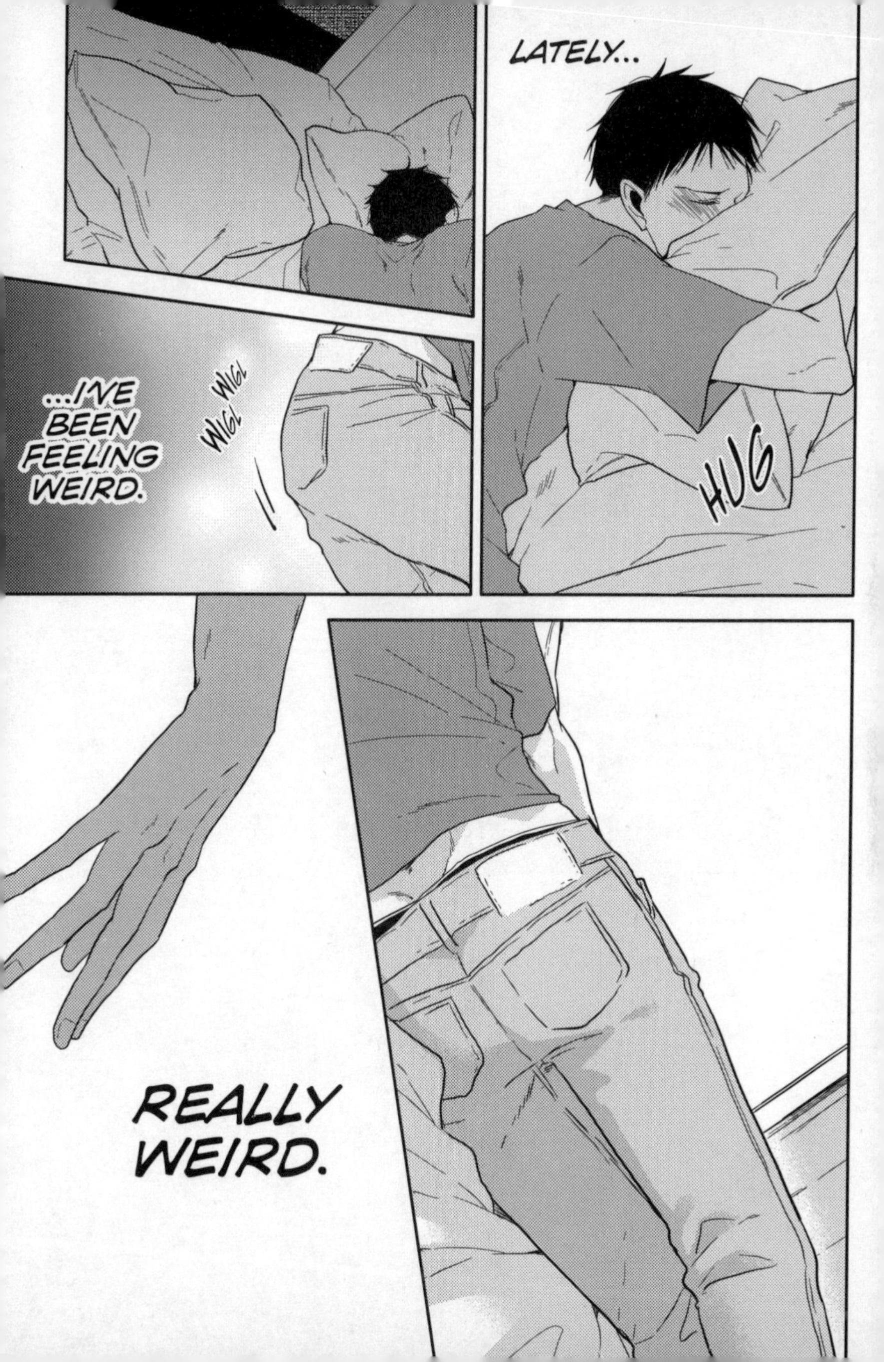
LATELY...
HUG
...I'VE BEEN FEELING WEIRD.
WIGL WIGL
REALLY WEIRD.

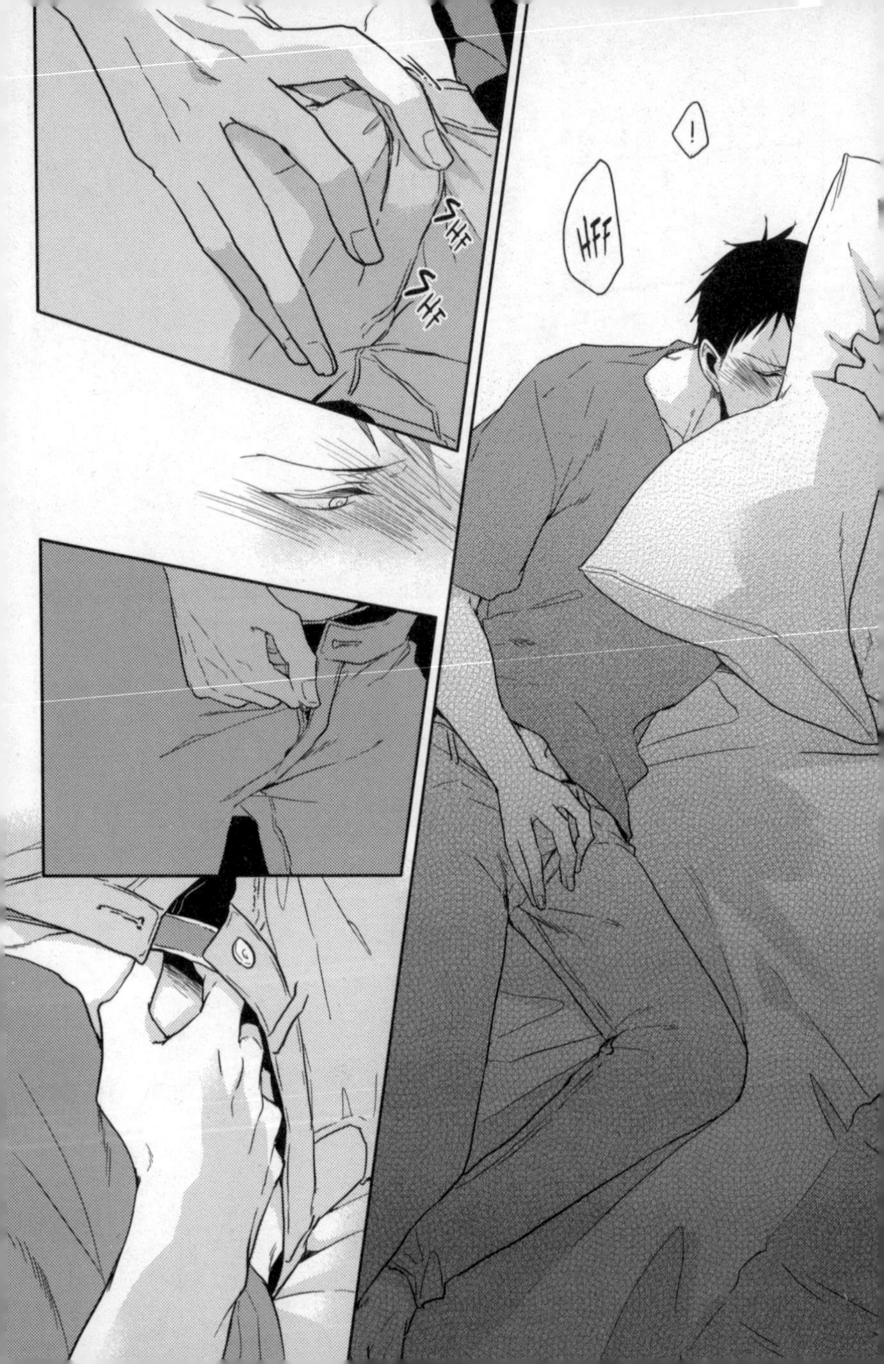
!
HFF
SHF
SHF

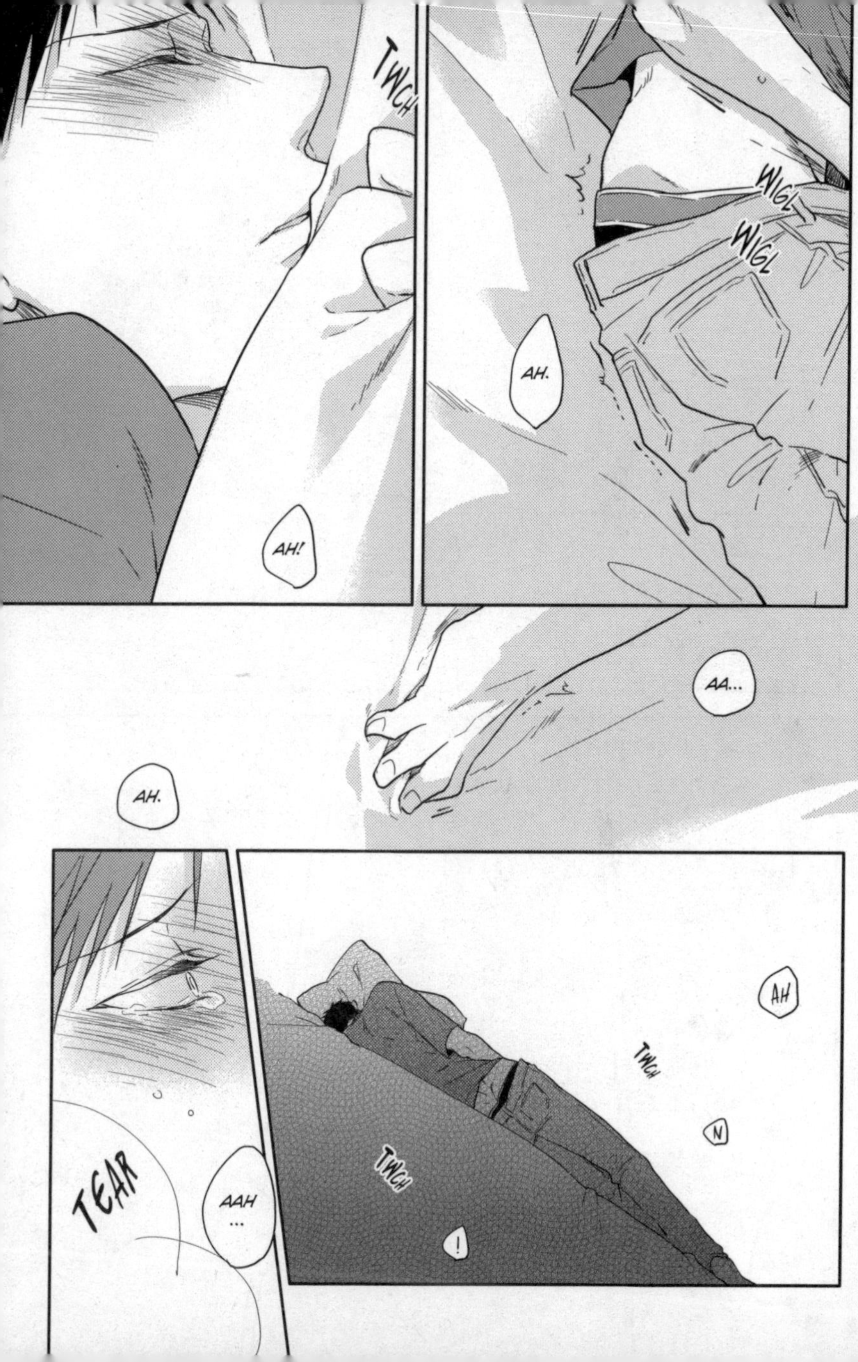
WIGL
WIGL
AH.
TWCH
AH!
AA...
AH.
AH
TWCH
N
TWCH
!
TEAR
AAH ...

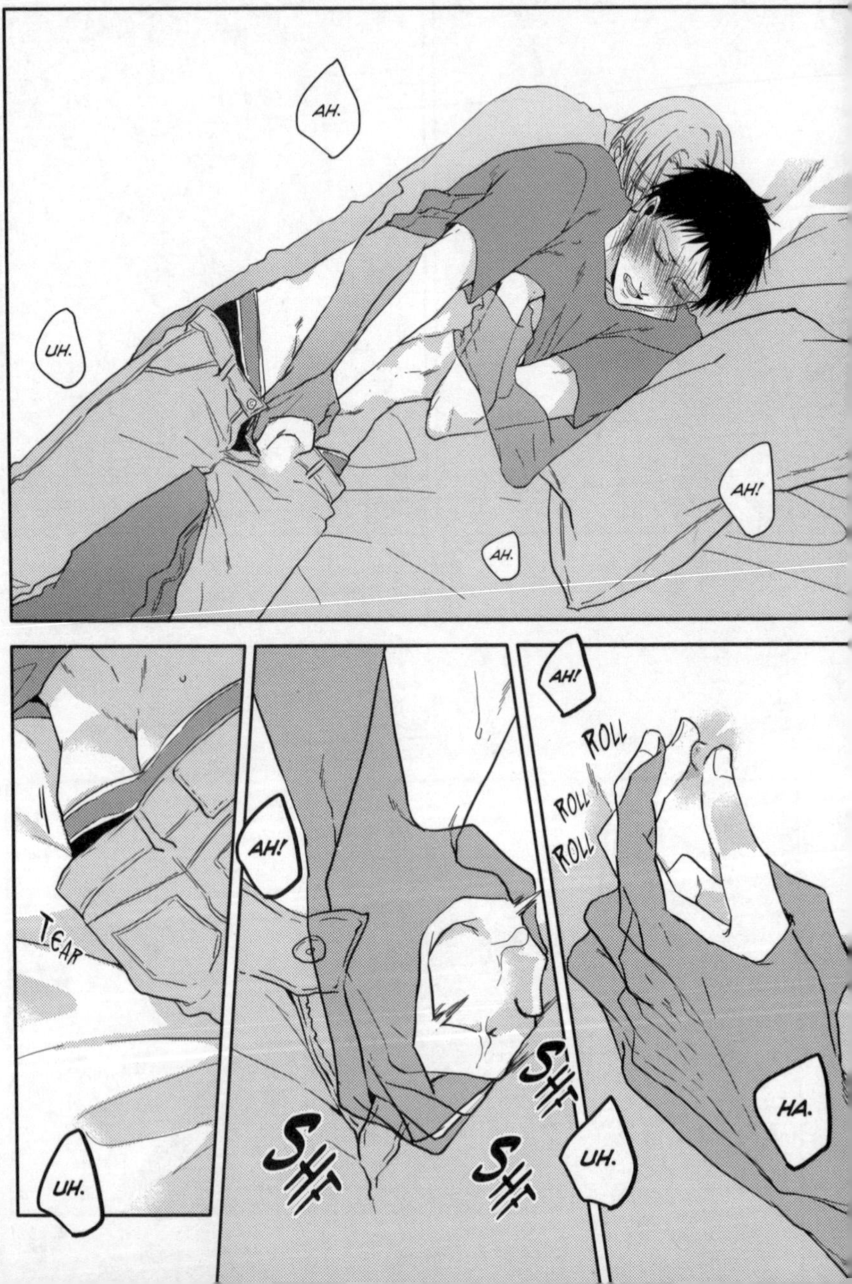
AH.
AH!
AH.
UH.
AH!
ROLL
ROLL
ROLL
HA.
UH.
SHF
SHF
AH!
SHF
TEAR
UH.

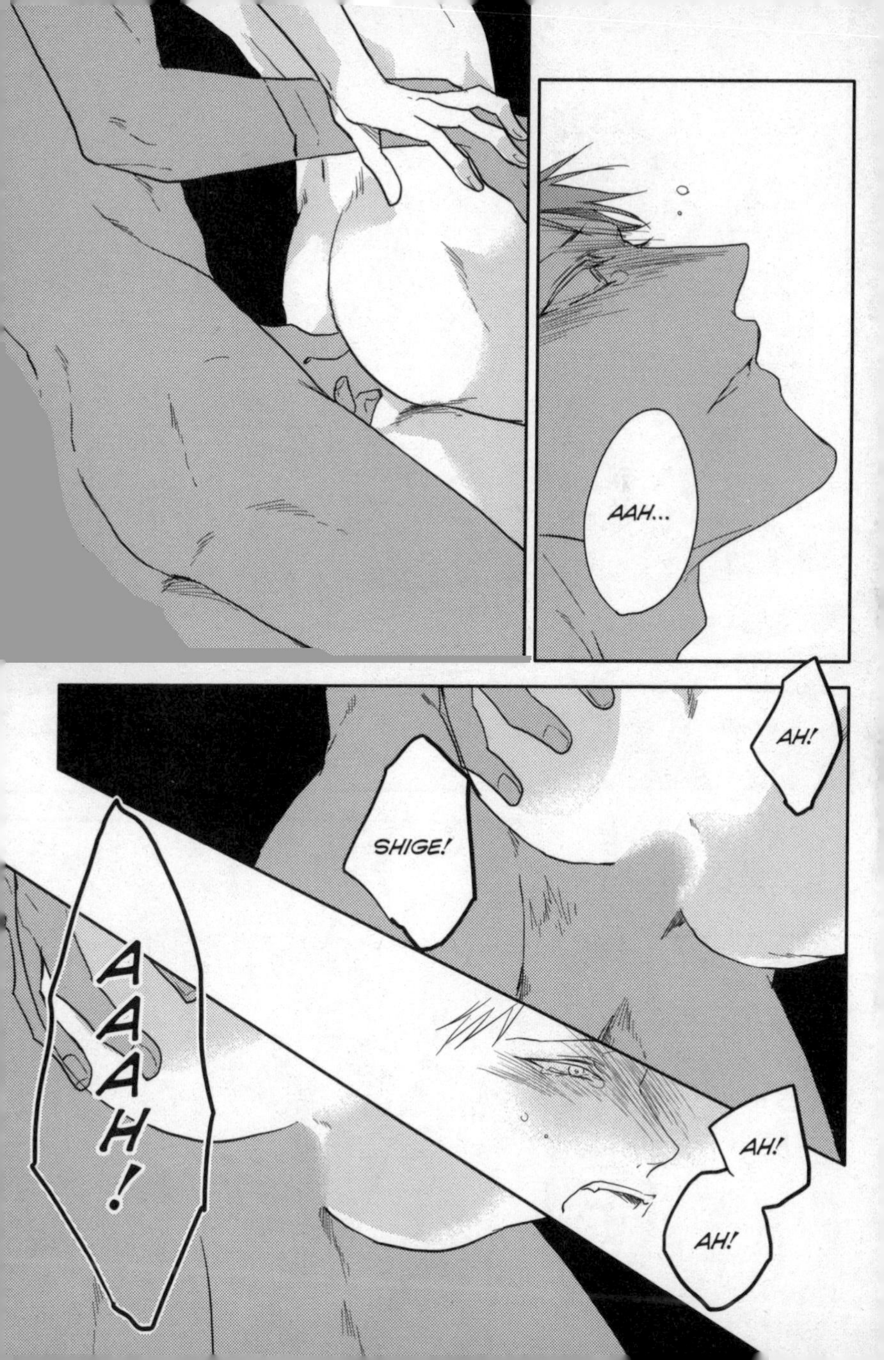
AAH...
AH!
SHIGE!
AH!
AH!
AAAAH!

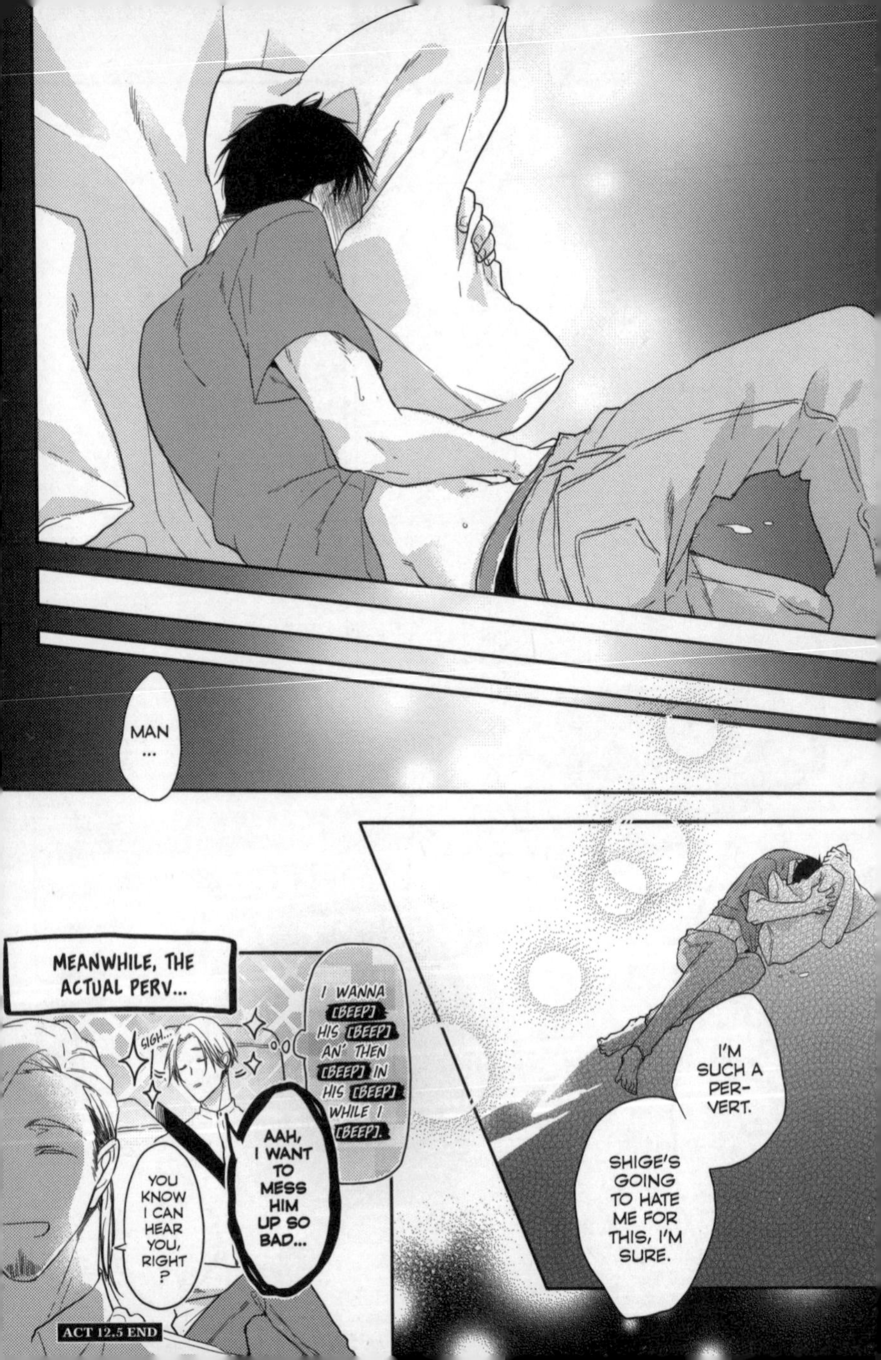
MAN ...
I'M SUCH A PER-VERT.
SHIGE'S GOING TO HATE ME FOR THIS, I'M SURE.
MEANWHILE, THE ACTUAL PERV...
I WANNA [BEEP] HIS [BEEP] AN' THEN [BEEP] IN HIS [BEEP] WHILE I [BEEP].
SIGH...
AAH, I WANT TO MESS HIM UP SO BAD...
YOU KNOW I CAN HEAR YOU, RIGHT?
ACT 12.5 END

AFTERWORD

HELLO. I'M SACHIMO, AND IT'S HARD TO BELIEVE THIS IS VOLUME 4 ALREADY. I WAS A LITTLE WORRIED SHIGE WOULD START GOING BALD FROM ALL THE STRESS, BUT SHIN ARRIVED TO GIVE HIM THE MOST EFFECTIVE HAIR TONIC THERE IS. AT LEAST, THAT'S WHAT THIS VOLUME FEELS LIKE TO ME.

I'LL DO MY BEST TO GET THE NEXT VOLUME FINISHED AS QUICKLY AS I CAN FOR YOU!

さちも.

SACHIMO

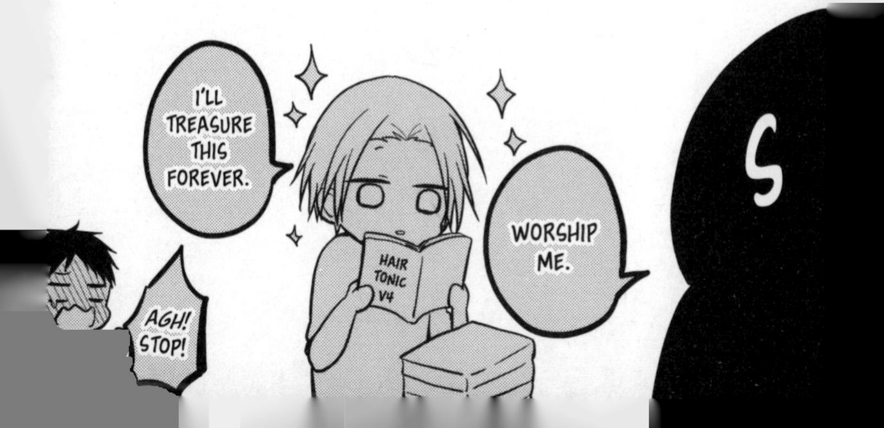
S
WORSHIP ME.
I'LL TREASURE THIS FOREVER.
HAIR TONIC V4
AGH! STOP!

About the Author

Sachimo
DOB August 17
Blood Type O
Born in Saitama Prefecture

Black or White
Volume 4
SuBLime Manga Edition

Story and Art by **Sachimo**

Translation—**Adrienne Beck**
Touch-Up Art and Lettering—**Deborah Fisher**
Cover and Graphic Design—**Shawn Carrico**
Editor—**Jennifer LeBlanc**

BLACK or WHITE Vol. 4
© Sachimo 2020
First published in Japan in 2020 by KADOKAWA CORPORATION, Tokyo.
English translation rights arranged with KADOKAWA CORPORATION, Tokyo.

ASUKA COMICS CL D X

Printed in the U.S.A.

Published by SuBLime Manga
P.O. Box 77010
San Francisco, CA 94107

10 9 8 7 6 5 4 3 2 1
First printing, June 2022

PARENTAL ADVISORY
BLACK OR WHITE is rated M for Mature and is recommended for mature readers. This volume contains graphic imagery and mature themes.

MATURE

SuBLimeManga.com

For more information

on all our products, along with the most up-to-date news on releases, series announcements, and contests, please visit us at:

 SuBLimeManga.com

 twitter.com/**SuBLimeManga**

 facebook.com/**SuBLimeManga**

 instagram.com/**SuBLimeManga**

 SuBLimeManga.tumblr.com